CLEP-12 COLLEGE-LEVEL EXAMINATION
PROGRAM SERIES

This is your
PASSBOOK for...

English Literature

Test Preparation Study Guide
Questions & Answers

NATIONAL LEARNING CORPORATION®

COPYRIGHT NOTICE

This book is SOLELY intended for, is sold ONLY to, and its use is RESTRICTED to individual, bona fide applicants or candidates who qualify by virtue of having seriously filed applications for appropriate license, certificate, professional and/or promotional advancement, higher school matriculation, scholarship, or other legitimate requirements of education and/or governmental authorities.

This book is NOT intended for use, class instruction, tutoring, training, duplication, copying, reprinting, excerption, or adaptation, etc., by:

1) Other publishers
2) Proprietors and/or Instructors of "Coaching" and/or Preparatory Courses
3) Personnel and/or Training Divisions of commercial, industrial, and governmental organizations
4) Schools, colleges, or universities and/or their departments and staffs, including teachers and other personnel
5) Testing Agencies or Bureaus
6) Study groups which seek by the purchase of a single volume to copy and/or duplicate and/or adapt this material for use by the group as a whole without having purchased individual volumes for each of the members of the group
7) Et al.

Such persons would be in violation of appropriate Federal and State statutes.

PROVISION OF LICENSING AGREEMENTS – Recognized educational, commercial, industrial, and governmental institutions and organizations, and others legitimately engaged in educational pursuits, including training, testing, and measurement activities, may address request for a licensing agreement to the copyright owners, who will determine whether, and under what conditions, including fees and charges, the materials in this book may be used them. In other words, a licensing facility exists for the legitimate use of the material in this book on other than an individual basis. However, it is asseverated and affirmed here that the material in this book CANNOT be used without the receipt of the express permission of such a licensing agreement from the Publishers. Inquiries re licensing should be addressed to the company, attention rights and permissions department.

All rights reserved, including the right of reproduction in whole or in part, in any form or by any means, electronic or mechanical, including photocopying, recording, or by any information storage and retrieval system, without permission in writing from the Publisher.

Copyright © 2025 by
National Learning Corporation

212 Michael Drive, Syosset, NY 11791
(516) 921-8888 • www.passbooks.com
E-mail: info@passbooks.com

PASSBOOK® SERIES

THE *PASSBOOK® SERIES* has been created to prepare applicants and candidates for the ultimate academic battlefield – the examination room.

At some time in our lives, each and every one of us may be required to take an examination – for validation, matriculation, admission, qualification, registration, certification, or licensure.

Based on the assumption that every applicant or candidate has met the basic formal educational standards, has taken the required number of courses, and read the necessary texts, the *PASSBOOK® SERIES* furnishes the one special preparation which may assure passing with confidence, instead of failing with insecurity. Examination questions – together with answers – are furnished as the basic vehicle for study so that the mysteries of the examination and its compounding difficulties may be eliminated or diminished by a sure method.

This book is meant to help you pass your examination provided that you qualify and are serious in your objective.

The entire field is reviewed through the huge store of content information which is succinctly presented through a provocative and challenging approach – the question-and-answer method.

A climate of success is established by furnishing the correct answers at the end of each test.

You soon learn to recognize types of questions, forms of questions, and patterns of questioning. You may even begin to anticipate expected outcomes.

You perceive that many questions are repeated or adapted so that you can gain acute insights, which may enable you to score many sure points.

You learn how to confront new questions, or types of questions, and to attack them confidently and work out the correct answers.

You note objectives and emphases, and recognize pitfalls and dangers, so that you may make positive educational adjustments.

Moreover, you are kept fully informed in relation to new concepts, methods, practices, and directions in the field.

You discover that you are actually taking the examination all the time: you are preparing for the examination by "taking" an examination, not by reading extraneous and/or supererogatory textbooks.

In short, this PASSBOOK®, used directedly, should be an important factor in helping you to pass your test.

NONTRADITIONAL EDUCATION

Students returning to school as adults bring more varied experience to their studies than do the teenagers who begin college shortly after graduating from high school. As a result, there are numerous programs for students with nontraditional learning curves. Hundreds of colleges and universities grant degrees to people who cannot attend classes at a regular campus or have already learned what the college is supposed to teach.

You can earn nontraditional education credits in many ways:
- Passing standardized exams
- Demonstrating knowledge gained through experience
- Completing campus-based coursework, and
- Taking courses off campus

Some methods of assessing learning for credit are objective, such as standardized tests. Others are more subjective, such as a review of life experiences.

With some help from four hypothetical characters – Alice, Vin, Lynette, and Jorge – this article describes nontraditional ways of earning educational credit. It begins by describing programs in which you can earn a high school diploma without spending 4 years in a classroom. The college picture is more complicated, so it is presented in two parts: one on gaining credit for what you know through course work or experience, and a second on college degree programs. The final section lists resources for locating more information.

Earning High School Credit

People who were prevented from finishing high school as teenagers have several options if they want to do so as adults. Some major cities have back-to-school programs that allow adults to attend high school classes with current students. But the more practical alternatives for most adults are to take the General Educational Development (GED) tests or to earn a high school diploma by demonstrating their skills or taking correspondence classes.

Of course, these options do not match the experience of staying in high school and graduating with one's friends. But they are viable alternatives for adult learners committed to meeting and, often, continuing their educational goals.

GED Program

Alice quit high school her sophomore year and took a job to help support herself, her younger brother, and their newly widowed mother. Now an adult, she wants to earn her high school diploma – and then go on to college. Because her job as head cook and her family responsibilities keep her busy during the day, she plans to get a high school equivalency diploma. She will study for, and take, the GED tests. Every year, about half a million adults earn their high school credentials this way. A GED diploma is accepted in lieu of a high school one by more than 90 percent of employers, colleges, and universities, so it is a good choice for someone like Alice.

The GED testing program is sponsored by the American Council on Education and State and local education departments. It consists of examinations in five subject areas: Writing, science, mathematics, social studies, and literature and the arts. The tests also measure skills such as analytical ability, problem solving, reading comprehension, and ability to understand and apply information. Most of the questions are multiple choice; the writing test includes an essay section on a topic of general interest.

Eligibility rules for taking the exams vary, but some states require that you must be at least 18. Tests are given in English, Spanish, and French. In addition to standard print, versions in large print, Braille, and audiocassette are also available. Total time allotted for the tests is 7 1/2 hours.

The GED tests are not easy. About one-fourth of those who complete the exams every year do not pass. Passing scores are established by administering the tests to a sample of graduating high school seniors. The minimum standard score is set so that about one-third of graduating seniors would not pass the tests if they took them.

Because of the difficulty of the tests, people need to prepare themselves to take them. Often, they start by taking the Official GED Practice Tests, usually available through a local adult education center. Centers are listed in your phone book's blue pages under "Adult Education," "Continuing Education," or "GED." Adult education centers also have information about GED preparation classes and self-study materials. Classes are generally arranged to accommodate adults' work schedules. National Learning Corporation publishes several study guides that aim to thoroughly prepare test-takers for the GED.

School districts, colleges, adult education centers, and community organizations have information about GED testing schedules and practice tests. For more information, contact them, your nearest GED testing center, or:

GED Testing Service
One Dupont Circle, NW, Suite 250
Washington, DC 20036-1163
1(800) 62-MY GED (626-9433)
(202) 939-9490

Skills Demonstration

Adults who have acquired high school level skills through experience might be eligible for the National External Diploma Program. This alternative to the GED does not involve any direct instruction. Instead, adults seeking a high school diploma must demonstrate mastery of 65 competencies in 8 general areas: Communication; computation; occupational preparedness; and self, social, consumer, scientific, and technological awareness.

Mastery is shown through the completion of the tasks. For example, a participant could prove competency in computation by measuring a room for carpeting, figuring out the amount of carpet needed, and computing the cost.

Before being accepted for the program, adults undergo an evaluation. Tests taken at one of the program's offices measure reading, writing, and mathematics abilities. A take-home segment includes a self-assessment of current skills, an individual skill evaluation, and an occupational interest and aptitude test.

Adults accepted for the program have weekly meetings with an assessor. At the meeting, the assessor reviews the participant's work from the previous week. If the task has not been completed properly, the assessor explains the mistake. Participants continue to correct their errors until they master each competency. A high school diploma is awarded upon proven mastery of all 65 competencies.

Fourteen States and the District of Columbia now offer the External Diploma Program. For more information, contact:
External Diploma Program
One Dupont Circle, NW, Suite 250
Washington, DC 20036-1193
(202) 939-9475

Correspondence and Distance Study
Vin dropped out of high school during his junior year because his family's frequent moves made it difficult for him to continue his studies. He promised himself at the time he dropped out that he would someday finish the courses needed for his diploma. For people like Vin, who prefer to earn a traditional diploma in a nontraditional way, there are about a dozen accredited courses of study for earning a high school diploma by correspondence, or distance study. The programs are either privately run, affiliated with a university, or administered by a State education department.

Distance study diploma programs have no residency requirements, allowing students to continue their studies from almost any location. Depending on the course of study, students need not be enrolled full time and usually have more flexible schedules for finishing their work. Selection of courses ranges from vo-tech to college prep, and some programs place different emphasis on the types of diplomas offered. University affiliated schools, for example, allow qualified students to take college courses along with their high school ones. Students can then apply the college credits toward a degree at that university or transfer them to another institution.

Taking courses by distance study is often more challenging and time consuming than attending classes, especially for adults who have other obligations. Success depends on each student's motivation. Students usually do reading assignments on their own. Written exercises, which they complete and send to an instructor for grading, supplement their reading material.

A list of some accredited high schools that offer diplomas by distance study is available free from the Distance Education and Training Council, formerly known as the National Home Study Council. Request the "DETC Directory of Accredited Institutions" from:
The Distance Education and Training Council
1601 18th Street, NW.
Washington, DC 20009-2529
(202) 234-5100

Some publications profiling nontraditional college programs include addresses and descriptions of several high school correspondence ones. See the Resources section at the end of this article for more information.

Getting College Credit For What You Know
Adults can receive college credit for prior coursework, by passing examinations, and documenting experiential learning. With help from a college advisor, nontraditional students should assess their skills, establish their educational goals, and determine the number of college credits they might be eligible for.

Even before you meet with a college advisor, you should collect all your school and training records. Then, make a list of all knowledge and abilities acquired through experience, no matter how irrelevant they seem to your chosen field. Next, determine your educational goals: What specific field do you wish to study? What kind of a degree do you want? Finally, determine how your past work fits into the field of study. Later on, you will evaluate educational programs to find one that's right for you.

People who have complex educational or experiential learning histories might want to have their learning evaluated by the Regents Credit Bank. The Credit Bank, operated by Regents College of the University of the State of New York, allows people to consolidate credits earned through college, experience, or other methods. Special assessments are available for Regents College enrollees whose knowledge in a specific field cannot be adequately evaluated by standardized exams. For more information, contact the Regents Credit Bank at:

Regents College
7 Columbia Circle
Albany, NY 12203-5159
(518) 464-8500

Credit For Prior College Coursework

When Lynette was in college during the 1970s, she attended several different schools and took a variety of courses. She did well in some classes and poorly in others. Now that she is a successful business owner and has more focus, Lynette thinks she should forget about her previous coursework and start from scratch. Instead, she should start from where she is.

Lynette should have all her transcripts sent to the colleges or universities of her choice and let an admissions officer determine which classes are applicable toward a degree. A few credits here and there may not seem like much, but they add up. Even if the subjects do not seem relevant to any major, they might be counted as elective credits toward a degree. And comparing the cost of transcripts with the cost of college courses, it makes sense to spend a few dollars per transcript for a chance to save hundreds, and perhaps thousands, of dollars in books and tuition.

Rules for transferring credits apply to all prior coursework at accredited colleges and universities, whether done on campus or off. Courses completed off campus, often called extended learning, include those available to students through independent study and correspondence. Many schools have extended learning programs; Brigham Young University, for example, offers more than 300 courses through its Department of Independent Study. One type of extended learning is distance learning, a form of correspondence study by technological means such as television, video and audio, CD-ROM, electronic mail, and computer tutorials. See the Resources section at the end of this article for more information about publications available from the National University Continuing Education Association.

Any previously earned college credits should be considered for transfer, no matter what the subject or the grade received. Many schools do not accept the transfer of courses graded below a C or ones taken more than a designated number of years ago. Some colleges and universities also have limits on the number of credits that can be transferred and applied toward a degree. But not all do. For example, Thomas Edison State College, New Jersey's State college for adults, accepts the transfer of all 120 hours of credit required for a baccalaureate degree – provided all the credits are transferred from regionally accredited schools, no more than 80 are at the junior college level, and the student's grades overall and in the field of study average out to C.

To assign credit for prior coursework, most schools require original transcripts. This means you must complete a form or send a written, signed request to have your transcripts released directly to a college or university. Once you have chosen the schools you want to apply to, contact the schools you attended before. Find out how much each transcript costs, and ask them to send your transcripts to the ones you are applying to. Write a letter that includes your name (and names used during attendance, if different) and dates of attendance, along with the names and addresses of the schools to which your transcripts should be sent. Include payment and mail to the registrar at the schools you have attended. The registrar's office will process your request and send an official transcript of your coursework to the colleges or universities you have designated.

Credit For Noncollege Courses

Colleges and universities are not the only ones that offer classes. Volunteer organizations and employers often provide formal training worth college credit. The American Council on Education has two programs that assess thousands of specific courses and make recommendations on the amount of college credit they are worth. Colleges and universities accept the recommendations or use them as guidelines.

One program evaluates educational courses sponsored by government agencies, business and industry, labor unions, and professional and voluntary organizations. It is the Program on Noncollegiate Sponsored Instruction (PONSI). Some of the training seminars Alice has participated in covered topics such as food preparation, kitchen safety, and nutrition. Although she has not yet earned her GED, Alice can earn college credit because of her completion of these formal job-training seminars. The number of credits each seminar is worth does not hinge on Alice's current eligibility for college enrollment.

The other program evaluates courses offered by the Army, Navy, Air Force, Marines, Coast Guard, and Department of Defense. It is the Military Evaluations Program. Jorge has never attended college, but the engineering technology classes he completed as part of his military training are worth college credit. And as an Army veteran, Jorge is eligible for a service that takes the evaluations one step further. The Army/American Council on Education Registry Transcript System (AARTS) will provide Jorge with an individualized transcript of American Council on Education credit recommendations for all courses he completed, the military occupational specialties (MOS's) he held, and examinations he passed while in the Army. All Army and National Guard enlisted personnel and veterans who enlisted after October 1981 are eligible for the transcript. Similar services are being considered by the Navy and Marine Corps.

To obtain a free transcript, see your Army Education Center for a 5454R transcript request form. Include your name, Social Security number, basic active service date, and complete address where you want the transcript sent. Mail your request to:

AARTS Operations Center
415 McPherson Ave.
Fort Leavenworth, KS 66027-1373

Recommendations for PONSI are published in *The National Guide to Educational Credit for Training Programs;* military program recommendations are in *The Guide to the Evaluation of Educational Experiences in the Armed Forces.* See the Resources section at the end of this article for more information about these publications.

Former military personnel who took a foreign language course through the Defense Language Institute may request course transcripts by sending their name, Social Security number, course title, duration of the course, and graduation date to:

Commandant, Defense Language Institute
Attn: ATFL-DAA-AR
Transcripts
Presidio of Monterey
Monterey, CA 93944-5006

Not all of Jorge's and Alice's courses have been assessed by the American Council on Education. Training courses that have no Council credit recommendation should still be assessed by an advisor at the schools they want to attend. Course descriptions, class notes, test scores, and other documentation may be helpful for comparing training courses to their college equivalents. An oral examination or other demonstration of competency might also be required.

There is no guarantee you will receive all the credits you are seeking – but you certainly won't if you make no attempt.

Credit By Examination

Standardized tests are the best-known method of receiving college credit without taking courses. These exams are often taken by high school students seeking advanced placement for college, but they are also available to adult learners. Testing programs and colleges and universities offer exams in a number of subjects. Two U.S. Government institutes have foreign language exams for employees that also may be worth college credit.

It is important to understand that receiving a passing score on these exams does not mean you get college credit automatically. Each school determines which test results it will accept, minimum scores required, how scores are converted for credit, and the amount of credit, if any, to be assigned. Most colleges and universities accept the American Council on Education credit recommendations, published every other year in the 250-page *Guide to Educational Credit by Examination*. For more information, contact:

The American Council on Education
Credit by Examination Program
One Dupont Circle, Suite 250
Washington, DC 20036-1193
(202) 939-9434

Testing programs:

You might know some of the five national testing programs by their acronyms or initials: CLEP, ACT PEP: RCE, DANTES, AP, and NOCTI. (The meanings of these initialisms are explained below.) There is some overlap among programs; for example, four of them have introductory accounting exams. Since you will not be awarded credit more than once for a specific subject, you should carefully evaluate each program for the subject exams you wish to take. And before taking an exam, make sure you will be awarded credit by the college or university you plan to attend.

CLEP (College-Level Examination Program), administered by the College Board, is the most widely accepted of the national testing programs; more than 2,800 accredited schools award credit for passing exam scores. Each test covers material taught in basic undergraduate courses. There are five general exams – English composition, humanities, college mathematics, natural sciences, and social sciences and history – and many subject exams. Most exams are entirely multiple-choice, but English composition exams may include an essay section. For more information, contact:

    CLEP
    P.O. Box 6600
    Princeton, NJ 08541-6600
    (609) 771-7865

ACT PEP: RCE (American College Testing Proficiency Exam Program: Regents College Examinations) tests are given in 38 subjects within arts and sciences, business, education, and nursing. Each exam is recommended for either lower- or upper-level credit. Exams contain either objective or extended response questions, and are graded according to a standard score, letter grade, or pass/fail. Fees vary, depending on the subject and type of exam. For more information or to request free study guides, contact:

    ACT PEP: Regents College Examinations
    P.O. Box 4014
    Iowa City, IA 52243
    (319) 337-1387
    (New York State residents must contact Regents College directly.)

DANTES (Defense Activity for Nontraditional Education Support) standardized tests are developed by the Educational Testing Service for the Department of Defense. Originally administered only to military personnel, the exams have been available to the public since 1983. About 50 subject tests cover business, mathematics, social science, physical science, humanities, foreign languages, and applied technology. Most of the tests consist entirely of multiple-choice questions. Schools determine their own administering fees and testing schedules. For more information or to request free study sheets, contact:

    DANTES Program Office
    Mail Stop 31-X
    Educational Testing Service
    Princeton, NJ 08541
    1(800) 257-9484

The AP (Advanced Placement) Program is a cooperative effort between secondary schools and colleges and universities. AP exams are developed each year by committees of college and high school faculty appointed by the College Board and assisted by consultants from the Educational Testing Service. Subjects include arts and languages, natural sciences, computer science, social sciences, history, and mathematics. Most tests are 2 or 3 hours long and include both multiple-choice and essay questions. AP courses are available to help students prepare for exams, which are offered in the spring. For more information about the Advanced Placement Program, contact:

    Advanced Placement Services
    P.O. Box 6671
    Princeton, NJ 08541-6671
    (609) 771-7300

NOCTI (National Occupational Competency Testing Institute) assessments are designed for people like Alice, who have vocational-technical skills that cannot be evaluated by other tests. NOCTI assesses competency at two levels: Student/job ready and teacher/experienced worker. Standardized evaluations are available for occupations such as auto-body repair, electronics, mechanical drafting, quantity food preparation, and upholstering. The tests consist of multiple-choice questions and a performance component. Other services include workshops, customized assessments, and pre-testing. For more information, contact:

NOCTI
500 N. Bronson Ave.
Ferris State University
Big Rapids, MI 49307
(616) 796-4699

Colleges and universities:

Many colleges and universities have credit-by-exam programs, through which students earn credit by passing a comprehensive exam for a course offered by the institution. Among the most widely recognized are the programs at Ohio University, the University of North Carolina, Thomas Edison State College, and New York University.

Ohio University offers about 150 examinations for credit. In addition, you may sometimes arrange to take special examinations in non-laboratory courses offered at Ohio University. To take a test for credit, you must enroll in the course. If you plan to transfer the credit earned, you also need written permission from an official at your school. Books and study materials are available, for a cost, through the university. Exams must be taken within 6 months of the enrollment date; most last 3 hours. You may arrange to take the exam off campus if you do not live near the university.

Ohio University is on the quarter-hour system; most courses are worth 4 quarter hours, the equivalent of 3 semester hours. For more information, contact:

Independent Study
Tupper Hall 302
Ohio University
Athens, OH 45701-2979
1(800) 444-2910
(614) 593-2910

The University of North Carolina offers a credit-by-examination option for 140 independent study (correspondence) courses in foreign languages, humanities, social sciences, mathematics, business administration, education, electrical and computer engineering, health administration, and natural sciences. To take an exam, you must request and receive approval from both the course instructor and the independent studies department. Exams must be taken within six months of enrollment, and you may register for no more than two at a time. If you are not near the University's Chapel Hill campus, you may take your exam under supervision at an accredited college, university, community college, or technical institute. For more information, contact:

Independent Studies
CB #1020, The Friday Center
UNC-Chapel Hill
Chapel Hill, NC 27599-1020
1(800) 862-5669 / (919) 962-1134

The Thomas Edison College Examination Program offers more than 50 exams in liberal arts, business, and professional areas. Thomas Edison State College administers tests twice a month in Trenton, New Jersey; however, students may arrange to take their tests with a proctor at any accredited American college or university or U.S. military base. Most of the tests are multiple choice; some also include short answer or essay questions. Time limits range from 90 minutes to 4 hours, depending on the exam. For more information, contact:

Thomas Edison State College
TECEP, Office of Testing and Assessment
101 W. State Street
Trenton, NJ 08608-1176
(609) 633-2844

New York University's Foreign Language Program offers proficiency exams in more than 40 languages, from Albanian to Yiddish. Two exams are available in each language: The 12-point test is equivalent to 4 undergraduate semesters, and the 16-point exam may lead to upper level credit. The tests are given at the university's Foreign Language Department throughout the year.

Proof of foreign language proficiency does not guarantee college credit. Some colleges and universities accept transcripts only for languages commonly taught, such as French and Spanish. Nontraditional programs are more likely than traditional ones to grant credit for proficiency in other languages.

For an informational brochure and registration form for NYU's foreign language proficiency exams, contact:

New York University
Foreign Language Department
48 Cooper Square, Room 107
New York, NY 10003
(212) 998-7030

Government institutes:

The Defense Language Institute and Foreign Service Institute administer foreign language proficiency exams for personnel stationed abroad. Usually, the tests are given at the end of intensive language courses or upon completion of service overseas. But some people – like Jorge, who knows Spanish – speak another language fluently and may be allowed to take a proficiency exam in that language before completing their tour of duty. Contact one of the offices listed below to obtain transcripts of those scores. Proof of proficiency does not guarantee college credit, however, as discussed above.

To request score reports from the Defense Language Institute for Defense Language Proficiency Tests, send your name, Social Security number, language for which you were tested, and, most importantly, when and where you took the exam to:

Commandant, Defense Language Institute
Attn: ATFL-ES-T
DLPT Score Report Request
Presidio of Monterey
Monterey, CA 93944-5006

To request transcripts of scores for Foreign Service Institute exams, send your name, Social Security number, language for which you were tested, and dates or year of exams to:

Foreign Service Institute
Arlington Hall
4020 Arlington Boulevard
Rosslyn, VA 22204-1500
Attn: Testing Office (Send your request to the attention of the testing office of the foreign language in which you were tested)

Credit For Experience

Experiential learning credit may be given for knowledge gained through job responsibilities, personal hobbies, volunteer opportunities, homemaking, and other experiences. Colleges and universities base credit awards on the knowledge you have attained, not for the experience alone. In addition, the knowledge must be college level; not just any learning will do. Throwing horseshoes as a hobby is not likely to be worth college credit. But if you've done research on how and where the sport originated, visited blacksmiths, organized tournaments, and written a column for a trade journal — well, that's a horseshoe of a different color.

Adults attempting to get credit for their experience should be forewarned: Having your experience evaluated for college credit is time-consuming, tedious work — not an easy shortcut for people who want quick-fix college credits. And not all experience, no matter how valuable, is the equivalent of college courses.

Requesting college credit for your experiential learning can be tricky. You should get assistance from a credit evaluations officer at the school you plan to attend, but you should also have a general idea of what your knowledge is worth. A common method for converting knowledge into credit is to use a college catalog. Find course titles and descriptions that match what you have learned through experience, and request the number of credits offered for those courses.

Once you know what credit to ask for, you must usually present your case in writing to officials at the college you plan to attend. The most common form of presenting experiential learning for credit is the portfolio. A portfolio is a written record of your knowledge along with a request for equivalent college credit. It includes an identification and description of the knowledge for which you are requesting credit, an explanatory essay of how the knowledge was gained and how it fits into your educational plans, documentation that you have acquired such knowledge, and a request for college credit. Required elements of a portfolio vary by schools but generally follow those guidelines.

In identifying knowledge you have gained, be specific about exactly what you have learned. For example, it is not enough for Lynette to say she runs a business. She must identify the knowledge she has gained from running it, such as personnel management, tax law, marketing strategy, and inventory review. She must also include brief descriptions about her knowledge of each to support her claims of having those skills.

The essay gives you a chance to relay something about who you are. It should address your educational goals, include relevant autobiographical details, and be well organized, neat, and convey confidence. In his essay, Jorge might first state his goal of becoming an engineer. Then he would explain why he joined the Army, where he got hands-on training and experience in developing and servicing electronic equipment.

This, he would say, led to his hobby of creating remote-controlled model cars, of which he has built 20. His conclusion would highlight his accomplishments and tie them to his desire to become an electronic engineer.

Documentation is evidence that you've learned what you claim to have learned. You can show proof of knowledge in a variety of ways, including audio or video recordings, letters from current or former employers describing your specific duties and job performance, blueprints, photographs or artwork, and transcripts of certifying exams for professional licenses and certification – such as Alice's certification from the American Culinary Federation. Although documentation can take many forms, written proof alone is not always enough. If it is impossible to document your knowledge in writing, find out if your experiential learning can be assessed through supplemental oral exams by a faculty expert.

Earning a College Degree

Nontraditional students often have work, family, and financial obligations that prevent them from quitting their jobs to attend school full time. Can they still meet their educational goals? Yes.

More than 150 accredited colleges and universities have nontraditional bachelor's degree programs that require students to spend little or no time on campus; over 300 others have nontraditional campus-based degree programs. Some of those schools, as well as most junior and community colleges, offer associate's degrees nontraditionally. Each school with a nontraditional course of study determines its own rules for awarding credit for prior coursework, exams, or experience, as discussed previously. Most have charges on top of tuition for providing these special services.

Several publications profile nontraditional degree programs; see the Resources section at the end of this article for more information. To determine which school best fits your academic profile and educational goals, first list your criteria. Then, evaluate nontraditional programs based on their accreditation, features, residency requirements, and expenses. Once you have chosen several schools to explore further, write to them for more information. Detailed explanations of school policies should help you decide which ones you want to apply to.

Get beyond the printed word – especially the glowing words each school writes about itself. Check out the schools you are considering with higher education authorities, alumni, employers, family members, and friends. If possible, visit the campus to talk to students and instructors and sit in on a few classes, even if you will be completing most or all of your work off campus. Ask school officials questions about such things as enrollment numbers, graduation rate, faculty qualifications, and confusing details about the application process or academic policies. After you have thoroughly investigated each prospective college or university, you can make an informed decision about which is right for you.

Accreditation

Accreditation is a process colleges and universities submit to voluntarily for getting their credentials. An accredited school has been investigated and visited by teams of observers and has periodic inspections by a private accrediting agency. The initial review can take two years or more.

Regional agencies accredit entire schools, and professional agencies accredit either specialized schools or departments within schools. Although there are no national accrediting standards, not just any accreditation will do. Countless "accreditation associations" have been invented by schools, many of which have no academic programs and sell phony degrees, to accredit themselves. But 6 regional and about 80 professional accrediting associations in the United States are recognized by the U.S. Department of Education or the Commission on Recognition of Postsecondary Accreditation. When checking accreditation, these are the names to look for. For more information about accreditation and accrediting agencies, contact:

>Institutional Participation Oversight Service Accreditation and State Liaison Division
>U.S. Department of Education
>ROB 3, Room 3915
>600 Independence Ave., SW
>Washington, DC 20202-5244
>(202) 708-7417

Because accreditation is not mandatory, lack of accreditation does not necessarily mean a school or program is bad. Some schools choose not to apply for accreditation, are in the process of applying, or have educational methods too unconventional for an accrediting association's standards. For the nontraditional student, however, earning a degree from a college or university with recognized accreditation is an especially important consideration. Although nontraditional education is becoming more widely accepted, it is not yet mainstream. Employers skeptical of a degree earned in a nontraditional manner are likely to be even less accepting of one from an unaccredited school.

Program Features

Because nontraditional students have diverse educational objectives, nontraditional schools are diverse in what they offer. Some programs are geared toward helping students organize their scattered educational credits to get a degree as quickly as possible. Others cater to those who may have specific credits or experience but need assistance in completing requirements. Whatever your educational profile, you should look for a program that works with you in obtaining your educational goals.

A few nontraditional programs have special admissions policies for adult learners like Alice, who plan to earn their GEDs but want to enroll in college in the meantime. Other features of nontraditional programs include individualized learning agreements, intensive academic counseling, cooperative learning and internship placement, and waiver of some prerequisites or other requirements – as well as college credit for prior coursework, examinations, and experiential learning, all discussed previously.

Lynette, whose primary goal is to finish her degree, wants to earn maximum credits for her business experience. She will look for programs that do not limit the number of credits awarded for equivalency exams and experiential learning. And since well-documented proof of knowledge is essential for earning experiential learning credits, Lynette should make sure the program she chooses provides assistance to students submitting a portfolio.

Jorge, on the other hand, has more credits than he needs in certain areas and is willing to forego some. To become an engineer, he must have a bachelor's degree; but because he is accustomed to hands-on learning, Jorge is interested in getting experience as he gains more technical skills. He will concentrate on finding schools with strong cooperative education, supervised fieldwork, or internship programs.

Residency Requirements

Programs are sometimes deemed nontraditional because of their residency requirements. Many people think of residency for colleges and universities in terms of tuition, with in-state students paying less than out-of-state ones. Residency also may refer to where a student lives, either on or off campus, while attending school.

But in nontraditional education, residency usually refers to how much time students must spend on campus, regardless of whether they attend classes there. In some nontraditional programs, students need not ever step foot on campus. Others require only a very short residency, such as one day or a few weeks. Many schools have standard residency requirements of several semesters but schedule classes for evenings or weekends to accommodate working adults.

Lynette, who previously took courses by independent study, prefers to earn credits by distance study. She will focus on schools that have no residency requirement. Several colleges and universities have nonresident degree completion programs for adults with some college credit. Under the direction of a faculty advisor, students devise a plan for earning their remaining credits. Methods for earning credits include independent study, distance learning, seminars, supervised fieldwork, and group study at arranged sites. Students may have to earn a certain number of credits through the degree-granting institution. But many programs allow students to take courses at accredited schools of their choice for transfer toward their degree.

Alice wants to attend lectures but has an unpredictable schedule. Her best course of action will be to seek out short residency programs that require students to attend seminars once or twice a semester. She can take courses that are televised and videotape them to watch when her schedule permits, with the seminars helping to ensure that she properly completes her coursework. Many colleges and universities with short residency requirements also permit students to earn some credits elsewhere, by whatever means the student chooses.

Some fields of study require classroom instruction. As Jorge will discover, few colleges and universities allow students to earn a bachelor's degree in engineering entirely through independent study. Nontraditional residency programs are designed to accommodate adults' daytime work schedules. Jorge should look for programs offering evening, weekend, summer, and accelerated courses.

Tuition and Other Expenses

The final decisions about which schools Alice, Jorge, and Lynette attend may hinge in large part on a single issue: Cost. And rising tuition is only part of the equation. Beginning with application fees and continuing through graduation fees, college expenses add up.

Traditional and nontraditional students have some expenses in common, such as the cost of books and other materials. Tuition might even be the same for some courses, especially for colleges and universities offering standard ones at unusual times. But for nontraditional programs, students may also pay fees for services such as credit or transcript review, evaluation, advisement, and portfolio assessment.

Students are also responsible for postage and handling or setup expenses for independent study courses, as well as for all examination and transcript fees for transferring credits. Usually, the more nontraditional the program, the more detailed the fees. Some schools charge a yearly enrollment fee rather than tuition for degree completion candidates who want their files to remain active.

Although tuition and fees might seem expensive, most educators tell you not to let money come between you and your educational goals. Talk to someone in the financial aid department of the school you plan to attend or check your library for publications about financial aid sources. The U.S. Department of Education publishes a guide to Federal aid programs such as Pell Grants, student loans, and work-study. To order the free 74-page booklet, *The Student Guide: Financial Aid from the U.S. Department of Education,* contact:

Federal Student Aid Information Center
P.O. Box 84
Washington, DC 20044
1 (800) 4FED-AID (433-3243)

Resources

Information on how to earn a high school diploma or college degree without following the usual routes is available from several organizations and in numerous publications. Information on nontraditional graduate degree programs, available for master's through doctoral level, though not discussed in this article, can usually be obtained from the same resources that detail bachelor's degree programs.

National Learning Corporation publishes study guides for all of these exams, for both general examinations and tests in specific subject areas. To order study guides, or to browse their catalog featuring more than 5,000 titles, visit NLC online at www.passbooks.com, or contact them by phone at (800) 632-8888.

Organizations

Adult learners should always contact their local school system, community college, or university to learn about programs that are readily available. The following national organizations can also supply information:

American Council on Education
One Dupont Circle
Washington, DC 20036-1193
(202) 939-9300

Within the American Council on Education, the Center for Adult Learning and Educational Credentials administers the National External Diploma Program, the GED Program, the Program on Noncollegiate Sponsored Instruction, the Credit by Examination Program, and the Military Evaluations Program.

College-Level Examination Program (CLEP)

1. WHAT IS CLEP?

CLEP stands for the College-Level Examination Program, sponsored by the College Board. It is a national program of credit-by-examination that offers you the opportunity to obtain recognition for college-level achievement. No matter when, where, or how you have learned – by means of formal or informal study – you can take CLEP tests. If the results are acceptable to your college, you can receive credit.

You may not realize it, but you probably know more than your academic record reveals. Each day you, like most people, have an opportunity to learn. In private industry and business, as well as at all levels of government, learning opportunities continually occur. If you read widely or intensively in a particular field, think about what you read, discuss it with your family and friends, you are learning. Or you may be learning on a more formal basis by taking a correspondence course, a television or radio course, a course recorded on tape or cassettes, a course assembled into programmed tests, or a course taught in your community adult school or high school.

No matter how, where, or when you gained your knowledge, you may have the opportunity to receive academic credit for your achievement that can be counted toward an undergraduate degree. The College-Level Examination Program (CLEP) enables colleges to evaluate your achievement and give you credit. A wide range of college-level examinations are offered by CLEP to anyone who wishes to take them. Scores on the tests are reported to you and, if you wish, to a college, employer, or individual.

2. WHAT ARE THE PURPOSES OF THE COLLEGE-LEVEL EXAMINATION PROGRAM?

The basic purpose of the College-Level Examination Program is to enable individuals who have acquired their education in nontraditional ways to demonstrate their academic achievement. It is also intended for use by those in higher education, business, industry, government, and other fields who need a reliable method of assessing a person's educational level.

Recognizing that the real issue is not how a person has acquired his education but what education he has, the College Level Examination Program has been designed to serve a variety of purposes. The basic purpose, as listed above, is to enable those who have reached the college level of education in nontraditional ways to assess the level of their achievement and to use the test results in seeking college credit or placement.

In addition, scores on the tests can be used to validate educational experience obtained at a nonaccredited institution or through noncredit college courses.

Some colleges and universities may use the tests to measure the level of educational achievement of their students, and for various institutional research purposes.

Other colleges and universities may wish to use the tests in the admission, placement, and guidance of students who wish to transfer from one institution to another.

Businesses, industries, governmental agencies, and professional groups now accept the results of these tests as a basis for advancement, eligibility for further training, or professional or semi-professional certification.

Many people are interested in the examination simply to assess their own educational progress and attainment.

The college, university, business, industry, or government agency that adopts the tests in the College-Level Examination Program makes its own decision about how it will use and interpret the test scores. The College Board will provide the tests, score them, and report the results either to the individuals who took the tests or the college or agency that administered them. It does NOT, and cannot, award college credit, certify college equivalency, or make recommendations regarding the standards these institutions should establish for the use of the test results.

Therefore, if you are taking the tests to secure credit from an institution, you should FIRST ascertain whether the college or agency involved will accept the scores. Each institution determines which CLEP tests it will accept for credit and the amount of credit it will award. If you want to take tests for college credit, first call, write, or visit the college you wish to attend to inquire about its policy on CLEP scores, as well as its other admission requirements.

The services of the program are also available to people who have been requested to take the tests by an employer, a professional licensing agency, a certifying agency, or by other groups that recognize college equivalency on the basis of satisfactory CLEP scores. You may, of course, take the tests SOLELY for your own information. If you do, your scores will be reported only to you.

While neither CLEP nor the College Board can evaluate previous credentials or award college credit, you will receive, with your scores, basic information to help you interpret your performance on the tests you have taken.

3. WHAT ARE THE COLLEGE-LEVEL EXAMINATIONS?

In order to meet different kinds of curricular organization and testing needs at colleges and universities, the College-Level Examination Program offers 35 different subject tests falling under five separate general categories: Composition and Literature, Foreign Languages, History and Social Sciences, Science and Mathematics, and Business.

4. WHAT ARE THE SUBJECT EXAMINATIONS?

The 35 CLEP tests offered by the College Board are listed below:

COMPOSITION AND LITERATURE:
- American Literature
- Analyzing and Interpreting Literature
- English Composition
- English Composition with Essay
- English Literature
- Freshman College Composition
- Humanities

FOREIGN LANGUAGES
- French
- German
- Spanish

HISTORY AND SOCIAL SCIENCES
- American Government
- Introduction to Educational Psychology
- History of the United States I: Early Colonization to 1877
- History of the United States II: 1865 to the Present
- Human Growth and Development
- Principles of Macroeconomics
- Principles of Microeconomics
- Introductory Psychology
- Social Sciences and History
- Introductory Sociology
- Western Civilization I: Ancient Near East to 1648
- Western Civilization II: 1648 to the Present

SCIENCE AND MATHEMATICS
- College Algebra
- College Algebra-Trigonometry
- Biology
- Calculus
- Chemistry
- College Mathematics
- Natural Sciences
- Trigonometry
- Precalculus

BUSINESS
- Financial Accounting
- Introductory Business Law
- Information Systems and Computer Applications
- Principles of Management
- Principles of Marketing

CLEP Examinations cover material taught in courses that most students take as requirements in the first two years of college. A college usually grants the same amount of credit to students earning satisfactory scores on the CLEP examination as it grants to students successfully completing the equivalent course.

Many examinations are designed to correspond to one-semester courses; some, however, correspond to full-year or two-year courses.

Each exam is 90 minutes long and, except for English Composition with Essay, is made up primarily of multiple-choice questions. Some tests have several other types of questions besides multiple choice. To see a more detailed description of a particular CLEP exam, visit www.collegeboard.com/clep.

The English Composition with Essay exam is the only exam that includes a required essay. This essay is scored by college English faculty designated by CLEP and does not require an additional fee. However, other Composition and Literature tests offer optional essays, which some college and universities require and some do not. These essays are graded by faculty at the individual institutions that require them and require an additional $10 fee. Contact the particular institution to ask about essay requirements, and check with your test center for further details.

All 35 CLEP examinations are administered on computer. If you are unfamiliar with taking a test on a computer, consult the CLEP Sampler online at www.collegeboard.com/clep. The Sampler contains the same tutorials as the actual exams and helps familiarize you with navigation and how to answer different types of questions.

Points are not deducted for wrong or skipped answers – you receive one point for every correct answer. Therefore it is best that an answer is supplied for each exam question, whether it is a guess or not. The number of correct answers is then converted to a formula score. This formula, or "scaled," score is determined by a statistical process called *equating*, which adjusts for slight differences in difficulty between test forms and ensures that your score does not depend on the specific test form you took or how well others did on the same form. The scaled scores range from 20 to 80 – this is the number that will appear on your score report.

To ensure that you complete all questions in the time allotted, you would probably be wise to skip the more difficult or perplexing questions and return to them later. Although the multiple-choice items in these tests are carefully designed so as not to be tricky, misleading, or ambiguous, on the other hand, they are not all direct questions of factual information. They attempt, in their way, to elicit a response that indicates your knowledge or lack of knowledge of the material in question or your ability or inability to use or interpret a fact or idea. Thus, you should concentrate on answering the questions as they appear to be without attempting to out-guess the testmakers.

5. WHAT ARE THE FEES?

The fee for all CLEP examinations is $55. Optional essays required by some institutions are an additional $10.

6. WHEN ARE THE TESTS GIVEN?

CLEP tests are administered year-round. Consult the CLEP website (www.collegeboard.com/clep) and individual test centers for specific information.

7. WHERE ARE THE TESTS GIVEN?

More than 1,300 test centers are located on college and university campuses throughout the country, and additional centers are being established to meet increased needs. Any accredited collegiate institution with an explicit and publicly available policy of credit by examination can become a CLEP test center. To obtain a list of these centers, visit the CLEP website at www.collegeboard.com/clep.

8. HOW DO I REGISTER FOR THE COLLEGE-LEVEL EXAMINATION PROGRAM?

Contact an individual test center for information regarding registration, scheduling and fees. Registration/admission forms can also be obtained on the CLEP website.

9. MAY I REPEAT THE COLLEGE-LEVEL EXAMINATIONS?

You may repeat any examination providing at least six months have passed since you were last administered this test. If you repeat a test within a period of time less than six months, your scores will be cancelled and your fees forfeited. To repeat a test, check the appropriate space on the registration form.

10. WHEN MAY I EXPECT MY SCORE REPORTS?

With the exception of the English Composition with Essay exam, you should receive your score report instantly once the test is complete.

11. HOW SHOULD I PREPARE FOR THE COLLEGE-LEVEL EXAMINATIONS?

This book has been specifically designed to prepare candidates for these examinations. It will help you to consider, study, and review important content, principles, practices, procedures, problems, and techniques in the form of varied and concrete applications.

12. QUESTIONS AND ANSWERS APPEARING IN THIS PUBLICATION

The College-Level Examinations are offered by the College Board. Since copies of past examinations have not been made available, we have used equivalent materials, including questions and answers, which are highly recommended by us as an appropriate means of preparing for these examinations.

If you need additional information about CLEP Examinations, visit www.collegeboard.com/clep.

THE COLLEGE-LEVEL EXAMINATION PROGRAM

How The Program Works

CLEP examinations are administered at many colleges and universities across the country, and most institutions award college credit to those who do well on them. The examinations provide people who have acquired knowledge outside the usual educational settings the opportunity to show that they have learned college-level material without taking certain college courses.

The CLEP examinations cover material that is taught in introductory-level courses at many colleges and universities. Faculties at individual colleges review the tests to ensure that they cover the important material taught in their courses. Colleges differ in the examinations they accept; some colleges accept only two or three of the examinations while others accept nearly all of them.

Although CLEP is sponsored by the College Board and the examinations are scored by Educational Testing Service (ETS), neither of these organizations can award college credit. Only accredited colleges may grant credit toward a degree. When you take a CLEP examination, you may request that a copy of your score report be sent to the college you are attending or plan to attend. After evaluating your scores, the college will decide whether or not to award you credit for a certain course or courses, or to exempt you from them. If the college gives you credit, it will record the number of credits on your permanent record, thereby indicating that you have completed work equivalent to a course in that subject. If the college decides to grant exemption without giving you credit for a course, you will be permitted to omit a course that would normally be required of you and to take a course of your choice instead.

What the Examinations Are Like

The examinations consist mostly of multiple-choice questions to be answered within a 90-minute time limit. Additional information about each CLEP examination is given in the examination guide and on the CLEP website.

Where To Take the Examinations

CLEP examinations are administered throughout the year at the test centers of approximately 1,300 colleges and universities. On the CLEP website, you will find a list of institutions that award credit for satisfactory scores on CLEP examinations. Some colleges administer CLEP examinations to their own students only. Other institutions administer the tests to anyone who registers to take them. If your college does not administer the tests, contact the test centers in your area for information about its testing schedule.

Once you have been tested, your score report will be available instantly. CLEP scores are kept on file at ETS for 20 years; and during this period, for a small fee, you may have your transcript sent to another college or to anyone else you specify. (Your scores will never be sent to anyone without your approval.)

APPROACHING A COLLEGE ABOUT CLEP

The following sections provide a step-by-step approach to learning about the CLEP policy at a particular college or university. The person or office that can best assist students desiring CLEP credit may have a different title at each institution, but the following guidelines will lead you to information about CLEP at any institution.

Adults returning to college often benefit from special assistance when they approach a college. Opportunities for adults to return to formal learning in the classroom are now widespread, and colleges and universities have worked hard to make this a smooth process for older students. Many colleges have established special service offices that are staffed with trained professionals who understand the kinds of problems facing adults returning to college. If you think you might benefit from such assistance, be sure to find out whether these services are available at your college.

How to Apply for College Credit

STEP 1. Obtain the General Information Catalog and a copy of the CLEP policy from the colleges you are considering. If you have not yet applied for admission, ask for an admissions application form too.

Information about admissions and CLEP policies can be obtained by contacting college admissions offices or finding admissions information on the school websites. Tell the admissions officer that you are a prospective student and that you are interested in applying for admission and CLEP credit. Ask for a copy of the publication in which the college's complete CLEP policy is explained. Also get the name and the telephone number of the person to contact in case you have further questions about CLEP.

At this step, you may wish to obtain information from external degree colleges. Many adults find that such colleges suit their needs exceptionally well.

STEP 2. If you have not already been admitted to the college you are considering, look at its admission requirements for undergraduate students to see if you can qualify.

This is an important step because if you can't get into college, you can't get college credit for CLEP. Nearly all colleges require students to be admitted and to enroll in one or more courses before granting the students CLEP credit.

Virtually all public community colleges and a number of four-year state colleges have open admission policies for in-state students. This usually means that they admit anyone who has graduated from high school or has earned a high school equivalency diploma.

If you think you do not meet the admission requirements, contact the admissions office for an interview with a counselor. Colleges do sometimes make exceptions, particularly for adult applicants. State why you want the interview and ask what documents you should bring with you or send in advance. (These materials may include a high school transcript, transcript of previous college work, completed application for admission, etc.) Make an extra effort to have all the information requested in time for the interview.

During the interview, relax and be yourself. Be prepared to state honestly why you think you are ready and able to do college work. If you have already taken CLEP examinations and scored high enough to earn credit, you have shown that you are able to do college work. Mention this achievement to the admissions counselor because it may increase your chances of being accepted. If you have not taken a CLEP examination, you can still improve your chances of being accepted by describing how your job training or independent study has helped prepare you for college-level work. Tell the counselor what you have learned from your work and personal experiences.

STEP 3. Evaluate the college's CLEP policy.

Typically, a college lists all its academic policies, including CLEP policies, in its general catalog. You will probably find the CLEP policy statement under a heading such as Credit-by-Examination, Advanced Standing, Advanced Placement, or External Degree Program. These sections can usually be found in the front of the catalog.

Many colleges publish their credit-by-examination policies in a separate brochure, which is distributed through the campus testing office, counseling center, admissions office, or registrar's office. If you find a very general policy statement in the college catalog, seek clarification from one of these offices.

Review the material in the section of this guide entitled Questions to Ask About a College's CLEP Policy. Use these guidelines to evaluate the college's CLEP policy. If you have not yet taken a CLEP examination, this evaluation will help you decide which examinations to take and whether or not to take the free-response or essay portion. Because individual colleges have different CLEP policies, a review of several policies may help you decide which college to attend.

STEP 4. If you have not yet applied for admission, do so early.

Most colleges expect you to apply for admission several months before you enroll, and it is essential that you meet the published application deadlines. It takes time to process your application for admission; and if you have yet to take a CLEP examination, it will be some time before the college receives and reviews your score report. You will probably want to take some, if not all, of the CLEP examinations you are interested in before you enroll so you know which courses you need not register for. In fact, some colleges require that all CLEP scores be submitted before a student registers.

Complete all forms and include all documents requested with your application(s) for admission. Normally, an admissions decision cannot be reached until all documents have been submitted and evaluated. Unless told to do so, do not send your CLEP scores until you have been officially admitted.

STEP 5. Arrange to take CLEP examination(s) or to submit your CLEP score(s).

You may want to wait to take your CLEP examinations until you know definitely which college you will be attending. Then you can make sure you are taking tests your college will accept for credit. You will also be able to request that your scores be sent to the college, free of charge, when you take the tests.

If you have already taken CLEP examinations, but did not have a copy of your score report sent to your college, you may request the College Board to send an official transcript at any time for a small fee. Use the Transcript Request Form that was sent to you with your score report. If you do not have the form, you may find it online at www.collegeboard.com/clep.

Your CLEP scores will be evaluated, probably by someone in the admissions office, and sent to the registrar's office to be posted on your permanent record once you are enrolled. Procedures vary from college to college, but the process usually begins in the admissions office.

STEP 6. Ask to receive a written notice of the credit you receive for your CLEP score(s).

A written notice may save you problems later, when you submit your degree plan or file for graduation. In the event that there is a question about whether or not you earned CLEP credit, you will have an official record of what credit was awarded. You may also need this verification of course credit if you go for academic counseling before the credit is posted on your permanent record.

STEP 7. Before you register for courses, seek academic counseling.

A discussion with your academic advisor can prevent you from taking unnecessary courses and can tell you specifically what your CLEP credit will mean to you. This step may be accomplished at the time you enroll. Most colleges have orientation sessions for new students prior to each enrollment period. During orientation, students are usually assigned an academic advisor who then gives them individual help in developing long-range plans and a course schedule for the next semester. In conjunction with this counseling, you may be asked to take some additional tests so that you can be placed at the proper course level.

External Degree Programs

If you have acquired a considerable amount of college-level knowledge through job experience, reading, or noncredit courses, if you have accumulated college credits at a variety of colleges over a period of years, or if you prefer studying on your own rather than in a classroom setting, you may want to investigate the possibility of enrolling in an external degree program. Many colleges offer external degree programs that allow you to earn a degree by passing examinations (including CLEP), transferring credit from other colleges, and demonstrating in other ways that you have satisfied the educational requirements. No classroom attendance is required, and the programs are open to out-of-state candidates as well as residents. Thomas A. Edison State College in New Jersey and Charter Oaks College in Connecticut are fully accredited independent state colleges; the New York program is part of the state university system and is also fully accredited. If you are interested in exploring an external degree, you can write for more information to:

Charter Oak College
The Exchange, Suite 171
270 Farmington Avenue
Farmington, CT 06032-1909

Regents External Degree Program
Cultural Education Center
Empire State Plaza
Albany, New York 12230

Thomas A. Edison State College
101 West State Street
Trenton, New Jersey 08608

Many other colleges also have external degree or weekend programs. While they often require that a number of courses be taken on campus, the external degree programs tend to be more flexible in transferring credit, granting credit-by-examination, and allowing independent study than other traditional programs. When applying to a college, you may wish to ask whether it has an external degree or weekend program.

Questions to Ask About a College's CLEP Policy

Before taking CLEP examinations for the purpose of earning college credit, try to find the answers to these questions:

1. Which CLEP examinations are accepted by this college?

A college may accept some CLEP examinations for credit and not others - possibly not the one you are considering. The English faculty may decide to grant college English credit based on the CLEP English Composition examination, but not on the Freshman College Composition examination. Or, the mathematics faculty may decide to grant credit based on the College Mathematics to non-mathematics majors only, requiring majors to take an examination in algebra, trigonometry, or calculus to earn credit. For these reasons, it is important that you know the specific CLEP tests for which you can receive credit.

2. Does the college require the optional free-response (essay) section as well as the objective portion of the CLEP examination you are considering?

Knowing the answer to this question ahead of time will permit you to schedule the optional essay examination when you register to take your CLEP examination.

3. Is credit granted for specific courses? If so, which ones?

You are likely to find that credit will be granted for specific courses and the course titles will be designated in the college's CLEP policy. It is not necessary, however, that credit be granted for a specific course in order for you to benefit from your CLEP credit. For instance, at many liberal arts colleges, all students must take certain types of courses; these courses may be labeled the core curriculum, general education requirements, distribution requirements, or liberal arts requirements. The requirements are often expressed in terms of credit hours. For example, all students may be required to take at least six hours of humanities, six hours of English, three hours of mathematics, six hours of natural science, and six hours of social science, with no particular courses in these disciplines specified. In these instances, CLEP credit may be given as 6 hrs. English credit or 3 hrs. Math credit without specifying for which English or mathematics courses credit has been awarded. In order to avoid possible disappointment, you should know before taking a CLEP examination what type of credit you can receive and whether you will only be exempted from a required course but receive no credit.

4. How much credit is granted for each examination you are considering, and does the college place a limit on the total amount of CLEP credit you can earn toward your degree?

Not all colleges that grant CLEP credit award the same amount for individual tests. Furthermore, some colleges place a limit on the total amount of credit you can earn through CLEP or other examinations. Other colleges may grant you exemption but no credit toward your degree. Knowing several colleges' policies concerning these issues may help you decide which college you will attend. If you think you are capable of passing a number of CLEP examinations, you may want to attend a college that will allow you to earn credit for all or most of them. For example, the state external degree programs grant credit for most CLEP examinations (and other tests as well).

5. What is the required score for earning CLEP credit for each test you are considering?

Most colleges publish the required scores or percentile ranks for earning CLEP credit in their general catalog or in a brochure. The required score may vary from test to test, so find out the required score for each test you are considering.

6. What is the college's policy regarding prior course work in the subject in which you are considering taking a CLEP test?

Some colleges will not grant credit for a CLEP test if the student has already attempted a college-level course closely aligned with that test. For example, if you successfully completed English 101 or a comparable course on another campus, you will probably not be permitted to receive CLEP credit in that subject, too. Some colleges will not permit you to earn CLEP credit for a course that you failed.

7. Does the college make additional stipulations before credit will be granted?

It is common practice for colleges to award CLEP credit only to their enrolled students. There are other stipulations, however, that vary from college to college. For example, does the college require you to formally apply for or accept CLEP credit by completing and signing a form? Or does the college require you to validate your CLEP score by successfully completing a more advanced course in the subject? Answers to these and other questions will help to smooth the process of earning college credit through CLEP.

The above questions and the discussions that follow them indicate some of the ways in which colleges' CLEP policies can vary. Find out as much as possible about the CLEP policies at the colleges you are interested in so you can choose a college with a policy that is compatible with your educational goals. Once you have selected the college you will attend, you can find out which CLEP examinations your college recognizes and the requirements for earning CLEP credit.

DECIDING WHICH EXAMINATIONS TO TAKE

If You're Taking the Examinations for College Credit or Career Advancement:

Most people who take CLEP examinations do so in order to earn credit for college courses. Others take the examinations in order to qualify for job promotions or for professional certification or licensing. It is vital to most candidates who are taking the tests for any of these reasons that they be well prepared for the tests they are taking so that they can advance as rapidly as possible toward their educational or career goals.

It is usually advisable that those who have limited knowledge in the subjects covered by the tests they are considering enroll in the college courses in which that material is taught. Those who are uncertain about whether or not they know enough about a subject to do well on a particular CLEP test will find the following guidelines helpful.

There is no way to predict if you will pass a particular CLEP examination, but answers to the questions under the seven headings below should give you an indication of whether or not you are likely to succeed.

1. Test Descriptions

Read the description of the test provided. Are you familiar with most of the topics and terminology in the outline?

2. Textbooks

Examine the suggested textbooks and other resource materials following the test descriptions in this guide. Have you recently read one or more of these books, or have you read similar college-level books on this subject? If you have not, read through one or more of the textbooks listed, or through the textbook used for this course at your college. Are you familiar with most of the topics and terminology in the book?

3. Sample Questions

The sample questions provided are intended to be typical of the content and difficulty of the questions on the test. Although they are not an exact miniature of the test, the proportion of the sample questions you can answer correctly should be a rough estimate of the proportion of questions you will be able to answer correctly on the test.

Answer as many of the sample questions for this test as you can. Check your answers against the correct answers. Did you answer more than half the questions correctly?

Because of variations in course content at different institutions, and because questions on CLEP tests vary from easy to difficult - with most being of moderate difficulty - the average student who passes a course in a subject can usually answer correctly about half the questions on the corresponding CLEP examination. Most colleges set their passing scores near this level, but some set them higher. If your college has set its required score above the level required by most colleges, you may need to answer a larger proportion of questions on the test correctly.

4. Previous Study

Have you taken noncredit courses in this subject offered by an adult school or a private school, through correspondence, or in connection with your job? Did you do exceptionally well in this subject in high school, or did you take an honors course in this subject?

5. Experience

Have you learned or used the knowledge or skills included in this test in your job or life experience? For example, if you lived in a Spanish-speaking country and spoke the language for a year or more, you might consider taking the Spanish examination. Or, if you have worked at a job in which you used accounting and finance skills, Principles of Accounting would be a likely test for you to take. Or, if you have read a considerable amount of literature and attended many art exhibits, concerts, and plays, you might expect to do well on the Humanities exam.

6. Other Examinations

Have you done well on other standardized tests in subjects related to the one you want to take? For example, did you score well above average on a portion of a college entrance examination covering similar skills, or did you obtain an exceptionally high score on a high school equivalency test or a licensing examination in this subject? Although such tests do not cover exactly the same material as the CLEP examinations and may be easier, persons who do well on these tests often do well on CLEP examinations, too.

7. Advice

Has a college counselor, professor, or some other professional person familiar with your ability advised you to take a CLEP examination?

If your answer was yes to questions under several of the above headings, you probably have a good chance of passing the CLEP examination you are considering. It is unlikely that you would have acquired sufficient background from experience alone. Learning gained through reading and study is essential, and you will probably find some additional study helpful before taking a CLEP examination.

If You're Taking the Examinations to Prepare for College

Many people entering college, particularly adults returning to college after several years away from formal education, are uncertain about their ability to compete with other college students. They wonder whether they have sufficient background for college study, and those who have been away from formal study for some time wonder whether they have forgotten how to study, how to take tests, and how to write papers. Such people may wish to improve their test-taking and study skills prior to enrolling in courses.

One way to assess your ability to perform at the college level and to improve your test-taking and study skills at the same time is to prepare for and take one or more CLEP examinations. You need not be enrolled in a college to take a CLEP examination, and you may have your scores sent only to yourself and later request that a transcript be sent to a college if you then decide to apply for credit. By reviewing the test descriptions and sample questions, you may find one or several subject areas in which you think you have substantial knowledge. Select one examination, or more if you like, and carefully read at least one of the textbooks listed in the bibliography for the test. By doing this, you will get a better idea of how much you know of what is usually taught in a college-level course in that subject. Study as much material as you can, until you think you have a good grasp of the subject matter. Then take the test at a college in your area. It will be several weeks before you receive your results, and you may wish to begin reviewing for another test in the meantime.

To find out if you are eligible for credit for your CLEP score, you must compare your score with the score required by the college you plan to attend. If you are not yet sure which college you will attend, or whether you will enroll in college at all, you should begin to follow the steps outlined. It is best that you do this before taking a CLEP test, but if you are taking the test only for the experience and to familiarize yourself with college-level material and requirements, you might take the test before you approach a college. Even if the college you decide to attend does not accept the test you took, the experience of taking such a test will enable you to meet with greater confidence the requirements of courses you will take.

You will find information about how to interpret your scores in WHAT YOUR SCORES MEAN, which you will receive with your score report, and which can also be found online at the CLEP website. Many colleges follow the recommendations of the American Council on Education (ACE) for setting their required scores, so you can use this information as a guide in determining how well you did. The ACE recommendations are included in the booklet.

If you do not do well enough on the test to earn college credit, don't be discouraged. Usually, it is the best college students who are exempted from courses or receive credit-by-examination. The fact that you cannot get credit for your score means that you should probably enroll in a college course to learn the material. However, if your score was close to the required score, or if you feel you could do better on a second try or after some additional study, you may retake the test after six months. Do not take it sooner or your score will not be reported and your fee will be forfeited.

If you do earn the score required to earn credit, you will have demonstrated that you already have some college-level knowledge. You will also have a better idea whether you should take additional CLEP examinations. And, what is most important, you can enroll in college with confidence, knowing that you do have the ability to succeed.

PREPARING TO TAKE CLEP EXAMINATIONS

Having made the decision to take one or more CLEP examinations, most people then want to know if it is worthwhile to prepare for them - how much, how long, when, and how should they go about it? The precise answers to these questions vary greatly from individual to individual. However, most candidates find that some type of test preparation is helpful.

Most people who take CLEP examinations do so to show that they have already learned the important material that is taught in a college course. Many of them need only a quick review to assure themselves that they have not forgotten some of what they once studied, and to fill in some of the gaps in their knowledge of the subject. Others feel that they need a thorough review and spend several weeks studying for a test. A few wish to take a CLEP examination as a kind of final examination for independent study of a subject instead of the college course. This last group requires significantly more study than those who only need to review, and they may need some guidance from professors of the subjects they are studying.

The key to how you prepare for CLEP examinations often lies in locating those skills and areas of prior learning in which you are strong and deciding where to focus your energies. Some people may know a great deal about a certain subject area, but may not test well. These individuals would probably be just as concerned about strengthening their test-taking skills as they are about studying for a specific test. Many mental and physical skills are used in preparing for a test. It is important not only to review or study for the examinations, but to make certain that you are alert, relatively free of anxiety, and aware of how to approach standardized tests. Suggestions on developing test-taking skills and preparing psychologically and physically for a test are given. The following section suggests ways of assessing your knowledge of the content of a test and then reviewing and studying the material.

Using This Study Guide

Begin by carefully reading the test description and outline of knowledge and skills required for the examination, if given. As you read through the topics listed there, ask yourself how much you know about each one. Also note the terms, names, and symbols that are mentioned, and ask yourself whether you are familiar with them. This will give you a quick overview of how much you know about the subject. If you are familiar with nearly all the material, you will probably need a minimum of review; however, if less than half of it is familiar, you will probably require substantial study to do well on the test.

If, after reviewing the test description, you find that you need extensive review, delay answering the sample question until you have done some reading in the subject. If you complete them before reviewing the material, you will probably look for the answers as you study, and then they will not be a good assessment of your ability at a later date.

If you think you are familiar with most of the test material, try to answer the sample questions.

Apply the test-taking strategies given. Keeping within the time limit suggested will give you a rough idea of how quickly you should work in order to complete the actual test.

Check your answers against the answer key. If you answered nearly all the questions correctly, you probably do not need to study the subject extensively. If you got about half the questions correct, you ought o review at least one textbook or other suggested materials on the subject. If you answered less than half the questions correctly, you will probably benefit from more extensive reading in the subject and thorough study of one or more textbooks. The textbooks listed are used at many colleges but they are not the only good texts. You will find helpful almost any standard text available to you., such as the textbook used at your college, or earlier editions of texts listed. For some examinations, topic outlines and textbooks may not be available. Take the sample tests in this book and check your answers at the end of each test. Check wrong answers.

Suggestions for Studying

The following suggestions have been gathered from people who have prepared for CLEP examinations or other college-level tests.

1. Define your goals and locate study materials

First, determine your study goals. Set aside a block of time to review the material provided in this book, and then decide which test(s) you will take. Using the suggestions, locate suitable resource materials. If a preparation course is offered by an adult school or college in your area, you might find it helpful to enroll.

2. Find a good place to study

To determine what kind of place you need for studying, ask yourself questions such as: Do I need a quiet place? Does the telephone distract me? Do objects I see in this place remind me of things I should do? Is it too warm? Is it well lit? Am I too comfortable here? Do I have space to spread out my materials? You may find the library more conducive to studying than your home. If you decide to study at home, you might prevent interruptions by other household members by putting a sign on the door of your study room to indicate when you will be available.

3. Schedule time to study

To help you determine where studying best fits into your schedule, try this exercise: Make a list of your daily activities (for example, sleeping, working, and eating) and estimate how many hours per day you spend on each activity. Now, rate all the activities on your list in order of their importance and evaluate your use of time. Often people are astonished at how an average day appears from this perspective. They may discover that they were unaware how large portions of time are spent, or they learn their time can be scheduled in alternative ways. For example, they can remove the least important activities from their day and devote that time to studying or another important activity.

4. Establish a study routine and a set of goals

In order to study effectively, you should establish specific goals and a schedule for accomplishing them. Some people find it helpful to write out a weekly schedule and cross out each study period when it is completed. Others maintain their concentration better by writing down the time when they expect to complete a study task. Most people find short periods of intense study more productive than long stretches of time. For example, they may follow a regular schedule of several 20- or 30-minute study periods with short breaks between them. Some people like to allow themselves rewards as they complete each study goal. It is not essential that you accomplish every goal exactly within your schedule; the point is to be committed to your task.

5. Learn how to take an active role in studying.

If you have not done much studying for some time, you may find it difficult to concentrate at first. Try a method of studying, such as the one outlined below, that will help you concentrate on and remember what you read.

    a. First, read the chapter summary and the introduction. Then you will know what to look for in your reading.

    b. Next, convert the section or paragraph headlines into questions. For example, if you are reading a section entitled, The Causes of the American Revolution, ask yourself: *What were the causes of the American Revolution?* Compose the answer as you read the paragraph. Reading and answering questions aloud will help you understand and remember the material.

c. Take notes on key ideas or concepts as you read. Writing will also help you fix concepts more firmly in your mind. Underlining key ideas or writing notes in your book can be helpful and will be useful for review. Underline only important points. If you underline more than a third of each paragraph, you are probably underlining too much.

d. If there are questions or problems at the end of a chapter, answer or solve them on paper as if you were asked to do them for homework. Mathematics textbooks (and some other books) sometimes include answers to some or all of the exercises. If you have such a book, write your answers before looking at the ones given. When problem-solving is involved, work enough problems to master the required methods and concepts. If you have difficulty with problems, review any sample problems or explanations in the chapter.

e. To retain knowledge, most people have to review the material periodically. If you are preparing for a test over an extended period of time, review key concepts and notes each week or so. Do not wait for weeks to review the material or you will need to relearn much of it.

Psychological and Physical Preparation

Most people feel at least some nervousness before taking a test. Adults who are returning to college may not have taken a test in many years or they may have had little experience with standardized tests. Some younger students, as well, are uncomfortable with testing situations. People who received their education in countries outside the United States may find that many tests given in this country are quite different from the ones they are accustomed to taking.

Not only might candidates find the types of tests and the kinds of questions on them unfamiliar, but other aspects of the testing environment may be strange as well. The physical and mental stress that results from meeting this new experience can hinder a candidate's ability to demonstrate his or her true degree of knowledge in the subject area being tested. For this reason, it is important to go to the test center well prepared, both mentally and physically, for taking the test. You may find the following suggestions helpful.

1. Familiarize yourself, as much as possible, with the test and the test situation before the day of the examination. It will be helpful for you to know ahead of time:

a. How much time will be allowed for the test and whether there are timed subsections.

b. What types of questions and directions appear on the examination.

c. How your test score will be computed.

d. How to properly answer the questions on the computer (See the CLEP Sample on the CLEP website)

e. In which building and room the examination will be administered. If you don't know where the building is, locate it or get directions ahead of time.

f. The time of the test administration. You might wish to confirm this information a day or two before the examination and find out what time the building and room will be open so that you can plan to arrive early.

g. Where to park your car or, if you wish to take public transportation, which bus or train to take and the location of the nearest stop.

h. Whether smoking will be permitted during the test.

i. Whether there will be a break between examinations (if you will be taking more than one on the same day), and whether there is a place nearby where you can get something to eat or drink.

2. Go to the test situation relaxed and alert. In order to prepare for the test:

a. Get a good night's sleep. Last minute cramming, particularly late the night before, is usually counterproductive.

b. Eat normally. It is usually not wise to skip breakfast or lunch on the day of the test or to eat a big meal just before the test.

c. Avoid tranquilizers and stimulants. If you follow the other directions in this book, you won't need artificial aids. It's better to be a little tense than to be drowsy, but stimulants such as coffee and cola can make you nervous and interfere with your concentration.

d. Don't drink a lot of liquids before the test. Having to leave the room during the test will disturb your concentration and take valuable time away from the test.

e. If you are inclined to be nervous or tense, learn some relaxation exercises and use them before and perhaps during the test.

3. Arrive for the test early and prepared. Be sure to:

a. Arrive early enough so that you can find a parking place, locate the test center, and get settled comfortably before testing begins. Allow some extra time in case you are delayed unexpectedly.

b. Take the following with you:

- Your completed Registration/Admission Form
- Two forms of identification – one being a government-issued photo ID with signature, such as a driver's license or passport
- Non-mechanical pencil
- A watch so that you can time your progress (digital watches are prohibited)
- Your glasses if you need them for reading or seeing the chalkboard or wall clock

c. Leave all books, papers, and notes outside the test center. You will not be permitted to use your own scratch paper; it will be provided. Also prohibited are calculators, cell phones, beepers, pagers, photo/copy devices, radios, headphones, food, beverages, and several other items.

d. Be prepared for any temperature in the testing room. Wear layers of clothing that can be removed if the room is too hot but will keep you warm if it is too cold.

4. When you enter the test room:

a. Sit in a seat that provides a maximum of comfort and freedom from distraction.

b. Read directions carefully, and listen to all instructions given by the test administrator. If you don't understand the directions, ask for help before test timing begins. If you must ask a question after the test has begun, raise your hand and a proctor will assist you. The proctor can answer certain kinds of questions but cannot help you with the test.

c. Know your rights as a test taker. You can expect to be given the full working time allowed for the test(s) and a reasonably quiet and comfortable place in which to work. If a poor test situation is preventing you from doing your best, ask if the situation can be remedied. If bad test conditions cannot be remedied, ask the person in charge to report the problem in the Irregularity Report that will be sent to ETS with the answer sheets. You may also wish to contact CLEP. Describe the exact circumstances as completely as you can. Be sure to include the test date and name(s) of the test(s) you took. ETS will investigate the problem to make sure it does not happen again, and, if the problem is serious enough, may arrange for you to retake the test without charge.

TAKING THE EXAMINATIONS

A person may know a great deal about the subject being tested, but not do as well as he or she is capable of on the test. Knowing how to approach a test is an important part of the testing process. While a command of test-taking skills cannot substitute for knowledge of the subject matter, it can be a significant factor in successful testing.

Test-taking skills enable a person to use all available information to earn a score that truly reflects his or her ability. There are different strategies for approaching different kinds of test questions. For example, free-response questions require a very different tack than do multiple-choice questions. Other factors, such as how the test will be graded, may also influence your approach to the test and your use of test time. Thus, your preparation for a test should include finding out all you can about the test so that you can use the most effective test-taking strategies.

Before taking a test, you should know approximately how many questions are on the test, how much time you will be allowed, how the test will be scored or graded, what types of questions and directions are on the test, and how you will be required to record your answers.

Taking Multiple-Choice Tests

1. Listen carefully to the instructions given by the test administrator and read carefully all directions before you begin to answer the questions.

2. Note the time that the test administrator starts timing the test. As you proceed, make sure that you are not working too slowly. You should have answered at least half the questions in a section when half the time for that section has passed. If you have not reached that point in the section, speed up your pace on the remaining questions.

3. Before answering a question, read the entire question, including all the answer choices. Don't think that because the first or second answer choice looks good to you, it isn't necessary to read the remaining options. Instructions usually tell you to select the best answer. Sometimes one answer choice is partially correct, but another option is better; therefore, it is usually a good idea to read all the answers before you choose one.

4. Read and consider every question. Questions that look complicated at first glance may not actually be so difficult once you have read them carefully.

5. Do not puzzle too long over any one question. If you don't know the answer after you've considered it briefly, go on to the next question. Make sure you return to the question later.

6. Make sure you record your response properly.

7. In trying to determine the correct answer, you may find it helpful to cross out those options that you know are incorrect, and to make marks next to those you think might be correct. If you decide to skip the question and come back to it later, you will save yourself the time of reconsidering all the options.

8. Watch for the following key words in test questions:

all	generally	never	perhaps
always	however	none	rarely
but	may	not	seldom
except	must	often	sometimes
every	necessary	only	usually

When a question or answer option contains words such as always, every, only, never, and none, there can be no exceptions to the answer you choose. Use of words such as often, rarely, sometimes, and generally indicates that there may be some exceptions to the answer.

9. Do not waste your time looking for clues to right answers based on flaws in question wording or patterns in correct answers. Professionals at the College Board and ETS put

a great deal of effort into developing valid, reliable, fair tests. CLEP test development committees are composed of college faculty who are experts in the subject covered by the test and are appointed by the College Board to write test questions and to scrutinize each question that is included on a CLEP test. Committee members make every effort to ensure that the questions are not ambiguous, that they have only one correct answer, and that they cover college-level topics. These committees do not intentionally include trick questions. If you think a question is flawed, ask the test administrator to report it, or contact CLEP immediately.

Taking Free-Response or Essay Tests

If your college requires the optional free-response or essay portion of a CLEP Composition and Literature exams, you should do some additional preparation for your CLEP test. Taking an essay test is very different from taking a multiple-choice test, so you will need to use some other strategies.

The essay written as part of the English Composition and Essay exam is graded by English professors from a variety of colleges and universities. A process called holistic scoring is used to rate your writing ability.

The optional free-response essays, on the other hand, are graded by the faculty of the college you designate as a score recipient. Guidelines and criteria for grading essays are not specified by the College Board or ETS. You may find it helpful, therefore, to talk with someone at your college to find out what criteria will be used to determine whether you will get credit. If the test requires essay responses, ask how much emphasis will be placed on your writing ability and your ability to organize your thoughts as opposed to your knowledge of subject matter. Find out how much weight will be given to your multiple-choice test score in comparison with your free-response grade in determining whether you will get credit. This will give you an idea where you should expend the greatest effort in preparing for and taking the test.

Here are some strategies you will find useful in taking any essay test:

1. Before you begin to write, read all questions carefully and take a few minutes to jot down some ideas you might include in each answer.

2. If you are given a choice of questions to answer, choose the questions you think you can answer most clearly and knowledgeably.

3. Determine in what order you will answer the questions. Answer those you find the easiest first so that any extra time can be spent on the more difficult questions.

4. When you know which questions you will answer and in what order, determine how much testing time remains and estimate how many minutes you will devote to each question. Unless suggested times are given for the questions or one question appears to require more or less time than the others, allot an equal amount of time to each question.

5. Before answering each question, indicate the number of the question as it is given in the test book. You need not copy the entire question from the question sheet, but it will be helpful to you and to the person grading your test if you indicate briefly the topic you are addressing – particularly if you are not answering the questions in the order in which they appear on the test.

6. Before answering each question, read it again carefully to make sure you are interpreting it correctly. Underline key words, such as those listed below, that often appear in free-response questions. Be sure you know the exact meaning of these words before taking the test.

analyze	demonstrate	enumerate	list
apply	derive	explain	outline
assess	describe	generalize	prove
compare	determine	illustrate	rank
contrast	discuss	interpret	show
define	distinguish	justify	summarize

If a question asks you to outline, define, or summarize, do not write a detailed explanation; if a question asks you to analyze, explain, illustrate, interpret, or show, you must do more than briefly describe the topic.

For a current listing of CLEP Colleges

where you can get credit and be tested, write:

CLEP, P.O. Box 6600, Princeton, NJ 08541-6600

Or e-mail: clep@ets.org, or call: (609) 771-7865

ENGLISH LITERATURE

Description of the Examination

The English Literature examination covers material usually taught in a two-semester course (or the equivalent) at the college level. The test is primarily concerned with major authors and literary works, but it also includes questions on some minor writers. Candidates are expected to be acquainted with common literary terms, such as metaphor and personification, and basic literary forms, such as the sonnet and the ballad.

In both coverage and approach, the examination resembles the historically organized survey of English literature offered by many colleges. It assumes that candidates have read widely and developed an appreciation of English literature, know the basic literary periods, and have a sense of the historical development of English literature.

The examination contains approximately 95 questions to be answered in 90 minutes. Any time candidates spend on tutorials and providing personal information is in addition to the actual testing time.

The CLEP English Literature exam also includes an optional essay section. Some schools require candidates to complete this section. Candidates should check with the school(s) of their choice to confirm whether the essay is required. This optional section requires candidates to demonstrate their ability to write clearly and effectively. Candidates respond to two of three essay topics. An essay on the first topic, a persuasive analysis of a poem, is required, and candidates are advised to spend 35 to 40 minutes on it. For the second essay, candidates choose one of two topics that presents a specific observation, position, or theme. Depending on the topic chosen, candidates choose any work by a particular author to appropriately support the claim or select works from a designated list provided. Candidates should plan to spend 50 to 55 minutes on the essay. All essays are scored by faculty at the school(s) where candidates send their reports.

Knowledge and Skills Required
The English Literature examination measures both knowledge and ability. The percentages below show the relative emphasis given to each; however, most questions draw on both.

35-40%   **Knowledge of:**
- Literary background Identification of authors
- Metrical patterns
- Literary references
- Literary terms

60-65%   **Ability to:**
- Analyze the elements of form in a literary passage
- Perceive meanings Identify tone and mood
- Follow patterns of imagery Identify characteristics of style
- Comprehend the reasoning in an excerpt of literary criticism

The examination deals with literature from Beowulf to the present. Familiarity with and understanding of major writers is expected, as is knowledge of literary periods and common literary terms, themes, and forms. Some of the questions on the examination ask candidates to identify the author of a representative quotation or to recognize the period in which an excerpt was written.

HOW TO TAKE A TEST

You have studied long, hard and conscientiously.

With your official admission card in hand, and your heart pounding, you have been admitted to the examination room.

You note that there are several hundred other applicants in the examination room waiting to take the same test.

They all appear to be equally well prepared.

You know that nothing but your best effort will suffice. The "moment of truth" is at hand: you now have to demonstrate objectively, in writing, your knowledge of content and your understanding of subject matter.

You are fighting the most important battle of your life—to pass and/or score high on an examination which will determine your career and provide the economic basis for your livelihood.

What extra, special things should you know and should you do in taking the examination?

I. YOU MUST PASS AN EXAMINATION

A. WHAT EVERY CANDIDATE SHOULD KNOW
Examination applicants often ask us for help in preparing for the written test. What can I study in advance? What kinds of questions will be asked? How will the test be given? How will the papers be graded?

B. HOW ARE EXAMS DEVELOPED?
Examinations are carefully written by trained technicians who are specialists in the field known as "psychological measurement," in consultation with recognized authorities in the field of work that the test will cover. These experts recommend the subject matter areas or skills to be tested; only those knowledges or skills important to your success on the job are included. The most reliable books and source materials available are used as references. Together, the experts and technicians judge the difficulty level of the questions.
Test technicians know how to phrase questions so that the problem is clearly stated. Their ethics do not permit "trick" or "catch" questions. Questions may have been tried out on sample groups, or subjected to statistical analysis, to determine their usefulness.
Written tests are often used in combination with performance tests, ratings of training and experience, and oral interviews. All of these measures combine to form the best-known means of finding the right person for the right job.

II. HOW TO PASS THE WRITTEN TEST

A. BASIC STEPS

1) Study the announcement

How, then, can you know what subjects to study? Our best answer is: "Learn as much as possible about the class of positions for which you've applied." The exam will test the knowledge, skills and abilities needed to do the work.

Your most valuable source of information about the position you want is the official exam announcement. This announcement lists the training and experience qualifications. Check these standards and apply only if you come reasonably close to meeting them. Many jurisdictions preview the written test in the exam announcement by including a section called "Knowledge and Abilities Required," "Scope of the Examination," or some similar heading. Here you will find out specifically what fields will be tested.

2) Choose appropriate study materials

If the position for which you are applying is technical or advanced, you will read more advanced, specialized material. If you are already familiar with the basic principles of your field, elementary textbooks would waste your time. Concentrate on advanced textbooks and technical periodicals. Think through the concepts and review difficult problems in your field.

These are all general sources. You can get more ideas on your own initiative, following these leads. For example, training manuals and publications of the government agency which employs workers in your field can be useful, particularly for technical and professional positions. A letter or visit to the government department involved may result in more specific study suggestions, and certainly will provide you with a more definite idea of the exact nature of the position you are seeking.

3) Study this book!

III. KINDS OF TESTS

Tests are used for purposes other than measuring knowledge and ability to perform specified duties. For some positions, it is equally important to test ability to make adjustments to new situations or to profit from training. In others, basic mental abilities not dependent on information are essential. Questions which test these things may not appear as pertinent to the duties of the position as those which test for knowledge and information. Yet they are often highly important parts of a fair examination. For very general questions, it is almost impossible to help you direct your study efforts. What we can do is to point out some of the more common of these general abilities needed in public service positions and describe some typical questions.

1) General information

Broad, general information has been found useful for predicting job success in some kinds of work. This is tested in a variety of ways, from vocabulary lists to questions about current events. Basic background in some field of work, such as sociology or economics, may be sampled in a group of questions. Often these are principles which have become familiar to most persons through exposure rather than through formal training. It is difficult to advise you how to study for these questions; being alert to the world around you is our best suggestion.

2) Verbal ability
An example of an ability needed in many positions is verbal or language ability. Verbal ability is, in brief, the ability to use and understand words. Vocabulary and grammar tests are typical measures of this ability. Reading comprehension or paragraph interpretation questions are common in many kinds of civil service tests. You are given a paragraph of written material and asked to find its central meaning.

IV. KINDS OF QUESTIONS

1. Multiple-choice Questions
Most popular of the short-answer questions is the "multiple choice" or "best answer" question. It can be used, for example, to test for factual knowledge, ability to solve problems or judgment in meeting situations found at work.
A multiple-choice question is normally one of three types:
- It can begin with an incomplete statement followed by several possible endings. You are to find the one ending which best completes the statement, although some of the others may not be entirely wrong.
- It can also be a complete statement in the form of a question which is answered by choosing one of the statements listed.
- It can be in the form of a problem – again you select the best answer.

Here is an example of a multiple-choice question with a discussion which should give you some clues as to the method for choosing the right answer:

When an employee has a complaint about his assignment, the action which will best help him overcome his difficulty is to
- A. discuss his difficulty with his coworkers
- B. take the problem to the head of the organization
- C. take the problem to the person who gave him the assignment
- D. say nothing to anyone about his complaint

In answering this question, you should study each of the choices to find which is best. Consider choice "A" – Certainly an employee may discuss his complaint with fellow employees, but no change or improvement can result, and the complaint remains unresolved. Choice "B" is a poor choice since the head of the organization probably does not know what assignment you have been given, and taking your problem to him is known as "going over the head" of the supervisor. The supervisor, or person who made the assignment, is the person who can clarify it or correct any injustice. Choice "C" is, therefore, correct. To say nothing, as in choice "D," is unwise. Supervisors have and interest in knowing the problems employees are facing, and the employee is seeking a solution to his problem.

2. True/False

3. Matching Questions
Matching an answer from a column of choices within another column.

V. RECORDING YOUR ANSWERS

Computer terminals are used more and more today for many different kinds of exams.

For an examination with very few applicants, you may be told to record your answers in the test booklet itself. Separate answer sheets are much more common. If this separate answer sheet is to be scored by machine – and this is often the case – it is highly important that you mark your answers correctly in order to get credit.

VI. BEFORE THE TEST

YOUR PHYSICAL CONDITION IS IMPORTANT

If you are not well, you can't do your best work on tests. If you are half asleep, you can't do your best either. Here are some tips:

1) Get about the same amount of sleep you usually get. Don't stay up all night before the test, either partying or worrying—DON'T DO IT!
2) If you wear glasses, be sure to wear them when you go to take the test. This goes for hearing aids, too.
3) If you have any physical problems that may keep you from doing your best, be sure to tell the person giving the test. If you are sick or in poor health, you relay cannot do your best on any test. You can always come back and take the test some other time.

Common sense will help you find procedures to follow to get ready for an examination. Too many of us, however, overlook these sensible measures. Indeed, nervousness and fatigue have been found to be the most serious reasons why applicants fail to do their best on civil service tests. Here is a list of reminders:

- Begin your preparation early – Don't wait until the last minute to go scurrying around for books and materials or to find out what the position is all about.
- Prepare continuously – An hour a night for a week is better than an all-night cram session. This has been definitely established. What is more, a night a week for a month will return better dividends than crowding your study into a shorter period of time.
- Locate the place of the exam – You have been sent a notice telling you when and where to report for the examination. If the location is in a different town or otherwise unfamiliar to you, it would be well to inquire the best route and learn something about the building.
- Relax the night before the test – Allow your mind to rest. Do not study at all that night. Plan some mild recreation or diversion; then go to bed early and get a good night's sleep.
- Get up early enough to make a leisurely trip to the place for the test – This way unforeseen events, traffic snarls, unfamiliar buildings, etc. will not upset you.
- Dress comfortably – A written test is not a fashion show. You will be known by number and not by name, so wear something comfortable.
- Leave excess paraphernalia at home – Shopping bags and odd bundles will get in your way. You need bring only the items mentioned in the official notice you received; usually everything you need is provided. Do not bring reference books to the exam. They will only confuse those last minutes and be taken away from you when in the test room.

- Arrive somewhat ahead of time – If because of transportation schedules you must get there very early, bring a newspaper or magazine to take your mind off yourself while waiting.
- Locate the examination room – When you have found the proper room, you will be directed to the seat or part of the room where you will sit. Sometimes you are given a sheet of instructions to read while you are waiting. Do not fill out any forms until you are told to do so; just read them and be prepared.
- Relax and prepare to listen to the instructions
- If you have any physical problem that may keep you from doing your best, be sure to tell the test administrator. If you are sick or in poor health, you really cannot do your best on the exam. You can come back and take the test some other time.

VII. AT THE TEST

The day of the test is here and you have the test booklet in your hand. The temptation to get going is very strong. Caution! There is more to success than knowing the right answers. You must know how to identify your papers and understand variations in the type of short-answer question used in this particular examination. Follow these suggestions for maximum results from your efforts:

1) Cooperate with the monitor

The test administrator has a duty to create a situation in which you can be as much at ease as possible. He will give instructions, tell you when to begin, check to see that you are marking your answer sheet correctly, and so on. He is not there to guard you, although he will see that your competitors do not take unfair advantage. He wants to help you do your best.

2) Listen to all instructions

Don't jump the gun! Wait until you understand all directions. In most civil service tests you get more time than you need to answer the questions. So don't be in a hurry. Read each word of instructions until you clearly understand the meaning. Study the examples, listen to all announcements and follow directions. Ask questions if you do not understand what to do.

3) Identify your papers

Civil service exams are usually identified by number only. You will be assigned a number; you must not put your name on your test papers. Be sure to copy your number correctly. Since more than one exam may be given, copy your exact examination title.

4) Plan your time

Unless you are told that a test is a "speed" or "rate of work" test, speed itself is usually not important. Time enough to answer all the questions will be provided, but this does not mean that you have all day. An overall time limit has been set. Divide the total time (in minutes) by the number of questions to determine the approximate time you have for each question.

5) Do not linger over difficult questions

If you come across a difficult question, mark it with a paper clip (useful to have along) and come back to it when you have been through the booklet. One caution if you do this – be sure to skip a number on your answer sheet as well. Check often to be sure that you have not lost your place and that you are marking in the row numbered the same as the question you are answering.

6) Read the questions

Be sure you know what the question asks! Many capable people are unsuccessful because they failed to read the questions correctly.

7) Answer all questions

Unless you have been instructed that a penalty will be deducted for incorrect answers, it is better to guess than to omit a question.

8) Speed tests

It is often better NOT to guess on speed tests. It has been found that on timed tests people are tempted to spend the last few seconds before time is called in marking answers at random – without even reading them – in the hope of picking up a few extra points. To discourage this practice, the instructions may warn you that your score will be "corrected" for guessing. That is, a penalty will be applied. The incorrect answers will be deducted from the correct ones, or some other penalty formula will be used.

9) Review your answers

If you finish before time is called, go back to the questions you guessed or omitted to give them further thought. Review other answers if you have time.

10) Return your test materials

If you are ready to leave before others have finished or time is called, take ALL your materials to the monitor and leave quietly. Never take any test material with you. The monitor can discover whose papers are not complete, and taking a test booklet may be grounds for disqualification.

VIII. EXAMINATION TECHNIQUES

1) Read the general instructions carefully. These are usually printed on the first page of the exam booklet. As a rule, these instructions refer to the timing of the examination; the fact that you should not start work until the signal and must stop work at a signal, etc. If there are any special instructions, such as a choice of questions to be answered, make sure that you note this instruction carefully.

2) When you are ready to start work on the examination, that is as soon as the signal has been given, read the instructions to each question booklet, underline any key words or phrases, such as least, best, outline, describe and the like. In this way you will tend to answer as requested rather than discover on reviewing your paper that you listed without describing, that you selected the worst choice rather than the best choice, etc.

3) If the examination is of the objective or multiple-choice type – that is, each question will also give a series of possible answers: A, B, C or D, and you are called upon to select the best answer and write the letter next to that answer on your answer paper – it is advisable to start answering each question in turn. There may be anywhere from 50 to 100 such questions in the three or four hours allotted and you can see how much time would be taken if you read through all the questions before beginning to answer any. Furthermore, if you

come across a question or group of questions which you know would be difficult to answer, it would undoubtedly affect your handling of all the other questions.

4) If the examination is of the essay type and contains but a few questions, it is a moot point as to whether you should read all the questions before starting to answer any one. Of course, if you are given a choice – say five out of seven and the like – then it is essential to read all the questions so you can eliminate the two that are most difficult. If, however, you are asked to answer all the questions, there may be danger in trying to answer the easiest one first because you may find that you will spend too much time on it. The best technique is to answer the first question, then proceed to the second, etc.

5) Time your answers. Before the exam begins, write down the time it started, then add the time allowed for the examination and write down the time it must be completed, then divide the time available somewhat as follows:
    - If 3-1/2 hours are allowed, that would be 210 minutes. If you have 80 objective-type questions, that would be an average of 2-1/2 minutes per question. Allow yourself no more than 2 minutes per question, or a total of 160 minutes, which will permit about 50 minutes to review.
    - If for the time allotment of 210 minutes there are 7 essay questions to answer, that would average about 30 minutes a question. Give yourself only 25 minutes per question so that you have about 35 minutes to review.

6) The most important instruction is to read each question and make sure you know what is wanted. The second most important instruction is to time yourself properly so that you answer every question. The third most important instruction is to answer every question. Guess if you have to but include something for each question. Remember that you will receive no credit for a blank and will probably receive some credit if you write something in answer to an essay question. If you guess a letter – say "B" for a multiple-choice question – you may have guessed right. If you leave a blank as an answer to a multiple-choice question, the examiners may respect your feelings but it will not add a point to your score. Some exams may penalize you for wrong answers, so in such cases only, you may not want to guess unless you have some basis for your answer.

7) Suggestions
    a. Objective-type questions
        1. Examine the question booklet for proper sequence of pages and questions
        2. Read all instructions carefully
        3. Skip any question which seems too difficult; return to it after all other questions have been answered
        4. Apportion your time properly; do not spend too much time on any single question or group of questions
        5. Note and underline key words – all, most, fewest, least, best, worst, same, opposite, etc.
        6. Pay particular attention to negatives
        7. Note unusual option, e.g., unduly long, short, complex, different or similar in content to the body of the question
        8. Observe the use of "hedging" words – probably, may, most likely, etc.

9. Make sure that your answer is put next to the same number as the question
10. Do not second-guess unless you have good reason to believe the second answer is definitely more correct
11. Cross out original answer if you decide another answer is more accurate; do not erase until you are ready to hand your paper in
12. Answer all questions; guess unless instructed otherwise
13. Leave time for review

b. Essay questions
1. Read each question carefully
2. Determine exactly what is wanted. Underline key words or phrases.
3. Decide on outline or paragraph answer
4. Include many different points and elements unless asked to develop any one or two points or elements
5. Show impartiality by giving pros and cons unless directed to select one side only
6. Make and write down any assumptions you find necessary to answer the questions
7. Watch your English, grammar, punctuation and choice of words
8. Time your answers; don't crowd material

8) Answering the essay question

Most essay questions can be answered by framing the specific response around several key words or ideas. Here are a few such key words or ideas:

M's: manpower, materials, methods, money, management
P's: purpose, program, policy, plan, procedure, practice, problems, pitfalls, personnel, public relations

a. Six basic steps in handling problems:
1. Preliminary plan and background development
2. Collect information, data and facts
3. Analyze and interpret information, data and facts
4. Analyze and develop solutions as well as make recommendations
5. Prepare report and sell recommendations
6. Install recommendations and follow up effectiveness

b. Pitfalls to avoid
1. Taking things for granted – A statement of the situation does not necessarily imply that each of the elements is necessarily true; for example, a complaint may be invalid and biased so that all that can be taken for granted is that a complaint has been registered
2. Considering only one side of a situation – Wherever possible, indicate several alternatives and then point out the reasons you selected the best one
3. Failing to indicate follow up – Whenever your answer indicates action on your part, make certain that you will take proper follow-up action to see how successful your recommendations, procedures or actions turn out to be
4. Taking too long in answering any single question – Remember to time your answers properly

EXAMINATION SECTION

EXAMINATION SECTION
TEST 1

DIRECTIONS: Each question or incomplete statement is followed by several suggested answers or completions. Select the one that BEST answers the question or completes the statement. *PRINT THE LETTER OF THE CORRECT ANSWER IN THE SPACE AT THE RIGHT.*

1. All public theatres were closed in England from

    A. 1616 - 1632
    B. 1642 - 1660
    C. 1664 - 1680
    D. 1680 - 1684

2.   I. VENUS AND ADONIS
    II. TIMON OF ATHENS
    III. THE RAPE OF LUCRECE
    IV. PERICLES, PRINCE OF TYRE
    Of the above, those that are Shakespeare's non-dramatic works are

    A. I, III   B. II, IV   C. I, II   D. III, IV

3. Samuel Butler's poem, HUDIBRAS, satirizes

    A. Cavaliers
    B. Roman Catholics
    C. Puritans
    D. The Established Church

4. Play and author are correctly paired in all of the following EXCEPT

    A. BUSSY D'AMBOIS - George Chapman
    B. EVERY MAN IN HIS HUMOUR - Ben Jonson
    C. THE SHOEMAKER'S HOLIDAY - Thomas Dekker
    D. THE KNIGHT OF THE BURNING PESTLE - John Webster

5.   I. William Shakespeare
    II. Thomas Kyd
    III. John Donne
    IV. Ben Jonson
    Contemporaries among those authors listed above are

    A. none   B. II, III, IV   C. I, II   D. all

6.   I. It espouses the idea of sacrificing the individual for the common good.
    II. It was originally written in English.
    III. It contains a number of animadversions.
    IV. It introduces actual persons, including the author.
    Of the above statements, those which are generally regarded as CORRECT with regard to Thomas More's UTOPIA are

    A. II, III, IV   B. I, III, IV   C. I, II, III   D. I, II, IV

7. "If thou be'est he - but oh how fallen! how changed From him! - who in the happy realms of light, Clothed with transcendent brightness, did'st outshine Myriads, though bright..."
    In Milton's PARADISE LOST, the above lines are spoken to

    A. Beelzebub by Satan
    B. Satan by Michael
    C. Lucifer by Gabriel
    D. Baal by God

8. Michael Drayton described the geography of England at great length in his poem
   - A. POLYOLBION
   - B. NYMPHIDIA
   - C. MUSOPHILUS
   - D. ARCADIA

9.
   - I. Wyatt
   - II. Drayton
   - III. Surrey
   - IV. Lyly

   Of the poets listed above, those included in TOTTEL'S MISCELLANY were
   - A. I, II
   - B. III, IV
   - C. I, III
   - D. II, III

10. Edmund Spenser attacked some shortcomings of his society in
    - A. AMORETTI
    - B. THE SHEPHERD'S CALENDAR
    - C. VIRGIL'S GNAT
    - D. MOTHER HUBBARD'S TALE

11. All of the following lines by John Milton are correctly paired with the titles of the works in which they appear EXCEPT
    - A. They hand in hand with wandring steps and slow,
      Through Eden took their solitary way - PARADISE LOST
    - B. And calm of mind all passion spent - SAMSON AGONISTES
    - C. Or if Virtue feeble were
      Heav'n itself would stoop to her - PARADISE REGAINED
    - D. At last he rose and twitched his Mantle blue
      Tomorrow to fresh Woods, and Pastures new - COMUS

12.
    - I. Tis with our judgments as our watches, none
      Go just alike, yet each believes his own
    - II. Those Rules of old discovered, not devised
      Are Nature still, but nature methodized
    - III. True wit is Nature to advantage dress'd
      What oft was thought, but ne'er so well express'd
    - IV. Be not the first by whom the new are tried
      Nor yet the last to lay the old aside

    Of the following lines, the ones attributed to the same author are
    - A. I, II, III
    - B. I, III, IV
    - C. II, IV
    - D. I, II, III, IV

13. The lines,

    "He is a portion of the loveliness
    Which once he made more lovely,"

    are from a poem written as a tribute to
    - A. Arthur Hugh Clough
    - B. John Keats
    - C. Percy Bysshe Shelley
    - D. Thomas Chatterton

14. "Timor mortis conturbat me," is the refrain of a poetic lament by
    - A. Geoffrey Chaucer
    - B. William Dunbar
    - C. John Gower
    - D. Robert Henryson

15. Which one of the following literary works is NOT correctly associated with its date?

    A. TOTTEL'S MISCELLANY - 1557
    B. SAMSON AGONISTES - 1642
    C. LYRICAL BALLADS - 1798
    D. POEMS BY TWO BROTHERS - 1827

16. *"I saw Eternity the other night
    Like a great Ring of pure and endless light"*
    These are the opening lines of a poem by

    A. John Donne   B. George Herbert
    C. Thomas Traherne   D. Henry Vaughan

17. What is the CORRECT chronological order of the following plays?
    I. GORBODUC
    II. RALPH ROISTER DOISTER
    III. RICHARD III
    IV. TAMBURLAINE
    The CORRECT answer is:

    A. I, II, III, IV   B. II, I, IV, III   C. III, II, I, IV   D. IV, III, II, I

18. *"What Song the Sirens sang, or what name Achilles assumed when he did himself among women, though puzzling questions, are not beyond all conjecture."*
    The author of this passage is

    A. Sir Thomas Browne   B. John Dryden
    C. John Milton   D. Izaak Walton

19. Which one of the following is NOT correctly associated with its author or authors?

    A. Beaumont and Fletcher - THE MAID'S TRAGEDY
    B. Ben Johnson - PHILASTER
    C. Marlowe and Nash - DIDO, QUEEN OF CARTHAGE
    D. Philip Massinger - A NEW WAY TO PAY OLD DEBTS

20. Which one of the following heroines is NOT correctly associated with the play in which she appears?

    A. Beatrice - MUCH ADO ABOUT NOTHING
    B. Helena - ALL'S WELL THAT ENDS WELL
    C. Isabella - MEASURE FOR MEASURE
    D. Perdita - LOVE'S LABOURS LOST

21. *"... and when a damp
    Fell round the path of Milton, in his hand
    The Thing became a trumpet, whence he blew
    Soul-animating strains - alas, too few!"*
    In these lines, the *Thing* referred to is

    A. Paradise Lost   B. sonnets
    C. pamphlets and tracts   D. Lycidas

22. JOURNAL OF THE PLAGUE YEAR was written by

   A. Joseph Addison
   B. Daniel Defoe
   C. John Evelyn
   D. Joseph Glanville

23. Which one of the following pseudonyms is INCORRECTLY paired with the actual name of the author?

   A. ELLIS BELL - Emily Bronte
   B. CADENUS - Jonathan Swift
   C. JOHN SINJOHN - E.M. Forster
   D. MICHAEL ANGELO TITMARSH - William Thackeray

24.
   I. THE DEVIL'S DISCIPLE - Don Juan after death philosophizes about life
   II. MAN AND SUPERMAN - A young man succumbs to the schemings of a woman
   III. CANDIDA - A woman decides between her clergyman husband and a young poet
   IV. HEARTBREAK HOUSE - A brigand escapes the law with the help of a lady

   The above plays by George Bernard Shaw are CORRECTLY described in

   A. I, II, III
   B. II, III
   C. I, IV
   D. I, II, IV

25. "All his novels present the losing struggle of individuals against the obscure power which moves the universe" BEST characterizes the work of

   A. George Meredith
   B. Arnold Bennett
   C. John Galsworthy
   D. Thomas Hardy

KEY (CORRECT ANSWERS)

1.	B	11.	C
2.	A	12.	D
3.	C	13.	B
4.	D	14.	B
5.	D	15.	B
6.	B	16.	D
7.	A	17.	B
8.	A	18.	A
9.	C	19.	B
10.	D	20.	D
21.	B		
22.	B		
23.	C		
24.	B		
25.	D		

TEST 2

DIRECTIONS: Each question or incomplete statement is followed by several suggested answers or completions. Select the one that BEST answers the question or completes the statement. *PRINT THE LETTER OF THE CORRECT ANSWER IN THE SPACE AT THE RIGHT.*

1. Which one of the following was NOT a poet laureate of England? 1.____

    A. Robert Browning
    B. Colley Cibber
    C. John Dryden
    D. William Wordsworth

2. The political figure represented by Achitophel in Dryden's ABSALOM AND ACHITOPHEL is 2.____

    A. Lord Chesterfield
    B. the Marquis of Halifax
    C. the Duke of Monmouth
    D. the Earl of Shaftesbury

3. "The poem shows that it was written in snatches rather than as a rounded entity. Jotted down as separate stanzas, some touching and some flatly banal, pieced and put together, it was, as the author said, a series of 'short swallow flights of song.' The phrase is fairly exact, for the long elegiac poem is actually a chain of lyrical quatrains which sometimes turn into epigrams." 3.____
This paragraph refers to

    A. ELEGY WRITTEN IN A COUNTRY CHURCHYARD
    B. IN MEMORIAM
    C. LYCIDAS
    D. THYRSIS

4. "They order," said I, "this matter better in France." The author of the book in which this line appears also wrote 4.____

    A. THE CASTLE OF OTRANTO
    B. CLARISSA
    C. MR. MIDSHIPMAN EASY
    D. TRISTRAM SHANDY

5. Which one of the following poets was NOT a member of the *graveyard school*? 5.____

    A. Robert Blair
    B. George Crabbe
    C. Thomas Gray
    D. Edward Young

6. Which one of the following ballads is attributable to a single author? 6.____

    A. CLERK SAUNDERS
    B. KEMP OWYNE
    C. LORD ULLIN'S DAUGHTER
    D. THE TWA SISTERS

7. Which one of the following pairs of plays was NOT written by the same author? 7.____

    A. THE RIVALS - THE SCHOOL FOR SCANDAL
    B. SHE STOOPS TO CONQUER - THE CRITIC
    C. ALL FOR LOVE - MARRIAGE-A-LA-MODE
    D. THE WAY OF THE WORLD - LOVE FOR LOVE

8. The MOST notable innovation in Samuel Johnson's A DICTIONARY OF THE ENGLISH LANGUAGE published in 1755 was 8.____

A. its attempt to record all words used in English
B. its attempt to list the etymology of each word
C. the inclusion of quotations to illustrate word meanings
D. the use of a phonetic alphabet to indicate pronunciation

9. The Flaming Tinman is a character in

    A. George Borrow's LAVENGRO
    B. Lewis Carroll's SYLVIE AND BRUNO
    C. Charles Kingsley's HEREWARD THE WAKE
    D. Thomas Peacock's THE MISFORTUNES OF ELPHIN

10. Madeline and Porphyro are the lovers whose tale is told in

    A. Byron's THE CORSAIR
    B. Coleridge's REMORSE
    C. Keats' THE EVE OF ST. AGNES
    D. Shelley's THE CENCI

11. The characteristic which the FAERIE QUEEN, CHILDE HAROLD, and THE EVE OF ST. AGNES have in common is that they

    A. were all written in the 19th century
    B. are all written in nine-line stanzas
    C. were all written to glorify a reigning monarch
    D. are all predominantly nature poems

12. The mysterious secret that Edward Rochester long kept from Jane Eyre was that

    A. he was in reality her half brother, and they could not marry
    B. his made first wife was still alive
    C. his fortune was founded on a swindle which might be exposed at any moment
    D. he was suffering from an incurable disease leading to blindness and possible insanity

13. Which one of the following characters is NOT correctly matched with the novel in which he appears?

    A. Thomas Gradgrind - HARD TIMES
    B. Harold Skimpole - LITTLE DORRIT
    C. Joseph Sedley - VANITY FAIR
    D. George Esmond - THE VIRGINIANS

14. IMAGINARY CONVERSATIONS, the major prose work of an author better known for his poetry, was written by

    A. Robert Browning
    B. Thomas DeQuincey
    C. Henry Austin Dobson
    D. Walter Savage Landor

15. George Meredith's MODERN LOVE differs from most sonnet sequences MOST markedly in that

    A. it was not written for publication but for private circulation
    B. the *sonnets* do not rhyme
    C. it was the occasion of a legal action for libel
    D. each *sonnet* contains sixteen, rather than fourteen, lines

16. Which of these writers are noted for their stories of fox hunting in England?
    I. Richard Blackmore
    II. J. Sheridan LeFanu
    III. Robert Surtees
    IV. George Whyte-Melville
    The CORRECT answer is:

    A. I, III   B. II, IV   C. I, IV   D. III, IV

17. Which one of the following was NOT written by Rudyard Kipling?

    A. "Drake he's in his hammock an' a thousand mile away, (Capten, art tha sleepin' there below?)"
    B. "So 'ere's to you, Fuzzy-Wuzzy, at your 'ome in the Soudan; You're a pore benighted 'eathen but a first class fightin' man."
    C. "For the Colonel's Lady an' Judy O'Grady Are sisters under their skins!"
    D. "When Earth's last picture is painted and the tubes are twisted and dried, When the oldest colours have faded, and the youngest critic has died,"

18. Which of the following writers are noted for their literary hoaxes?
    I. Thomas Chatterton
    II. Hartley Coleridge
    III. H.H. Furness
    IV. James Macphersen
    The CORRECT answer is:

    A. I, II   B. II, III   C. I, IV   D. III, IV

19. The association of which one of the following with Ellen Ternan is generally believed to have influenced the characterization of his later heroines?

    A. Samuel Butler   B. Charles Dickens
    C. George Gissing   D. William Thackeray

20. *"When thou at the random grim forge, powerful amidst peers, Didst fettle for the great gray dray horse his bright and battering sandal!"*
    These lines were written by

    A. Robert Bridges   B. Gerard Manley Hopkins
    C. Dante Gabriel Rossetti   D. Francis Thompson

21. The seven line stanza or rime royal used by Chaucer in some of the CANTERBURY TALES has been successfully used in several poems by

    A. Ernest Dowson   B. Robinson Jeffers
    C. John Masefield   D. Edwin Arlington Robinson

22. *"O, my Luve's like a red, red rose
    That's newly sprung in June;
    O' my Luve's like the melodie
    That's sweetly played in tune!"*
    These lines of poetry are written in the measure called

    A. archaic   B. dactylic   C. iambic   D. trochaic

23. Gabriel Oak, Angel Clare, and Diggory Venn are all characters in the works of

    A. Arnold Bennett
    B. Joseph Conrad
    C. Thomas Hardy
    D. Hugh Walpole

24. In John Galsworthy's THE FORSYTE SAGA, Irene Forsyte's lover, Philip Bosinney,

    A. eloped with Irene to America
    B. was run over in the fog and killed
    C. broke off the affair with Irene and married the wealthy June Forsyte
    D. shot himself on Soames Forsyte's front steps

25. In James Joyce's ULYSSES, the character Blazes Boylan is the

    A. fictional representation of Joyce's father
    B. rejected suitor of Leopold Bloom's daughter
    C. young man who plays Telemachus to Bloom's Ulysses
    D. lover of Molly Bloom

KEY (CORRECT ANSWERS)

1. A
2. D
3. B
4. D
5. B

6. C
7. B
8. C
9. A
10. C

11. B
12. B
13. B
14. D
15. D

16. D
17. A
18. C
19. B
20. B

21. C
22. C
23. C
24. B
25. D

TEST 3

DIRECTIONS: Each question or incomplete statement is followed by several suggested answers or completions. Select the one that BEST answers the question or completes the statement. *PRINT THE LETTER OF THE CORRECT ANSWER IN THE SPACE AT THE RIGHT.*

1. Which one of the following short stories is NOT correctly matched with its author? 1.____

   A. ENOCH SOAMES - Max Beerbohm
   B. THE TILLOTSON BANQUET - Aldous Huxley
   C. ARABY - Katherine Mansfield
   D. THE OUTSTATION - Somerset Maugham

2. "The patriots found in his characters and incidents an insult to the Irish nation ... and they expressed their disapproval in noisy violence that carried the author's name far into the intelligent world outside." 2.____
   The critic refers here to the disorder that greeted the presentation of

   A. Synge's THE PLAYBOY OF THE WESTERN WORLD
   B. O'Casey's JUNO AND THE PAYCOCK
   C. Yeats' THE COUNTESS CATHLEEN
   D. Robinson's THE WHITEHEADED BOY

3.
   I. TOXOPHILUS - archery 3.____
   II. AREOPAGITICA - diplomacy
   III. PSEUDODOXIA EPIDEMICA - superstitions
   IV. THE ANATOMY OF MELANCHOLY - elegiac poetry
   V. THE SACRED WOOD - mythology

   The literary works listed above and their MAIN themes are correctly paired in

   A. I, III   B. II, IV   C. I, V   D. II, V

4. Beowulf destroyed Grendel by 4.____

   A. piercing his heart with a spear
   B. crushing him to death
   C. tearing his arm from its socket
   D. cutting off his head

5. Phrase, and author with whom it is associated, are correctly paired in all of the following EXCEPT 5.____

   A. willing suspension of disbelief - Coleridge
   B. rhyme ... the invention of a barbarous age - Milton
   C. true ease in writing comes from art, not chance - Pope
   D. the charm of novelty to the things of every day - Poe

6. All the following writers are correctly associated with literary movements indicated EXCEPT 6.____

   A. Edward Pusey - OXFORD MOVEMENT
   B. Dante Gabriel Rossetti - PRE-RAPHAELITE BROTHERHOOD
   C. Edward Young - GRAVEYARD SCHOOL
   D. James Whitcomb Riley - TRANSCENDENTALISM

7. In his shorter poems, Robert Browning treats all the following subjects EXCEPT

   A. the scholar's quest for knowledge
   B. the betrayal of a painter's genius
   C. worldliness among the old clergy
   D. the flaying of the soul for its shortcomings

8. The author of ULALUME implemented his critical theories as editor of

   A. CORNHILL MAGAZINE
   B. SOUTHERN LITERARY MESSENGER
   C. NORTH AMERICAN REVIEW
   D. EDINBURGH REVIEW

9. The Church of Rome, the Church of England, and the Protestant dissenters are all satirized in Swift's

   A. THE BATTLE OF THE BOOKS   B. BICKERSTAFF PAPERS
   C. A TALE OF A TUB   D. A MODEST PROPOSAL

10.
   I. Anacreon - Roman lyric poet
   II. Jane Shore - condemned as a witch
   III. Mabinogion - Welsh tales of King Arthur
   IV. Ossian - legendary Gaelic warrior
   V. Lilith - wife of Cain
   VI. Acheron - river of the infernal regions

   Of the above, names of literary import and descriptive phrases are all appropriately paired EXCEPT

   A. III only   B. II, IV, VI
   C. I, V   D. III, IV, V, VI

11. Madame Eglantine is a character in

   A. EVELINA   B. GAMMER GURTON'S NEEDLE
   C. MOLL FLANDERS   D. THE CANTERBURY TALES

12. Each of the following Shakespearean quotations and the character it refers to are correctly paired EXCEPT

   A. "The glass of fashion and the mould of form" - Hamlet
   B. "This dead butcher and his fiend-like queen" - Macbeth
   C. "A king of shreds and patches" - Claudius
   D. "Rude am I in my speech,
      And little bless'd with the soft phrase of peace" - Henry V

13. The expression *in a Pickwickian sense* carries the connotation of

   A. cleverly-phrased, satirical innuendoes
   B. droll, philosophic witticisms
   C. uncomplimentary epithets jestingly used
   D. highly pedantic, ambiguous utterances

14.
   I. Byron - *"To the glory that was Greece,
       And the grandeur that was Rome"*
   II. Swinburne - *"That even the weariest river
        Winds somewhere safe to sea"*
   III. Dowson - *"I have been faithful to thee,
         Cynara, in my fashion"*
   IV. Shelley - *"I arise from dreams of thee
         In the first sweet sleep of night"*

   Author and quotation are CORRECTLY matched in

   A. I, II, III   B. II, III, IV
   C. I, III, IV   D. I, II, IV

15. The hero and his old philosopher friend escape to Egypt from Abyssinia and study the various conditions of men's lives, searching for a formula of happiness, in

   A. MARIUS THE EPICUREAN   B. CANDIDE
   C. RASSELAS   D. EUPHUES

16. A NOVEL WITHOUT A HERO is the subtitle for

   A. EMMA
   B. VANITY FAIR
   C. TESS OF THE D'URBERVILLES
   D. THE WAY OF ALL FLESH

17. Byron's ENGLISH BARDS AND SCOTCH REVIEWERS was a vigorous attack on the critics of his

   A. CHILDE HAROLD   B. DON JUAN
   C. THE VISION OF JUDGMENT   D. HOURS OF IDLENESS

18. All of the following are characters in works by Ben Jonson, EXCEPT

   A. Sir Epicure Mammon   B. Morose
   C. Mosca   D. Sir Oliver Surface

19.
   I. FIRST FOLIO OF SHAKESPEARE PLAYS - 1623
   II. PARADISE LOST - 1643
   III. PAMELA - 1782
   IV. LYRICAL BALLADS - 1789
   V. LEAVES OF GRASS - 1855
   VI. A FAREWELL TO ARMS - 1929

   Literary work and date of publication, within five years before or after, are CORRECTLY paired above in

   A. I, II, IV, V   B. I, III, V, VI
   C. II, III, IV, V   D. I, IV, V, VI

20. The *intellectual Declaration of Independence* in America was expressed in a notable speech by the author of

   A. THE CONDUCT OF LIFE   B. THE GOLDEN DAY
   C. THE CROSS OF GOLD   D. DEMOCRATIC VISTAS

21. In this famous murder case, after the two halves of Rome have given their opinions on the story of Pompilia, comes the impartial opinion of

    A. Caponsacchi   B. Tertium Quid
    C. The Pope   D. Abt Vogler

22.
    I. Layamon
    II. John Gower
    III. Robert Wace of Jersey
    IV. John Masefield
    V. Emily Dickinson
    VI. Thomas Hardy

Of the above writers, those who wrote extensively on the material of the Arthurian Legend are

    A. II, IV, V, VI   B. I, III, IV
    C. I, II, III, V   D. III, V, VI

23.
    I. Baron Tweedsmuir - John Buchan
    II. Baroness Karen Blixen-Finecke - Isak Dinesen
    III. Viscount St. Albans - Alfred Tennyson
    IV. Earl of Beaconsfield - Francis Bacon
    V. Fourth Earl of Chesterfield - Philip Dormer Stanhope

Of the above, appellation of distinction (hereditary or acquired) and author's name are CORRECTLY paired in

    A. I, II, V   B. I, III, IV
    C. II, IV, V   D. II, III, V

24. The one of the following popularly known as DARWIN'S BULLDOG is

    A. Alfred Lord Tennyson   B. Bertrand Russell
    C. Thomas Henry Huxley   D. Pierre Simon LaPlace

25. ART FOR ART'S SAKE expresses the prevailing literary philosophy of

    A. Alfred Lord Tennyson   B. Robert Browning
    C. Oscar Wilde   D. John Davidson

KEY (CORRECT ANSWERS)

1.	C		11.	D
2.	A		12.	D
3.	C		13.	C
4.	A		14.	B
5.	B		15.	C
6.	B		16.	B
7.	D		17.	D
8.	B		18.	D
9.	C		19.	D
10.	C		20.	A

21. B
22. B
23. A
24. C
25. C

TEST 4

DIRECTIONS: Each question or incomplete statement is followed by several suggested answers or completions. Select the one that BEST answers the question or completes the statement. *PRINT THE LETTER OF THE CORRECT ANSWER IN THE SPACE AT THE RIGHT.*

1. Anglo-Saxon poetry is appropriately characterized by all of the following statements EXCEPT

    A. it generally has internal as well as end rime
    B. each line is divided into two well-defined parts
    C. each line has four or fewer accented syllables
    D. it is alliterative

2. Of the British and American authors below, the pair which are NOT contemporaries is

    A. Algernon Swinburne - Walt Whitman
    B. Edgar Allan Poe - William Wordsworth
    C. Benjamin Franklin - Samuel Johnson
    D. John Milton - William Cullen Bryant

3. Author, title, and subject are properly related in each of the following EXCEPT

    A. Shelley - ADONAIS - John Keats
    B. Swinburne - AVE ATQUE VALE - Charles Baudelaire
    C. Milton - LYCIDAS - Edward King
    D. Tennyson - IN MEMORIAM - Arthur Hugh Clough

4.
    I. Thomas Overbury - characters
    II. Sir Thomas Malory - Arthurian romance
    III. Geoffrey of Monmouth - history of Britain
    IV. John Lyly - translator of Vergil
    V. Sir Thomas Wyatt - sonnets
    VI. Thomas Nash - interludes

    Each of the above writers is appropriately paired with the subject or the literary form for which he has gained literary prominence EXCEPT

    A. I, IV   B. II, III   C. I, VI   D. IV, VI

5.
    I. Henry Fleming - soldier
    II. Kate Hardcastle - barmaid
    III. Jurgen - pawnbroker
    IV. Billy Budd - seaman
    V. C.J. Stryver - lawyer
    VI. Bottom - tinker

    Of the above, literary character and occupation are correctly paired in all EXCEPT

    A. I, III   B. II, VI   C. V only   D. IV only

6. In Pater's STUDIES IN THE HISTORY OF THE RENAISSANCE, there is an oft-quoted description of

    A. THE ANGELUS by Manet
    B. THE LAUGHING CAVALIER by Hals
    C. THE NIGHT WATCH by Rembrandt
    D. MONA LISA by da Vinci

7. The quotations, *"Scorn not the sonnet"* and *"A sonnet is a moment's monument,"* are, respectively, from poems by

    A. Milton and Millay
    B. Spenser and Sidney
    C. Shakespeare and Keats
    D. Wordsworth and Rossetti

8. Of the following, the tenet which was NOT in accord with neo-classic eighteenth century practice in literature was

    A. ancient writers are worthy of imitation
    B. literature is fundamentally concerned with moral truths
    C. the most enduring literature comes from man's probing into the infinite
    D. adherence to form and convention is commendable literary practice

9. The INCORRECT item about Orm's ORMULUM among the following is that it

    A. contains a predominance of words derived from Norman-French
    B. is a metrical paraphrase of the Gospels
    C. was written about 1150 and 1250 A.D.
    D. has notable philologic value as a key to English pronunciation of the times

10. The one of the following quotations NOT CORRECTLY matched with its author is

    A. "Yet ah, that Spring should vanish with the Rose!" - Edward Fitzgerald
    B. "My soul that lingers sighing
        About the glimmering weirs" - A. E. Housman
    C. "Was this the face that launched a thousand ships?" - Christopher Marlowe
    D. "There midnight's all a glimmer, and noon a purple glow" - Alfred Noyes

11. *"Founder and chief exemplar of the 'Satanic school' of poetry"* is a description which MOST appropriately applies to

    A. John Webster
    B. Lord Byron
    C. Samuel Taylor Coleridge
    D. Robert Southey

12. Among the following works, all were uncompleted EXCEPT

    A. THE MYSTERY OF EDWIN DROOD - Dickens
    B. PARADISE REGAINED - Milton
    C. KUBLA KHAN - Coleridge
    D. HYPERION - Keats

13. Thomas Tyrwhitt is noted in the history of literature for his

    A. deciphering of the Rosetta Stone
    B. exposing the literary forgeries in early ballads
    C. discovery of ballad manuscripts
    D. important edition of CANTERBURY TALES

14.
   I. "Tired with all these, for restful death I cry"
   II. "Much have I traveled in the realms of gold"
   III. "Come sleep! O sleep, the certain knot of peace"
   IV. "Milton! thou shouldst be living at this hour"
   V. "Euclid alone has looked on beauty bare"
   VI. "Be with me, Beauty, for the fire is dying"

   The six lines of poetry above are opening lines of sonnets written, respectively, by

   A. Shakespeare, Keats, Sidney, Wordsworth, Millay, Masefield
   B. Keats, Millay, Shakespeare, Masefield, Wordsworth, Sidney
   C. Sidney, Masefield, Millay, Wordsworth, Keats, Shakespeare
   D. Millay, Wordsworth, Sidney, Keats, Masefield, Shakespeare

15. The process by which the images in a great poet's creation were drawn from various sources is reconstructed in

   A. THE DEFENCE OF POESIE
   B. THE POETIC PRINCIPLE
   C. THE ROAD TO XANADU
   D. THE FINE FRENZY

16. *"I am a part of all that I have met"*
   "Old age hath yet his honor and his toil"
   Tennyson's lines quoted above are

   A. both from ULYSSES
   B. both from IN MEMORIAM
   C. from ULYSSES and IN MEMORIAM, respectively
   D. from neither poem mentioned in (C) above

17. The following description,
   "He is famed in English literature for having written masterpieces in four literary types: prose fiction, drama, poetry, essay,"
   appropriately applies to

   A. Thomas Hardy
   B. William Butler Yeats
   C. William Cowper
   D. Oliver Goldsmith

18. Of the following quotations, the one NOT from Thoreau is

   A. "It would be glorious to see mankind at leisure for once."
   B. "Most of the luxuries, and many of the so-called comforts of life are not only not indispensable, but positive hindrances to the elevation of mankind."
   C. "The mass of men lead lives of quiet desperation."
   D. "To be great is to be misunderstood."

19.
   I. Epigrams - Ben Jonson
   II. Odes - John Skelton
   III. Eclogues - Edmund Spenser
   IV. Elegies - Walter Savage Landor
   V. Emblems - Francis Quarles

   Of the above, literary form and author who was an important practitioner of it are correctly matched EXCEPT

   A. I, III   B. II, IV   C. III, V   D. I, IV

20. *"If thou appear untouched by solemn thought,*
Thy nature is not therefore less divine:
Thou liest in Abraham's bosom all the year,
And worship'st at the Temple's inner shrine,
God being with thee when we know it not."
The lines above were written by

   A. Shelley
   C. Spenser
   B. Wordsworth
   D. Keats

21. The death of John Keats was generally said to have been hastened by a harsh criticism of his

   A. ENDYMION in Blackwood's
   B. HYPERION in The Quarterly
   C. THE EVE OF ST. AGNES in The Review
   D. LAMIA in The Rambler

22. The following first lines of songs, the singers, and the plays in which they appear, all are correctly grouped in each of the following EXCEPT

   A. "Full fathom five thy father lies" - Ariel - THE TEMPEST
   B. "Who is Silvia? what is she" - Petruchio - TAMING OF THE SHREW
   C. "Blow, blow, thou winter wind" - Amiens - AS YOU LIKE IT
   D. "And let me the canakin clink, clink" - Iago - OTHELLO

23. *"Whoever wishes to attain an English style, familiar but not coarse, and elegant but not ostentatious, must give his days and nights to the volumes of _____."*
The writer whose name completes the quotation above is

   A. Addison   B. Swift   C. Lamb   D. Pater

24. *"Come live with me and be my love"* and the reply beginning, *"If all the world and love were young,"* were written, respectively, by

   A. Christopher Marlowe and Ben Jonson
   B. Christopher Marlowe and Sir Walter Raleigh
   C. Ben Jonson and Sir Walter Raleigh
   D. Sir Philip Sidney and Ben Jonson

25. The FIRST book printed in English was

   A. LE RECUEIL DBS HISTOIRES DE TROYE
   B. CONFESSIO AMANTIS
   C. THE SHIP OF FOOLS
   D. THE PEARL

KEY (CORRECT ANSWERS)

1.	A	11.	B
2.	D	12.	B
3.	D	13.	D
4.	D	14.	A
5.	B	15.	C
6.	D	16.	A
7.	D	17.	D
8.	C	18.	D
9.	A	19.	B
10.	D	20.	B

21. A
22. B
23. A
24. B
25. A

TEST 5

DIRECTIONS: Each question or incomplete statement is followed by several suggested answers or completions. Select the one that BEST answers the question or completes the statement. *PRINT THE LETTER OF THE CORRECT ANSWER IN THE SPACE AT THE RIGHT.*

1. The English dialect which won a commanding position over other English dialects in use in the Middle English period was

    A. East Midland
    B. West Midland
    C. Northumbrian
    D. Kentish

    1.____

2. The century of greatest influx of French words into the English language was the

    A. 11th   B. 12th   C. 13th   D. 14th

    2.____

3. The evolution of the word meanings of *knave* and *vulgar* provides an example of the language process of

    A. degeneration
    B. agglutination
    C. folk etymology
    D. duplication

    3.____

4. The one of the following words that is NOT of French origin is

    A. judge   B. apparel   C. church   D. campaign

    4.____

5. In the period after the Norman Conquest, English was officially adopted as the language of the English courts in

    A. 1158   B. 1215   C. 1294   D. 1362

    5.____

6. The word element *xeno* means

    A. universal   B. yellow   C. hateful   D. strange

    6.____

7. The pronouns *they, their, them* came into the English language from the

    A. Celtic
    B. Anglo-Saxon
    C. Scandinavian
    D. Norman-French

    7.____

8. Authors and women of consequence in their lives are correctly paired in all of the following EXCEPT

    A. Percy Bysshe Shelley - Anne Milbank
    B. John Keats - Fanny Brawne
    C. Thomas Carlyle - Jane Welsh
    D. Nathaniel Hawthorne - Sophia Peabody

    8.____

9. Each of the following works is correctly paired with the description accompanying it EXCEPT

    A. COLIN CLOUTS COME HOME AGAIN - Spenser's eulogy to John Skelton
    B. ASTROPHEL - pastoral elegy to the memory of Sidney
    C. THE SHEPHERD'S CALENDAR - Colin Clout's love is spurned by Rosalind
    D. THE FAERIE QUEENE - twelve books contemplated; only six completed

    9.____

10. THE ANGLO-SAXON CHRONICLE was

    A. discontinued immediately after the Norman Conquest
    B. continued at Peterborough until 1154
    C. written in French after 1215 under the supervision of the court
    D. translated into Latin under the direction of Cambrensis

11. I. LADY WINDERMERE'S FAN - a mother sacrifices her own reputation to save her daughter's
    II. MRS. WARREN'S PROFESSION - a mother marries a man she despises to provide her daughter with means for an education
    III. THE WIDOW IN THE BYE STREET - a mother tries to rear her son as a model boy, but he commits murder
    IV. PRIDE AND PREJUDICE - a scheming and ambitious father seeks to marry off his daughters for his own profit

    In the above, the two titles and themes CORRECTLY matched are

    A. I, III   B. II, IV   C. I, IV   D. II, III

12. Of the following, the item INCORRECTLY identified is

    A. THE GOLDEN BOUGH - a study of folklore
    B. UPANISHADS - Hindu philosophical treatises
    C. ROWLEY POEMS - Chatterton's hoax
    D. DRAPIER'S LETTERS - epistolary novel

13. Author and well-known characterization are correctly paired in all of the following EXCEPT

    A. William Shakespeare - FANCY'S CHILD
    B. John Milton - ORGAN VOICE OF ENGLAND
    C. Lord Byron - PILGRIM OF ETERNITY
    D. John Keats - WELL OF ENGLISH UNDEFILED

14. Of the following Shakespearean plays, all have been made into operas EXCEPT

    A. MACBETH   B. KING LEAR
    C. OTHELLO   D. MERRY WIVES OF WINDSOR

15. "And though that he were worthy, he was wys,
    And of his port as mecke as is a mayde
    He nevere yet no vileyne ne sayde
    In al his lyfe unto no maner wight."

    In the above lines, Chaucer describes the

    A. Squire   B. Monk   C. Knight   D. Poor parson

16. I. Helen Gardner - art
    II. Standard and Poor - business
    III. Sir George Grove - music
    IV. Thomas Bulfinch - law
    V. Edith Granger - drama
    VI. David Ewen - opera

    Of the above writer or editors of standard reference works, all are correctly matched with their recognized fields EXCEPT

    A. I, II, VI   B. IV, V   C. II, IV, VI   D. III, V

17.
   I. Reign of James I of England
   II. War of the Roses
   III. Sir Thomas Wyatt
   IV. Geoffrey Chaucer
   V. The Protectorate

   The CORRECT chronological order of the events and persons above, beginning with the earliest, is

   A. I, IV, II, III, V
   B. IV, II, I, III, V
   C. IV, II, III, I, V
   D. II, IV, III, V, I

18.
   I. Fra Lippo Lippi
   II. Andrea del Sarto
   III. The Englishman in Italy
   IV. The Bishop Orders His Tomb at St. Praxed's
   V. A Grammarian's Funeral

   Of the poems by Browning listed above, those with an Italian Renaissance setting are

   A. I, II, III, IV
   B. I, II, IV, V
   C. II, III, IV, V
   D. I, III, IV, V

19.
   I. REMEMBRANCE OF THINGS PAST
   II. THE WHIPS OF TIME
   III. EYELESS IN GAZA
   IV. STRATAGEMS AND SPOILS
   V. DEATH BE NOT PROUD

   Of the above book titles, those which are phrases found in the writings of Shakespeare are

   A. I, II, IV
   B. II, III, IV
   C. I, III, V
   D. III, IV, V

20. All of the following names are correctly identified with their descriptions EXCEPT

   A. PASTON LETTERS - valuable 17th century source for historical novels
   B. AREOPAGUS - literary group, including Spenser, to reform English versification
   C. MARPRELATE CONTROVERSY - Puritan attack on the Church of England
   D. ANCRENE RIWLE - 13th century prose manual of religious counsel

21. Literary works and the inns which play a part in their setting are correctly paired in all the items below EXCEPT

   A. Three Jolly Pigeons - SHE STOOPS TO CONQUER
   B. Admiral Benbow - TREASURE ISLAND
   C. Wayside - A NIGHT AT AN INN
   D. Tabard - CANTERBURY TALES

22. The aesthetes of FIN DE SIECLE England were satirized in

   A. THE HOUND OF HEAVEN
   B. PATIENCE
   C. THE GREAT TRADITION
   D. PRAETERITA

23. All of the following words and their settings are correctly paired EXCEPT

    A. Beowulf - Sweden and Denmark
    B. The Marble Faun - Greece
    C. Ulysses - Ireland
    D. Sohrab and Rustum - Persia

24.
    I. Philip Sidney
    II. Edmund Spenser
    III. George Crabbe
    IV. Ben Jonson
    V. Samuel Daniel

    Of the above, all wrote sonnet sequences EXCEPT

    A. I, III, V   B. III, IV
    C. I, II, V   D. II, IV

25. Shaw's doctrine of the LIFE FORCE as a power that seeks a higher and better existence is expounded in all of the following EXCEPT

    A. HEARTBREAK HOUSE   B. YOU NEVER CAN TELL
    C. BACK TO METHUSELAH   D. MAN AND SUPERMAN

KEY (CORRECT ANSWERS)

1.	A	11.	A
2.	D	12.	D
3.	A	13.	C
4.	C	14.	B
5.	D	15.	C
6.	D	16.	B
7.	C	17.	C
8.	A	18.	B
9.	A	19.	A
10.	B	20.	A

21. C
22. B
23. B
24. B
25. B

EXAMINATION SECTION
TEST 1

DIRECTIONS: Each question or incomplete statement is followed by several suggested answers or completions. Select the one that BEST answers the question or completes the statement. *PRINT THE LETTER OF THE CORRECT ANSWER IN THE SPACE AT THE RIGHT.*

1. Sidney's ASTROPHEL AND STELLA, Spenser's AMORETTI, and Rossetti's HOUSE OF LIFE have in common their   1.____

    A. structure as sonnet sequences
    B. publication in the Elizabethan Age
    C. use of the Spenserian stanza
    D. euphuistic prose

2. A play of George Bernard Shaw's, the theme of which is the conflict of the sexes, is   2.____

    A. ARMS AND THE MAN
    B. THE DEVIL'S DISCIPLE
    C. MAN AND SUPERMAN
    D. CAPTAIN BRASSBOUND'S CONVERSION

3. Of the following works, the one LEAST sympathetic toward its *"Utopian"* civilization is   3.____

    A. More's UTOPIA
    B. Bacon's THE NEW ATLANTIS
    C. Huxley's BRAVE NEW WORLD
    D. Bellamy's LOOKING BACKWARD

4. Elia was the pseudonym of   4.____

    A. William Hazlitt   B. Charles Lamb
    C. Thomas DeQuincy   D. Walter Savage Landor

5. The poem, MY LAST DUCHESS, is a(n)   5.____

    A. dramatic monologue   B. pastoral
    C. ode   D. elegy

6. A long poem, the theme of which is the spiritual sterility of the twentieth century, was written by   6.____

    A. Hart Crane   B. T.S. Eliot
    C. James Joyce   D. Wallace Stevens

7. The phrase *"sweetness and light"* is used by and associated with   7.____

    A. John Ruskin   B. Matthew Arnold
    C. Charles Lamb   D. Joseph Addison

8. In the category of comedy is the work entitled   8.____

    A. TITUS ANDRONICUS   B. THE DUCHESS OF MALFI
    C. THE RIVALS   D. ALL FOR LOVE

9. All of the following poems are elegies EXCEPT

   A. IN MEMORIAM
   B. ADONAIS
   C. THYRSIS
   D. IL PENSEROSO

10. The line, *"Fool," said my muse to me, "look in thy heart and write,"* is from a poem by

    A. William Shakespeare
    B. Ben Jonson
    C. Sir Philip Sidney
    D. Christopher Marlowe

11. All of the following are by Wordsworth EXCEPT

    A. TINTERN ABBEY
    B. THE PRISONER OF CHILLON
    C. THE EXCURSION
    D. THE SOLITARY REAPER

12. All of the following groups are described in Gulliver's Travels EXCEPT

    A. Erewhonians
    B. Yahoos
    C. Brobdingnagians
    D. Houyhnhnms

13. The author of THE PLAYBOY OF THE WESTERN WORLD also wrote

    A. JUNO AND THE PAYCOCK
    B. CATHLEEN NI HOULIHAN
    C. RIDERS TO THE SEA
    D. THE INFORMER

14. Of the following novels, the one which bitterly attacks the smugness and hypocrisy of Victorian family life is

    A. THE MOON AND SIXPENCE
    B. SONS AND LOVERS
    C. NEW GRUB STREET
    D. THE WAY OF ALL FLESH

15. The writer whose declared purpose was *"to justify the ways of God to men"* was

    A. Jonathan Edwards
    B. John Bunyan
    C. Matthew Arnold
    D. John Milton

16. Of the following, the MOST appropriate adjective to describe Keats' EVE OF ST. AGNES is

    A. didactic
    B. expository
    C. sensuous
    D. realistic

17. All of the following writers are known as authors of the historic novel EXCEPT

    A. Charles Reade
    B. Rafael Sabatini
    C. William Thackeray
    D. Jane Austen

18. All of the following are examples of allegory EXCEPT

    A. THE VICAR OF WAKEFIELD
    B. THE VISION CONCERNING PIERS PLOWMAN
    C. THE FAERIE QUEENE
    D. EVERYMAN

19. The author of THE SHORTEST WAY WITH DISSENTERS also wrote

    A. A MODEST PROPOSAL
    B. ROBINSON CRUSOE
    C. THE DUNCIAD
    D. THE BLOODY TENENT

20. All of the following characters are from the same novel EXCEPT

    A. Uriah Heep
    B. Mr. Murdstone
    C. Mrs. Bardell
    D. Dora Spenlow

21. The writer NOT correctly associated with a place indicated is

    A. Pope - Twickenham
    B. Arnold - The Lake Country
    C. Scott - Abbotsford
    D. Carlyle - Craigenputtock

22. A novel in which the hero suffers from a physical deformity which seriously affects his self-confidence is

    A. HOW GREEN WAS MY VALLEY
    B. OF HUMAN BONDAGE
    C. THE CITADEL
    D. THE MAN OF PROPERTY

23. The author of REYNARD THE FOX also wrote

    A. THE HOUND OF HEAVEN
    B. MEMOIRS OF A FOX-HUNTING MAN
    C. DAUBER
    D. ON THIS ISLAND

24. ALL FOR LOVE is a retelling of the story of

    A. Hero and Leander
    B. Anthony and Cleopatra
    C. Pyramus and Thisbe
    D. Elizabeth and Essex

25. A novel in which the chief character tries to atone for an early act of cowardice is

    A. THE ORDEAL OF RICHARD FEVEREL
    B. THE MAYOR OF CASTERBRIDGE
    C. CLAYHANGER
    D. LORD JIM

KEY (CORRECT ANSWERS)

1.	A		11.	B
2.	C		12.	A
3.	C		13.	C
4.	B		14.	D
5.	A		15.	D
6.	B		16.	C
7.	B		17.	D
8.	C		18.	A
9.	D		19.	B
10.	C		20.	C

21. B
22. B
23. C
24. B
25. D

TEST 2

DIRECTIONS: Each question or incomplete statement is followed by several suggested answers or completions. Select the one that BEST answers the question or completes the statement. *PRINT THE LETTER OF THE CORRECT ANSWER IN THE SPACE AT THE RIGHT.*

1. Tennyson's THE PRINCESS deals with   1.____

   A. the English royal family
   B. woman's proper sphere in life
   C. a sailing vessel
   D. the joys and sorrows of a pre-adolescent girl

2. Of the following works, the one MOST closely paralleling Milton's own life is   2.____

   A. PARADISE LOST   B. SAMSON AGONISTES
   C. COMUS   D. LYCIDAS

3. The author of THYRSIS also wrote   3.____

   A. ATALANTA IN CALYDON   B. CULTURE AND ANARCHY
   C. SESAME AND LILIES   D. THE EARTHLY PARADISE

4. Of the following, the one NOT a satirical poem is   4.____

   A. THE VISION OF JUDGMENT
   B. THE MEDAL
   C. A NEW WAY TO PAY OLD DEBTS
   D. THE DUNCIAD

5. An uncanny atmosphere plays little part in the novel   5.____

   A. CASTLE OF OTRANTO   B. EDWIN DROOD
   C. THE MYSTERIES OF UDOLPHO D. CLARISSA HARLOWE

6. The world-weary, disillusioned, moody, defiant hero was characteristically used in works by   6.____

   A. William Wordsworth   B. Alfred Tennyson
   C. George Gordon Byron   D. William Collins

7. Sir Roger de Coverley is a character appearing in   7.____

   A. THE SPECTATOR   B. THE EXAMINER
   C. THE CITIZEN OF THE WORLD D. THE RAMBLER

8. All of the following writers had first-hand acquaintanceship with the sea EXCEPT   8.____

   A. John Masefield   B. Jonathan Swift
   C. Mark Twain   D. James Fenimore Cooper

9. All of the following lines are from the same work EXCEPT   9.____

   A. Parting is such sweet sorrow
   B. Take, O take those lips away
   C. A plague on both your houses
   D. What's in a name? A rose by any other name would smell as sweet

10. The rhyme scheme aba, bcb, cdc, etc. is used in

    A. terza rima
    B. the rondel
    C. the Spenserian stanza
    D. the Shakespearean sonnet

11. The use of the heroic couplet is one of the characteristics of the poetry of

    A. John Milton
    B. Alexander Pope
    C. William Shakespeare
    D. Carl Sandburg

12. Of the following lines quoted from poems, all are representative of the Cavalier spirit EXCEPT

    A. Why so pale and wan, fond lover?
    B. Bright star, would I were steadfast as thou are...
    C. I could not love thee dear so much...
    D. Go, lovely rose,...

13. Clym Yeobright is a character in

    A. THE LIGHT THAT FAILED
    B. MOBY DICK
    C. KING SOLOMON'S MINES
    D. THE RETURN OF THE NATIVE

14. *"Whatever is, is right"* is a quotation from

    A. THE CASTLE OF INDOLENCE
    B. THE TASK
    C. PIPPA PASSES
    D. ESSAY ON MAN

15. The person referred to in the line, *"Good night, sweet prince,"* is

    A. Romeo B. Macbeth C. Hamlet D. Othello

16. Among the following writers, the one generally recognized as the creator of the historical novel is

    A. Jane Austen
    B. Charles Dickens
    C. Sir Walter Scott
    D. George Eliot

17. Micawber, in Dickens' novel, DAVID COPPERFIELD, is famous for his

    A. despair
    B. humbleness
    C. optimism
    D. efficiency

18. An author and region NOT correctly associated are

    A. Hardy and Wessex
    B. Faulkner and Yoknopatawpha
    C. Cabell and Poictesme
    D. Aldous Huxley and the Five Towns

19. All of the following appear in THE CANTERBURY TALES as narrators or characters EXCEPT

    A. Griselda
    B. Lady Meed
    C. Palamon
    D. The Wife of Bath

20. Much of the poetry of Robert Browning exhibits all of the following qualities to a considerable degree EXCEPT a(n)   20._____

    A. optimistic faith in mankind
    B. clarity and directness of style
    C. innate sense of drama
    D. knowledge of relatively obscure events of medieval and classical times

21. The poetry of Dante, Gabriel Rossetti, in its imagery and fantasy, is MOST like that of   21._____

    A. Spenser   B. Shelley
    C. Milton   D. Walter De La Mare

22. Chaucer's English is called   22._____

    A. Anglo-Saxon   B. Old English
    C. Middle English   D. Modern English

23. The Imagist poets were guided by all of the following principles EXCEPT: 23._____

    A. Poetry must present a fixed image
    B. Poetry must deal only with serious themes
    C. Poetry should use the language of common speech
    D. Poetry may use new rhythms to present new moods

24. The contributions to the sonnet form are listed correctly in all of the following cases EXCEPT   24._____

    A. Wordsworth - revived interest in the sonnet
    B. Milton - used the Italian form of the sonnet
    C. Elizabeth B. Browning - translated sonnets from other languages
    D. Wyatt and Surrey - introduced the sonnet into English poetry

25. Of the following, the heroine NOT correctly associated with a play is   25._____

    A. Beatrice - MUCH ADO ABOUT NOTHING
    B. Viola - TWELFTH NIGHT
    C. Cordelia - THE TEMPEST
    D. Desdemona - OTHELLO

KEY (CORRECT ANSWERS)

1.	B		11.	B
2.	B		12.	B
3.	B		13.	D
4.	C		14.	D
5.	D		15.	C
6.	C		16.	C
7.	A		17.	C
8.	B		18.	D
9.	B		19.	B
10.	A		20.	B

21. A
22. C
23. B
24. C
25. C

TEST 3

DIRECTIONS: Each question or incomplete statement is followed by several suggested answers or completions. Select the one that BEST answers the question or completes the statement. *PRINT THE LETTER OF THE CORRECT ANSWER IN THE SPACE AT THE RIGHT.*

1. Of the following, the writer whose prose style differs MOST markedly from that of the others is   1.____

    A. Samuel Johnson
    B. Francis Bacon
    C. Philip Sidney
    D. Sir Thomas Browne

2. The statement about the nature of poetry that can be MOST properly attributed to Wordsworth is: 2.____

    A. A poem is the statement of emotion recollected in tranquility
    B. One of the chief purposes of poetry is to make the strange and mysterious seem real and acceptable
    C. A poem should produce a single emotional effect
    D. Poetry is a criticism of life under conditions fixed by the laws of poetic truth and beauty

3. The creator of Jeanie Deans also created the character   3.____

    A. Elizabeth Bennett
    B. Amy Robsart
    C. Amelia Sedley
    D. Eustacia Vye

4. Improperly grouped with the others from the standpoint of the author's purpose and literary technique is   4.____

    A. SARTOR RESARTUS
    B. GULLIVER'S TRAVELS
    C. EREWHON
    D. THE GOLDEN BOUGH

5. Greene and Nash are properly identified with   5.____

    A. THE UNIVERSITY WITS
    B. THE GRAVEYARD SCHOOL
    C. THE ESSAYISTS
    D. EUPHUES

6. King Alfred is MOST renowned in legend for his stand against the   6.____

    A. Picts   B. Jutes   C. Danes   D. Normans

7. John Wyclif is sometimes called the father of English prose because of his   7.____

    A. speeches to the Lollards
    B. translation of the Bible
    C. Voyages and Travels
    D. Pearl

8. The word *scop* is NOT allied in meaning to the word   8.____

    A. gleeman
    B. herald
    C. minstrel
    D. minnesinger

9. The technique of the dramatic monologue is NOT used in

   A. MY LAST DUCHESS
   B. INCIDENT OF THE FRENCH CAMP
   C. RABBI BEN EZRA
   D. PARACELSUS

10. Of the following plays, the one NOT written by Marlowe is

    A. KING JOHN   B. FAUSTUS
    C. THE JEW OF MALTA   D. TAMBURLAINE

11. G.K. Chesterton did NOT

    A. create the Father Brown stories
    B. make extensive use of paradox and antithesis
    C. champion the cause of TREMENDOUS TRIFLES
    D. become a disciple of H.G. Wells

12. The author of HILDA LESSWAYS also wrote

    A. TONO-BUNGAY   B. PETER GRIMES
    C. CLAYHANGER   D. THE CROCK OF GOLD

13. Apart from his verse, the author of A SHROPSHIRE LAD is noted for his

    A. classical scholarship
    B. support of Disraeli's concept of EMPIRE
    C. contributions to the Irish Literary Renaissance
    D. identification with the sea

14. MOST prominently identified with the origin of the Abbey Theatre is

    A. Douglas Hyde   B. Lady Gregory
    C. A.E.   D. James Stephens

15. It is NOT true that Stevenson

    A. married an American widow
    B. traveled with a donkey
    C. translated the ARABIAN NIGHTS
    D. wrote THE BLACK ARROW

16. Considered to be the MOST representative of Victorian England is the author of

    A. PIPPA PASSES   B. THE PRINCESS
    C. SARTOR RESARTUS   D. DOVER BEACH

17. The author of THE COTTER'S SATURDAY NIGHT did NOT write the line

    A. "Owad some Pow'r the giftie gie us"
    B. "God moves in a mysterious way"
    C. "Flow gently, sweet Afton"
    D. "My Mary from my soul was torn"

18. Lamb and Hazlitt were PRIMARILY

    A. biographers
    B. essayists
    C. lyricists
    D. dilettantes

19. Of the following, the one MOST influential in forming Wordsworth's poetic philosophy was

    A. Southey
    B. Shelley
    C. Coleridge
    D. Mary B. Hutchinson

20. The novel, HOW GREEN WAS MY VALLEY, deals CHIEFLY with

    A. life in Cardiff
    B. Welsh coal miners
    C. a Welsh schoolboy and his schoolmistress
    D. Welsh folklore

21. Of the following pairs, the one NOT correctly matched is

    A. Percy Bysshe Shelley - Harriet Westbrook
    B. Thomas Carlyle - Jane Welsh
    C. Edgar Allan Poe - Virginia Dare
    D. Nathaniel Hawthorne - Sophia Peabody

22. The author of SALTWATER BALLADS also wrote

    A. DAUBER
    B. GLORY ROAD
    C. THE BARREL ORGAN
    D. IOLANTHE

23. Of the following, the one which should be omitted from a gallery of Dickensian characters is

    A. Betsy Trotwood
    B. Kate Nickleby
    C. Amelia Sedley
    D. Mrs. Bardell

24. *Hebraism* is Matthew Arnold's term for

    A. aesthetic living
    B. culture and anarchy
    C. sweetness and light
    D. moral education

25. The author of FINNEGAN'S WAKE also wrote

    A. PORTRAIT OF THE ARTIST AS A YOUNG MAN
    B. THE BABINOGION
    C. THE NIGHT RIDERS
    D. LOST HORIZON

KEY (CORRECT ANSWERS)

1.	B		11.	D
2.	A		12.	C
3.	B		13.	A
4.	D		14.	B
5.	A		15.	C
6.	C		16.	B
7.	B		17.	B
8.	B		18.	B
9.	D		19.	C
10.	A		20.	B

21. C
22. A
23. C
24. D
25. A

TEST 4

DIRECTIONS: Each question or incomplete statement is followed by several suggested answers or completions. Select the one that BEST answers the question or completes the statement. *PRINT THE LETTER OF THE CORRECT ANSWER IN THE SPACE AT THE RIGHT.*

1. Mrs. Malaprop is famous for her 1._____

   A. beauty
   B. patronage of the arts
   C. mistreatment of the English language
   D. friendship with Sydney

2. Of the following, the one who had the MOST profound effect upon young Irish poets was 2._____

   A. William B. Yeats
   B. Seumas O'Sullivan
   C. Padraic Colum
   D. Liam O'Flaherty

3. Of the following, the one MOST closely related to Jane Austen's work is 3._____

   A. Gothic romance
   B. English country society
   C. intricate plot structure
   D. the Five Towns

4. Alexander Pope did NOT write 4._____

   A. DRAPIER'S LETTERS
   B. THE DUNCIAD
   C. ESSAY ON MAN
   D. THE RAPE OF THE LOCK

5. RIME ROYAL was so named because of its use by 5._____

   A. James I
   B. Edward II
   C. Henry V
   D. Richard II

6. Wyatt and Surrey are perhaps BEST known for their 6._____

   A. introduction into England on new verse forms
   B. discovery of Scottish ballads
   C. translation of More's UTOPIA
   D. influence on the sonnets of Shakespeare

7. The approximate date of publication of the King James version of the Bible is USUALLY considered to be 7._____

   A. 1625   B. 1558   C. 1564   D. 1611

8. MOST closely associated with the production of early mystery and morality plays were 8._____

   A. traveling players
   B. the Savoyards
   C. the guilds
   D. the pamphleteers

9. The author of THE NIGGER OF THE NARCISSUS, although identified with English literature, was by nationality 9._____

   A. Greek   B. Norwegian   C. Polish   D. Italian

10. The fictional detective paired with the WRONG creator is

    A. Sherlock Holmes - A. Conan Doyle
    B. Hercule Poirot - Agatha Christie
    C. Mr. Moto - John Marquand
    D. Reggie Fortune - G.K. Chesterton

11. Mention of the Tabard Inn should remind one of

    A. THE HOUSE OF FAME   B. TROILUS AND CRESSIDA
    C. THE CANTERBURY TALES   D. THE ROMAUNT OF THE ROSE

12. A theme MOST often reiterated in George Eliot's novels is

    A. scholasticism   B. landlord absenteeism
    C. love and marriage   D. the frivolity of the court

13. The novel, THE ORDEAL OF RICHARD FEVEREL, deals principally with

    A. woman's emancipation   B. education
    C. politics   D. egotism

14. The novel, UNDER THE GREENWOOD TREE, has for its setting

    A. Wessex   B. Devonshire
    C. Cornwall   D. Thrums

15. A series of historical novels about England's sea exploits during the Napoleonic Wars has been written around

    A. Captain Bartlett   B. Lord Jim
    C. Horatio Hornblower   D. Captain Bligh

16. Of the following titles, the one which is IMPROPERLY grouped with the other three is

    A. LORD RANDAL   B. BARBARA ALLAN
    C. ALEXANDER'S FEAST   D. SIR PATRICK SPENS

17. *"Beauty is truth, truth beauty"* was the philosophy of the author of

    A. BRIGHT STAR   B. CAIN
    C. PROMETHEUS UNBOUND   D. THE RECLUSE

18. The line which follows *"Shall I compare thee to a summer's day?"* is

    A. "Rough winds do shake the darling buds of May"
    B. "But thy eternal summer shall not fade"
    C. "When in eternal lines to time thou growest"
    D. "Thou art more lovely and more temperate"

19. *"Who is Silvia?"* may be found in

    A. TWELFTH NIGHT   B. CYMBELINE
    C. TWO GENTLEMEN OF VERONA   D. THE TEMPEST

20. Spenser's work is NOT especially noted for its

    A. intricate allegory
    B. imaginative beauty

C. reproduction of homely idioms
D. moral purpose and seriousness

21. The character who speaks the line, *"Come live with me and be my love,"* is a(n)   21.____

    A. elf   B. shepherd   C. ploughman   D. prince

22. Of the following authors and poems, the ones IMPROPERLY paired are   22.____

    A. Byron - THE PRISONER OF CHILLON
    B. Scott - THE CORSAIR
    C. Shelley - OZYMANDIAS
    D. Keats - EVE OF ST. AGNES

23. *"They also serve who only stand and wait"* is from Milton's   23.____

    A. ON HIS BLINDNESS   B. ON SHAKESPEARE
    C. L'ALLEGRO   D. COMUS

24. The lines   24.____
    "Whan that Aprille with his shoures sote
    The droghte of Marche hath perced to the rote"
    are from

    A. Spenser   B. Dryden   C. Ascham   D. Chaucer

25. George Eliot wrote   25.____

    A. CALLISTA   B. ROMOLA
    C. RAMONA   D. CLYTEMNESTRA

KEY (CORRECT ANSWERS)

1.	C	11.	C
2.	C	12.	B
3.	B	13.	B
4.	A	14.	A
5.	A	15.	C
6.	A	16.	C
7.	D	17.	A
8.	C	18.	D
9.	C	19.	C
10.	C	20.	C

21. B
22. B
23. A
24. D
25. B

TEST 5

DIRECTIONS: Each question or incomplete statement is followed by several suggested answers or completions. Select the one that BEST answers the question or completes the statement. *PRINT THE LETTER OF THE CORRECT ANSWER IN THE SPACE AT THE RIGHT.*

1. *"Grow old along with me! The best is yet to be"* was written by

    A. Matthew Arnold
    B. W.E. Henley
    C. Robert Browning
    D. Alfred Tennyson

    1._____

2. The line which CORRECTLY follows *"Life's but a walking shadow, a poor player"* is

    A. "His acts being seven stages"
    B. "Full of sound and bombast, spouting rhymes"
    C. "That struts and frets his hour upon the stage"
    D. "A mouthing mountebank, niggard of talent"

    2._____

3. *".....Her voice was ever soft, Gentle, and low, an excellent thing in woman"* is a quotation from

    A. KING LEAR
    B. TWO GENTLEMEN OF VERONA
    C. ROMEO AND JULIET
    D. MEASURE FOR MEASURE

    3._____

4. Horton and Bunhill are places associated with

    A. Joseph Addison
    B. John Bunyan
    C. John Milton
    D. William Congreve

    4._____

5. A critic who felt strongly that poets should not attribute human feelings to inanimate objects was

    A. George Saintsbury
    B. John Ruskin
    C. Thomas Love Peacock
    D. Matthew Arnold

    5._____

6. The heroine of THE MILL ON THE FLOSS

    A. left the country when her lover married
    B. lived out her life alone in the mill
    C. met death by drowning
    D. ran away to Spain with her lover

    6._____

7. The angel Ithuriel, in PARADISE LOST, exposed deceit by means of a

    A. graven ring
    B. magic spear
    C. golden sword
    D. special shibboleth

    7._____

8. Charles Lamb's difficulty with his sister Mary stemmed from her

    A. greater reputation
    B. periodic fits of madness
    C. personal hatred
    D. refusal to collaborate with him

    8._____

9. In SHE STOOPS TO CONQUER, Tony Lumpkin

   A. was a writer of serious plays
   B. married his cousin for her money
   C. saved his stepfather from drowning
   D. made two strangers think his stepfather's house was an inn

10. Arnold Bennett's MOST significant work deals with

    A. the Wessex Country
    B. the Five Towns
    C. unusual exploits of outstanding men
    D. old Celtic legends

11. One of the chief contributors of the poems in TOTTEL'S MISCELLANY was

    A. William Shakespeare
    B. Ben Jonson
    C. Thomas Wyatt
    D. Christopher Marlowe

12. Of the following novels by H.G. Wells, the one which is NOT properly classed *as scientific fiction* is

    A. THE TIME MACHINE
    B. THE FOOD OF THE GODS
    C. TONO-BUNGAY
    D. THE SLEEPER AWAKES

13. In Chaucer's CANTERBURY TALES, the pilgrims are traveling to the shrine of Saint

    A. Thomas à Becket
    B. Thomas Aquinas
    C. George of England
    D. Michael

14. A sonnet sequence named ASTROPHEL AND STELLA was written by

    A. John Lyly
    B. Sir Philip Sydney
    C. Edmund Spenser
    D. Samuel Daniel

15. The rhyme scheme of a Shakespearean sonnet is

    A. a b b a a b b a c d e c d e
    B. a b b a a b b a c d c d c d
    C. a b a b c d c d e f e f g g
    D. a b a b c d c d e f g e f g

16. Of the following, the one NOT written by Dryden is

    A. THE DUNCIAD
    B. THE MEDAL
    C. MAC FLECKNOE
    D. RELIGIO LAICI

17. Alexander Pope translated THE ILIAD into

    A. blank verse
    B. rhymed couplets
    C. ballad meter
    D. free verse

18. In form, Milton's LYCIDAS is a(n)

    A. masque
    B. elegy
    C. sonnet sequence
    D. epic

19. Shelley's ADONAIS commemorates the death of

   A. Lamb B. Byron C. Wordsworth D. Keats

20. From 1850 to 1892, England's poet laureate was

   A. Wordsworth B. Southey
   C. Tennyson   D. Browning

21. Browning's THE RING AND THE BOOK is a series of

   A. satires B. dramatic monologues
   C. lyrics   D. sonnets

22. Credit for being the earliest English comedy goes to

   A. RALPH ROISTER DOISTER
   B. GAMMER GURTON'S NEEDLE
   C. MASTER PIERRE PATELIN
   D. FRIAR BACON AND FRIAR BUNGAY

23. Richard Burbage was renowned as a

   A. Shakespearean actor
   B. 17th century playwright
   C. 18th century scenic designer
   D. Restoration Comedy actor

24. During the middle part of the 18th century, David Garrick was manager of the _____ Theatre.

   A. Drury Lane   B. Globe
   C. Covent Garden D. Platform

25. Tony Lumpkin is a character in a play written by

   A. Christopher Marlowe B. John Dryden
   C. Oliver Goldsmith   D. William Shakespeare

KEY (CORRECT ANSWERS)

1.	C	11.	C
2.	C	12.	C
3.	A	13.	A
4.	C	14.	B
5.	B	15.	C
6.	C	16.	A
7.	B	17.	B
8.	B	18.	B
9.	D	19.	D
10.	B	20.	C

21. B
22. A
23. A
24. A
25. C

EXAMINATION SECTION
TEST 1

DIRECTIONS: Each question or incomplete statement is followed by several suggested answers or completions. Select the one that BEST answers the question or completes the statement. *PRINT THE LETTER OF THE CORRECT ANSWER IN THE SPACE AT THE RIGHT.*

1. Of the following, the one NOT basically a poet is 1.____

    A. Evelyn Waugh
    B. John Masefield
    C. W.H. Auden
    D. Stephen Spender

2. Of the following, the writer NOT connected with the Celtic Renaissance is 2.____

    A. Lord Dunsany
    B. William Butler Keats
    C. Lady Gregory
    D. Sir James Barrie

3. Of the following, the one who was a famous essayist of the Elizabethan period is 3.____

    A. The Earl of Chesterfield
    B. Sir Francis Bacon
    C. William Hazlitt
    D. Sir William Temple

4. Elia was the pseudonym of 4.____

    A. George Saintsbury
    B. Thomas DeQuincey
    C. Thomas B. Macaulay
    D. Charles Lamb

5. Joseph Addison contributed many essays to THE SPECTATOR, a publication which he conducted in conjunction with 5.____

    A. Jonathan Swift
    B. John Dryden
    C. Richard Steele
    D. Samuel Johnson

6. Alexander Pope's ESSAY ON CRITICISM differs from MOST modern essays in that it is 6.____

    A. devoted to a literary subject
    B. written in verse form
    C. based upon a controversial theme
    D. an expression of the author's own opinions

7. The title of Samuel Butler's satirical poem about the Puritans is 7.____

    A. THE DUNCIAD
    B. HUDIBRAS
    C. SOHRAB AND RUSTUM
    D. BEPPO

8. Lady Gregory was CLOSELY associated with the 8.____

    A. Gaiety Theatre
    B. Abbey Theatre
    C. Globe Theatre
    D. Old Vic

9. The character of a social climber is portrayed in 9.____

    A. KENILWORTH
    B. VANITY FAIR
    C. GUY MANNERING
    D. ELMER GANTRY

43

10. A handkerchief is regarded as evidence of a wife's faithlessness in

    A. LOVE'S LABOUR'S LOST   B. THE MERRY WIVES OF WINDSOR
    C. THE TAMING OF THE SHREW D. OTHELLO

11. Shaw's famous prefaces may be said to find a precedent in

    A. Hugo's CROMWELL
    B. Schiller's DEATH OF WALLENSTEIN
    C. Dumas' DAME AUX CAMELIAS
    D. Lope de Vega's THE SHEEP WELL

12. The story of Prometheus has been interpreted by

    A. Aeschylus and Shelley   B. Sophocles and Keats
    C. Euripedes and Shelley   D. Homer and Keats

13. The Bodleian Library is

    A. a collection of rare manuscripts at Oxford
    B. a repository of incubula at Cambridge
    C. the original source of the Folger Library
    D. a specialized collection of medieval ballads

14. In Book II of PARADISE LOST, the fallen angels decide to

    A. make one last attack on Heaven's high towers
    B. live in *ignoble ease and peaceful sloth*
    C. seek mediation between God and themselves
    D. try to strike at God indirectly

15. A savagely realistic picture of village life is presented in

    A. Crabbe's THE VILLAGE
    B. Goldsmith's THE DESERTED VILLAGE
    C. Burn's THE COTTER'S SATURDAY NIGHT
    D. Cowper's THE TASK

16. Of the following plot situations, all appear in a Shakespearean play EXCEPT a

    A. baby girl is abandoned on the shore of Bohemia
    B. Roman noble marries the sister of his rival for power
    C. tinker kills a treasonable general and leads an army to victory
    D. girl disguised as a man is challenged to a duel

17. An examination of the roots of organized charity is the central point in

    A. MAJOR BARBARA   B. CANDIDA
    C. MAN AND SUPERMAN   D. THE DOCTOR'S DILEMMA

18. In a famous sonnet, John Keats paid tribute to a translation of a classic made by a(n)

    A. Irish poet
    B. Elizabethan dramatist
    C. contemporary essayist
    D. fifteenth century religious writer

19. John Dryden has often been accused of

   A. having a weak prose style
   B. timeserving
   C. writing flabby satirical poems
   D. inflexibility and unwillingness to experiment

20. Beatrix Castlewood is a character in both

   A. HENRY ESMOND and THE VIRGINIANS
   B. HENRY ESMOND and VANITY FAIR
   C. VANITY FAIR and PENDENNIS
   D. PENDENNIS and THE VIRGINIANS

21. In George Meredith's THE EGOIST, Sir Willoughby Patterne

   A. loses both Constantia Durham and Clara Middleton
   B. comes to his senses after his first defeat and successfully woos Clara
   C. finds in Laetitia Dale the indifference that piques his interest
   D. is self-effacing, despite his wealth and position

22. Tennyson's THE PRINCESS was good-naturedly satirized by

   A. Robert Browning   B. W.S. Gilbert
   C. Jerome K. Jerome   D. Ernest Dowson

23. Of the following, each is for the MOST part autobiographical EXCEPT

   A. FAR AWAY AND LONG AGO - Hudson
   B. THE SUMMING UP - Maugham
   C. GRACE ABOUNDING - John Bunyan
   D. THE CROCK OF GOLD - James Stephens

24. The expression *an acute study in the consciousness of lost honor* is BEST applied to

   A. THE OLD WIVES' TALES - Arnold Bennett
   B. LORD JIM - Joseph Conrad
   C. JUSTICE - John Galsworthy
   D. THE BELOVED VAGABOND - William Locke

25. In the essay AES TRIPLEX, Stevenson reflects upon

   A. the difficulties faced by a writer
   B. the pleasures of walking
   C. man's courage in the face of death
   D. the brevity of literary fame

KEY (CORRECT ANSWERS)

1.	A	11.	A
2.	D	12.	A
3.	B	13.	A
4.	D	14.	D
5.	C	15.	A
6.	B	16.	C
7.	B	17.	A
8.	B	18.	B
9.	B	19.	B
10.	D	20.	A

21. A
22. B
23. D
24. B
25. C

TEST 2

DIRECTIONS: Each question or incomplete statement is followed by several suggested answers or completions. Select the one that BEST answers the question or completes the statement. *PRINT THE LETTER OF THE CORRECT ANSWER IN THE SPACE AT THE RIGHT.*

1. A poet who frequently drew his material from ancient and medieval legends is 1._____

    A. Ralph Hodgson
    B. John Henry Newman
    C. William Norris
    D. James Thompson (1834-1882)

2. Character and novel are correctly matched in each of the following pairs EXCEPT: 2._____

    A. Sophia Western - TOM JONES
    B. Matthew Bramble - HUMPHREY CLINKER
    C. Uncle Toby - TRISTRAM SHANDY
    D. Amy Robsart - THE VICAR OF WAKEFIELD

3. Milton's COMUS is indebted in part to the 3._____

    A. story of Dido, from THE AENEID
    B. Circe myth, in THE ODYSSEY
    C. Andromache episode, in THE ILIAD
    D. tale of Paolo and Francesca, in THE DIVINE COMEDY

4. Each of the following elegies is correctly matched with its subject EXCEPT: 4._____

    A. THYRSIS - Arthur Hugh Clough
    B. ASTROPHEL - Edmund Spenser
    C. LYCIDAS - Edward King
    D. IN MEMORIAM - Arthur Hallam

5. THE HEART OF THE MATTER, by Graham Greene, has as its MAIN character a 5._____

    A. British official in a small African town
    B. missionary among the aborigines of the Amazon
    C. convict-settler in Australia
    D. wealthy plantation owner in the new Indonesia

6. A priest, Father Brown, is the detective in a series of stories by 6._____

    A. Erle Stanley Gardner   B. A. Conan Doyle
    C. Hilaire Belloc   D. G.K. Chesterton

7. THE CASTLE OF OTRANTO is a good example of the 7._____

    A. gothic novel   B. pastoral romance
    C. philosophical tale   D. sociological novel

47

8. Although he wrote many novels about his own era, Charles Reade is BEST known for his book,

    A. ALTON LOCKS
    B. PASSIONATE PILGRIM
    C. THE CLOISTER AND THE HEARTH
    D. WESTWARD HO!

9. A sequel to HENRY ESMOND is

    A. PENDENNIS   B. THE NEWCOMES
    C. VANITY FAIR   D. THE VIRGINIANS

10. David Copperfield's first wife was

    A. Agnes Wickfield   B. Dora Spenlow
    C. Little Em'ly   D. Rosa Dartle

11. The author of TRISTRAM SHANDY also wrote

    A. TRAVELS WITH A DONKEY
    B. A SENTIMENTAL JOURNEY
    C. TRAVEL DIARY OF A PHILOSOPHER
    D. THE BIBLE IN SPAIN

12. Of the following novels, the one NOT in epistolary form is

    A. SIR CHARLES GRANDISON   B. PAMELA
    C. HUMPHREY CLINKER   D. MOLL FLANDERS

13. A.E. Housman is noted for his poems about

    A. London   B. Shropshire
    C. Isle of Man   D. Scotland

14. The writer among the following who was NOT a physician is

    A. Lytton Strachey   B. A.J. Cronin
    C. Oliver Wendell Holmes   D. Somerset Maugham

15. The lines,
    ...my purpose holds
    To sail beyond the sunset, and the baths
    Of all the western stars, until I die,
are from

    A. THE PASSING OF ARTHUR   B. ULYSSES
    C. THE FORSAKEN MERMAN   D. ONE WORD MORE

16. Of the following novels, the one which has NOT been filmed is

    A. THE KEYS OF THE KINGDOM   B. GREAT EXPECTATIONS
    C. THE EGOIST   D. TREASURE ISLAND

17. Of the following poems, the one which does NOT commemorate a dead friend is

    A. IN MEMORIAM   B. OZYMANDIAS
    C. ADONAIS   D. LYCIDAS

18. In A MODEST PROPOSAL, Swift ironically suggested   18.____

    A. revising currency   B. compulsory marriage
    C. cooking babies   D. educational reform

19. The name NOT usually associated with that of Dr. Johnson is   19.____

    A. Mrs. Thrale   B. Sir Joshua Reynolds
    C. Gainsborough   D. Boswell

20. Prominent as interpreters of Shakespearean roles on the stage have been all of the following EXCEPT   20.____

    A. John Gielgud   B. Leslie Howard
    C. Robert Morley   D. Maurice Evans

21. Of the following pairs, the one in which the items are INCORRECTLY matched is: 21.____

    A. Katherine Mansfield - Yorkshire
    B. Hardy - Wessex
    C. Bennett - The Five Towns
    D. Barrie - Thrums

22. The hero has a clubfoot in   22.____

    A. TONO-BUNGAY   B. OLD WIVES' TALE
    C. OF HUMAN BONDAGE   D. THE MAN OF PROPERTY

23. Murder is NOT an important item in the plot of   23.____

    A. WINTERSET   B. TRIFLES
    C. GREEN PASTURES   D. HOMECOMING

24. In the line, *And gladly wolde he lerne, and gladly teche,* Chaucer wrote of the   24.____

    A. Pardoner   B. Knight   C. Clerk   D. Squire

25. Of the following, the one which is NOT the title of a poem by Masefield is   25.____

    A. LORD HIM   B. THE EVERLASTING MERCY
    C. DAUBER   D. THE WIDOW IN THE BYE ST.

KEY (CORRECT ANSWERS)

1.	C	11.	B
2.	D	12.	D
3.	B	13.	B
4.	B	14.	A
5.	A	15.	B
6.	D	16.	C
7.	A	17.	B
8.	C	18.	C
9.	D	19.	C
10.	B	20.	C

21. A
22. C
23. C
24. C
25. A

TEST 3

DIRECTIONS: Each question or incomplete statement is followed by several suggested answers or completions. Select the one that BEST answers the question or completes the statement. *PRINT THE LETTER OF THE CORRECT ANSWER IN THE SPACE AT THE RIGHT.*

1. *To-morrow and to-morrow, and to-morrow,*
   Creeps in this petty pace from day to day
   was spoken by

   A. Hamlet B. King Lear
   C. Macbeth D. Henry V

   1.____

2. Of the following English authors, the one who NEVER lived or traveled in America was

   A. Rudyard Kipling B. Robert Louis Stevenson
   C. T.S. Eliot D. George Eliot

   2.____

3. *Look'd at each other with a wild surmise,*
   Silent, upon a peak in Darien
   are lines from the poetry of

   A. Shelley B. Keats
   C. Wordsworth D. Byron

   3.____

4. *My purpose was to imitate, and, as far as possible, to adopt the very language of men* was a poetic creed expressed by

   A. Poe B. Coleridge
   C. Whitman D. Wordsworth

   4.____

5. The one of the following places NOT the scene of one of Jane Austen's novels is

   A. Northanger Abbey B. Mansfield Park
   C. Barchester Towers D. Hertfordshire

   5.____

6. The line, *And the night shall be filled with music,* is from the poetry of

   A. Byron B. Wordsworth
   C. Longfellow D. Burns

   6.____

7. The lines,
   That men may rise on stepping-stones
   Of their dead selves to higher things,
   were written by

   A. Matthew Arnold B. William Cullen Bryant
   C. Robert Browning D. Alfred Tennyson

   7.____

8. The lines,
   Life, like a dome of many-coloured glass,
   Stains the white radiance of eternity,
   appear in

   A. HYPERION B. IN MEMORIAM
   C. ADONAIS D. LYCIDAS

   8.____

9. Lines in Shakespeare's plays suggested all of the following titles of books EXCEPT

   A. BRIEF CANDLES
   B. FAME IS THE SPUR
   C. BOTH YOUR HOUSES
   D. TOLD BY AN IDIOT

10. The death of a favorite cat was described by the author of

    A. TO A HOUSE
    B. THE TIGER
    C. ELEGY WRITTEN IN A COUNTRY CHURCHYARD
    D. OWL AND THE PUSSYCAT

11. THE PRELUDE, by Wordsworth, deals in part with

    A. his experiences in France during the Revolution
    B. an early love affair
    C. the childhood of Michael
    D. his thoughts concerning life after death

12. Roderick Random, Peregrine Pickle, and Humphrey Clinker were all created by

    A. Laurence Sterne
    B. Tobias Smollett
    C. Thomas Fielding
    D. Daniel Defoe

13. Redemption through love is the theme of

    A. ALASTOR
    B. HYPERION
    C. THE VISION OF SIR LAUNFAL
    D. DAYS OF ANCIENT ROME

14. In RABBI BEN EZRA, Browning

    A. affirms his faith in the future
    B. discusses the tenets of Judaism
    C. tells of his experience in a synagogue
    D. writes of a journey to religious shrines

15. *Here lies one whose name was write in water* is the epitaph of

    A. Christopher Marlowe
    B. John Keats
    C. Lord Byron
    D. Robert Louis Stevenson

16. A realistic picture of the daily life of coal miners is given in

    A. PENDENNIS
    B. CRANFORD
    C. CALIBAN IN THE COAL MINES
    D. SONS AND LOVERS

17. The line, *A thing of beauty is a joy forever,* is the beginning of the poem

    A. ODE TO A NIGHTINGALE
    B. ODE ON A GRECIAN URN
    C. ENDYMION
    D. THE EVE OF ST. AGNES

18. The one of the following who is the heroine of a novel is

   A. Mary Godwin
   B. Clarissa Harlowe
   C. Lucy Gray
   D. Kate Hardcastle

19. The one of the following in which the central character is NOT a cripple is

   A. RICHARD III
   B. OF HUMAN BONDAGE
   C. ADAM BEDE
   D. GLASS MENAGERIE

20. All of the following were famous letter writers EXCEPT

   A. Lord Chesterfield
   B. Samuel Richardson
   C. Horace Walpole
   D. George Eliot

21. The one of the following NOT a Restoration playwright is

   A. John Dryden
   B. Richard Brinsley Sheridan
   C. William Wycherley
   D. William Congreve

22. The one of the following critical judgments made of Shakespeare was that he

   A. is the first great painter of character because he is the first great observer of it among European writers
   B. was not of an age but for all time
   C. is the only English poet who sustains the so-called grand style
   D. was the strongest poet of the age of prose

23. In the ODE TO A NIGHTINGALE, Keats

   A. says that truth is beauty
   B. speaks of the eternality in a thing of beauty
   C. asks to be taught the song of the bird
   D. gives voice to a premonition of premature death

24. *This above all: to thine own self be true* was advice given by

   A. Jacques   B. Polonius   C. Banquo   D. Portia

25. The one of the following NOT a play by Shakespeare is

   A. TITUS ANDRONICUS
   B. TROILUS AND CRESSIDA
   C. TIMON OF ATHENS
   D. VENUS AND ADONIS

KEY (CORRECT ANSWERS)

1.	C	11.	A
2.	D	12.	B
3.	B	13.	C
4.	C	14.	A
5.	C	15.	B
6.	C	16.	D
7.	D	17.	C
8.	C	18.	B
9.	B	19.	C
10.	C	20.	D

21. B
22. B
23. D
24. B
25. D

TEST 4

DIRECTIONS: Each question or incomplete statement is followed by several suggested answers or completions. Select the one that BEST answers the question or completes the statement. *PRINT THE LETTER OF THE CORRECT ANSWER IN THE SPACE AT THE RIGHT.*

1. COLLEGES OF UNREASON represented a satirical reference to imperfect educational institutions in 1.____
    - A. EREWHON
    - B. THE REPUBLIC
    - C. BRAVE NEW WORLD
    - D. A TRAVELER FROM ALTRURIA

2. The one of the following NOT a collection of letters is 2.____
    - A. JOURNAL TO STELLA
    - B. JOURNAL OF THE PLAGUE YEAR
    - C. PAMELA
    - D. EVELINA

3. The Augustan Age in English literature marks the triumph of 3.____
    - A. Romanticism
    - B. Naturalism
    - C. Neo-classicism
    - D. Humanism

4. The great London fire of 1666 was minutely described by 4.____
    - A. John Bunyan
    - B. John Milton
    - C. Alexander Pope
    - D. Samuel Pepys

5. The one of the following NOT a quotation from Shakespeare is: 5.____
    - A. And spite of pride, in erring reason's spite,
      One truth is clear, whatever is, is right.
    - B. The time is out of joint; O, cursed spite,
      That ever I was born to set it right!
    - C. Her voice was ever soft, gentle, and low, an excellent thing in woman.
    - D. Come what come may,
      Time and the hour runs through the roughest day.

6. The novel in which NONE of the action takes place on a South Seas island is 6.____
    - A. TYPEE
    - B. PITCAIRN ISLAND
    - C. THE MOON AND SIXPENSE
    - D. GREEN MANSIONS

7. *This was the noblest Roman of them all* was a tribute paid to 7.____
    - A. Caesar   B. Brutus   C. Cassius   D. Portia

8. A shipwreck causes a reversal of social status in 8.____
    - A. ADRIFT ON AN ICE FLOE
    - B. THE ADMIRABLE CRICHTON
    - C. MAN AND SUPERMAN
    - D. HOTEL UNIVERSE

9. The quotation, *It is not so deep as a well nor so wide as a church-door,* is from

   A. MACBETH
   B. AS YOU LIKE IT
   C. ROMEO AND JULIET
   D. A MIDSUMMER NIGHT'S DREAM

10. John Shand, in Barrie's play, WHAT EVERY WOMAN KNOWS,

    A. loved Maggie at first sight
    B. ran away with the Countess
    C. became a member of Parliament
    D. refused to carry out his contract with Maggie's brother

11. In DAVID COPPERFIELD, Uriah Keep

    A. married Emily
    B. ran away with Dora
    C. taught David to play a musical instrument
    D. wanted to marry Agnes

12. Of the following, the one containing an INCORRECT description is

    A. Jaques - a melancholy man
    B. Nerissa - a female servant-confidante
    C. Launcelot Gobbo - a witty, clownish servant
    D. Henry V - a scheming villain of a king

13. Sir James M. Barrie gives his characters *a second chance* to relive and improve their lives in

    A. THE LITTLE MINISTER
    B. PETER PAN
    C. THE TWELVE-POUND LOOK
    D. DEAR BRUTUS

14. All of the following poems were written for particular occasions EXCEPT

    A. CONCORD HYMN
    B. RECESSIONAL
    C. PROTHALAMION
    D. CHRISTABEL

15. That we reap what we sow, that *character is fate,* is a DOMINANT theme in the novels of

    A. Emily Bronte
    B. Charles Kingsley
    C. George Eliot
    D. Anthony Trollope

16. Of the following, all are sonnet sequences EXCEPT

    A. AMORETTI
    B. ASTROPHEL AND STELLA
    C. THE HOUSE OF LIFE
    D. EPITHALAMION

17. All of the following were Pre-Raphaelites EXCEPT

    A. Dante Gabriel Rossetti
    B. John Everett Millais
    C. William Henry Davies
    D. William Holman Hunt

18. The name of William Sansom is PROMINENT as that of

    A. the author of several excellent historical novels
    B. an English short story writer and novelist
    C. an incisive literary critic in the tradition of Dr. Johnson
    D. an iconoclastic expatriate glorying in a *decadent art*

19. Aldous Huxley's works show a(n)

    A. continuation of the bitter cynicism of his earlier novels
    B. interest in oriental religion as a solution to the world's ills
    C. materialistic and mechanistic philosophy of living
    D. preoccupation with the scientific principles of Thomas Henry Huxley

20. Donizetti's opera, LUCIA DI LAMMERMOOR, is based upon a novel by the author who created the character

    A. John Ridd
    B. Sophia Baines
    C. Wendy Darling
    D. Keanie Deans

21. Ruskin's SESAME: OF KINGS' TREASURES deals PRINCIPALLY with the

    A. value of an enlightened citizenry to a liberal monarch
    B. questions of what to read and how to read
    C. duty of governments to subsidize the production of the true *kings* of a nation - its writers
    D. effect of nineteenth century economic policies on the workers of the world

22. Screwtape, of THE SCREWTAPE LETTERS, by C.S. Lewis, is a

    A. demon
    B. defrocked clergyman
    C. martian
    D. misanthropic banker

23. The *playboy of the Western World* loses stature with the community when

    A. he tries to murder his father
    B. he betrays the love of Pegeen
    C. his father reappears
    D. he flees after the first attack on his father

24. Dryden's ALL FOR LOVE deals with the same subject matter as

    A. CYMBELINE
    B. CORIOLANUS
    C. ANTONY AND CLEOPATRA
    D. ROMEO AND JULIET

25. THE ROAD TO XANADU is a

    A. biography of Coleridge
    B. sequel to CHRISTABEL
    C. romantic adventure story
    D. study of the workings of the imagination

KEY (CORRECT ANSWERS)

1.	A	11.	D
2.	B	12.	D
3.	C	13.	D
4.	D	14.	D
5.	A	15.	C
6.	D	16.	D
7.	B	17.	C
8.	B	18.	B
9.	C	19.	B
10.	C	20.	D

21.	B
22.	A
23.	C
24.	C
25.	D

TEST 5

DIRECTIONS: Each question or incomplete statement is followed by several suggested answers or completions. Select the one that BEST answers the question or completes the statement. *PRINT THE LETTER OF THE CORRECT ANSWER THE SPACE AT THE RIGHT.*

1. A tale of love and betrayal during the Trojan War is told by BOTH

    A. John Lyly and George Moore
    B. Ben Jonson and Edmund Spenser
    C. Shakespeare and Chaucer
    D. Keats and Tennyson

    1.____

2. THE WAKEFIELD CYCLE is the name given to

    A. a series of medieval mystery plays
    B. a tapestry depicting England at the time of William the Conqueror
    C. a collection of plays with Wakefield as the setting
    D. folk ballads collected by Bishop Thomas Percy

    2.____

3. Allan Quatermain is the creation of

    A. George Du Maurier
    B. Rider Haggard
    C. John Buchan
    D. Sheridan Le Fanu

    3.____

4. *He was not of an age, but for all time!* was

    A. Wordsworth's tribute to Milton
    B. Jonson's tribute to Shakespeare
    C. Sandburg's tribute to Lincoln
    D. Keat's tribute to Homer

    4.____

5. The lines,
    Will no one tell me what she sings?
    Perhaps the plaintive numbers flow
    For old, unhappy, far-off things
    And battles long ago,
    are from a poem by the author of

    A. TIGER! TIGER! BURNING BRIGHT
    B. MICHAEL
    C. MARY MORISON
    D. PROMETHEUS UNBOUND

    5.____

6. The lines,
    Speak of me as I am; nothing extenuate
    Nor set down aught in malice; then must you speak
    Of one that lov'd not wisely but too well,
    are from

    A. KING LEAR
    B. OTHELLO
    C. ROMEO AND JULIET
    D. JULIUS CAESAR

    6.____

59

7. The quotation,
   What's time? Leave Now for dogs and apes!
   Man has forever,
   is from a poem by

   A. Tennyson B. Swinburne
   C. Browning D. Arthur Hugh Clough

8. The expression *between two worlds* comes from a famous poem by

   A. Elizabeth Barrett Browning
   B. Swinburne
   C. Dante Gabriel Rossetti
   D. Matthew Arnold

9. A remarkable psychological study of Coleridge's KUBLA KHAN and ANCIENT MARINER was written by

   A. J. Forster   B. H.D. Traill
   C. G.E. Saintsbury D. J.L. Lowes

10. The Oxford movement which influenced literary thought was founded by

    A. John Keble   B. Edward Puesey
    C. William Ward   D. John Henry Newman

11. In PATIENCE, Gilbert and Sullivan satirized the

    A. imperialism of Kipling   B. didacticism of Tennyson
    C. aestheticism of Wilde   D. idealism of Yeats

12. The definitive biography of John Milton was written by

    A. Mark Patterson B. Walter Raleigh
    C. Richard Garnet D. David Masson

13. Macaronic verse is a term loosely applied to any form of verse which

    A. mingles two or more languages
    B. deals with the manners and morals of the aristocracy
    C. has Italian romance for its theme
    D. the author interlards with personal comments

14. The author of SHROPSHIRE LAD was eminent as a(n)

    A. astronomer   B. Latinist
    C. mathematician D. barrister

15. ONE WORD MORE was written by

    A. Byron B. Browning C. Tennyson D. Arnold

16. The names of Wyatt and Surrey loom large in the Renaissance period because

    A. of their introduction into English of foreign verse forms
    B. their position in court circles enabled them to foster their own publications
    C. they lived long enough to establish permanently a definite school of English poetry
    D. they devoted themselves exclusively to English life and thought

17. The title of the piece which was said to have made *Gay rich and Rich gay* was   17.____

    A. POLLY   B. FABLES
    C. THE BEGGAR'S OPERA   D. THE SHEPERD'S WEEK

18. Jeanie Deans is a character in Scott's   18.____

    A. GUY MANNERING   B. THE HEART OF MIDLOTHIAN
    C. OLD MORTALITY   D. ROB ROY

19. The regular Pindaric Ode was FIRST used in England by   19.____

    A. John Dryden   B. Abraham Cowley
    C. Ben Jonson   D. Thomas Gray

20. The life and death of Thomas à Becket was the subject of a play by   20.____

    A. Paul Vincent Carroll   B. J.M. Barrie
    C. John Synge   D. T.S. Eliot

21. The one person who, with William Butler Yeats, was MOST instrumental in the founding of the Irish National Theatre was   21.____

    A. Sean O'Casey   B. Lady Gregory
    C. James Stephens   D. George Moore

22. The importance of Francis Bacon in English culture rests on the fact that   22.____

    A. his philosophical works were the first of their kind to be written in English
    B. he provided the scientific method which was to overcome the Aristotelian tyranny of authority
    C. his essays, so like Montaigne's in their style and substance, were influential in establishing the English prose form
    D. he continued the idealistic reform inaugurated by Sir Thomas Morley in his great Latin work, the NEW ATLANTIS

23. The characteristic division of the Elizabethan tragedy into five acts may be traced to the influence of   23.____

    A. the earlier miracle plays which proved the fountain head of English dramaturgy
    B. the ancient Greek tragedies upon which the Renaissance seized with avidity as the quintessence of form
    C. Seneca, whose tragedies were regarded as models of dramaturgical skills
    D. the French playwrights who in turn found their authority in Aristotle

24. TIMBER by Ben Jonson was   24.____

    A. the first English grammar, written to restrain the license of the Elizabethan poets intoxicated with their power
    B. one of the salacious masques written for the court of James I
    C. a poetic defense of the classical moderation which Jonson represented
    D. a collection of notes and reflections on miscellaneous subjects for the greater part adapted from Latin writers

25. In its final form, ENDYMION, by John Keats, 25.____
   A. is a finished, highly polished piece, regarded with pride and equanimity by its author
   B. is a work of an immature genius, with emphasis upon sensation rather than thought
   C. is an almost perfect example of that rara avis, a long poem dashed off in the heat of poetic inspiration
   D. was described by him in his preface as a feverish attempt, rather than a deed accomplished

KEY (CORRECT ANSWERS)

1.	C	11.	C
2.	A	12.	D
3.	B	13.	A
4.	B	14.	B
5.	B	15.	B
6.	B	16.	A
7.	C	17.	C
8.	D	18.	B
9.	D	19.	B
10.	A	20.	D

21. B
22. B
23. B
24. D
25. D

EXAMINATION SECTION
TEST 1

DIRECTIONS: Each question or incomplete statement is followed by several suggested answers or completions. Select the one that BEST answers the question or completes the statement. *PRINT THE LETTER OF THE CORRECT ANSWER IN THE SPACE AT THE RIGHT.*

1. A CORRECT statement about the Old English ballads would be that　　1._____

    A. they were first collated and printed by Caxton
    B. they are usually perfect in metrical pattern and rhyme
    C. their subject matter includes domestic tragedies, historical events, and tales of outlaws
    D. literary scholars have finally reached agreement as to how they might have been composed

2. Of the following statements about THE VISION OF PIERS PLOWMAN, the LEAST accurate statement is that　　2._____

    A. it dates from the eleventh century
    B. it is probably the work of more than one man
    C. the verse is alliterative
    D. it attacks many of the vices of the times

3. In MUCH ADO ABOUT NOTHING, Dogberry, the constable, is noteworthy for his　　3._____

    A. malicious performance of duty
    B. melodious singing voice
    C. susceptibility to amorous maidens
    D. abuse of the English language

4. In TAMBURLAINE THE GREAT by Christopher Marlowe, the hero may be accurately characterized as　　4._____

    A. bloodthirsty and inhuman
    B. harsh at times but calm and dignified
    C. gracious to his captives
    D. weak and sniveling when captured

5. All of the following are properly matched with songs that they sing EXCEPT　　5._____

    A. Ariel: *Full fathom five thy father lies*
    B. Benedict: *The God of love*
    　　　　　That sits above
    C. Ophelia: *How should I your true love know*
    D. Puck: *Tell me where is fancy bred*

6. Ben Jonson's comedies of humor were marked by　　6._____

    A. dances and songs
    B. clever caricature
    C. romantic tone
    D. well-rounded characterization

7. All of the following are well known as writers of religious verse EXCEPT

    A. George Herbert   B. William Cowper
    C. Christina Rossetti   D. Edmund Waller

8. Of the following, the statement LEAST applicable to Dryden is that

    A. his prose style was clear, lucid, and orderly
    B. his couplets were more flexible and varied than those of Pope
    C. his dramas broke away from the conventions of the Restoration theatre
    D. ABSALOM AND ACHITOPHEL and THE MEDAL are both satires on political themes

9. Of the following characters from THE CANTERBURY TALES, the one who is INCORRECTLY described is:

    A. The Clerk: But all be that he was a philosophre,
                      Yet hadde he but litol gold in cofre.
    B. The Knight: Syngynge he was, or floytynge, al the days
                       He was as fresh as is the month of May.
    C. The Parson: This noble ensample to his sheep he yaf,
                       That first he wroghte, and afterward he taughte.
    D. The Monk: He was a lord ful fat and in good poynt.

10. BERMUDAS by Andrew Marvell concerns the arrival at the islands of

    A. shipwrecked sailors   B. religious exiles
    C. marauding pirates   D. Columbus' expedition

11. The poet who advised his readers to *go and catch a falling star* was

    A. John Dryden   B. Robert Herrick
    C. Ben Jonson   D. John Donne

12. *He wrote with flippant grace* is a description that BEST characterizes

    A. Samuel Daniel in CARE CHARMER SLEEP
    B. John Donne in his sonnet, DEATH
    C. Leigh Hunt in ABOU BEN ADHEM
    D. Thomas Carew in DISDAIN RETURNED

13. Alfred Tennyson was to Arthur Hallam as John Milton was to

    A. Oliver Cromwell   B. Cyriac Skinner
    C. Edward King   D. Henry Vaughan

14. The poetry of John Donne is often marred by

    A. conventional imagery   B. lack of real emotion
    C. Latinized diction   D. harsh versification

15. *This morning I took my wife toward Westminster by water and landed her at Whitefriars with 5 pounds to buy her a petticoat, and I to the Privy Seal.*
This passage comes from the writings of

    A. Defoe   B. Addison   C. Pepys   D. Evelyn

16. *God tempers the wind to the shorn lamb* is a line from 16.____

    A. the KING JAMES BIBLE
    B. A SENTIMENTAL JOURNEY by Sterne
    C. AS YOU LIKE IT by Shakespeare
    D. POEMS OF INNOCENCE by Blake

17. *Little fly*
They summer's play
My careless hand
Has brushed away.
The lines quoted are from a poem by 17.____

    A. John Suckling   B. Emily Dickinson
    C. H.D.   D. William Blake

18. Samuel Johnson's contributions to THE RAMBLER were MAINLY 18.____

    A. installments which were later published as RASSELAS
    B. didactic and allegorical selections in narrative form
    C. essays on literature, manners, and morals
    D. poetic translations of classical writers like Juvenal

19. The Scriblerus Club included, among others, 19.____

    A. Richard Steel, Jonathan Swift, Joseph Addison
    B. Joseph Addison, Matthew Prior, John Dennis
    C. Alexander Pope, Dr. Arbuthnot, Jonathan Swift
    D. Williams Collins, Richard Steele, John Gay

20. *I am now to record a very curious incident in...life which fell under my own observation; of which pars magna fui and which I am persuaded will, with the liberal-minded, be much to his credit.*
The above passage was written by 20.____

    A. Maurois about Shelley   B. Strachey about Essex
    C. Boswell about Johnson   D. Jonson about Shakespeare

21. The poem TO MARY by William Cowper was written to 21.____

    A. Mary Wollstonecraft   B. Mary Morrison
    C. Mary Unwin   D. Mary Stuart

22. THE BEGGAR'S OPERA by John Gay was 22.____

    A. a satire on Italian opera
    B. a first-rate example of popular sentimental comedy
    C. unsuccessful during Gay's lifetime
    D. a glorification of William Pitt

23. A novel by Tobias Smollett which describes life on a British warship is 23.____

    A. PEREGRINE PICKLE   B. FERDINAND, COUNT FATHOM
    C. HUMPHREY CLINKER   D. RODERICK RANDOM

24. RURAL RIDES was the title given by William Cobbett to his collection of 24.____

   A. essays B. poems
   C. short stories D. letters

25. An IMPORTANT idea expressed in the preface to Wordsworth and Coleridge's LYRICAL 25.____
    BALLADS in 1798 was that

   A. poems should be written on the principle of art for art's sake
   B. there is a special language for poetry as distinguished from the language of prose
   C. all good poetry is the spontaneous overflow of powerful feelings
   D. the most fitting subject for poetry is the death of a beautiful woman

---

KEY (CORRECT ANSWERS)

1.	C	11.	D
2.	A	12.	D
3.	D	13.	C
4.	A	14.	D
5.	D	15.	C
6.	B	16.	B
7.	D	17.	D
8.	C	18.	C
9.	B	19.	C
10.	B	20.	C

21. C
22. A
23. D
24. A
25. C

TEST 2

DIRECTIONS: Each question or incomplete statement is followed by several suggested answers or completions. Select the one that BEST answers the question or completes the statement. *PRINT THE LETTER OF THE CORRECT ANSWER IN THE SPACE AT THE RIGHT.*

1. Of the following statements, the one LEAST applicable to Byron is that   1.____

    A. his narrative poetry is highly melodramatic
    B. he had a great admiration for Pope
    C. his poetry is often an overfrank expose of his own emotions
    D. he planned and revised his poems carefully

2. A quality INCORRECTLY associated with a character from Dickens' novels is   2.____

    A. optimism - Uriah Heep
    B. hypocrisy - Pecksniff
    C. self-sacrifice - Sidney Carton
    D. benevolence - Mr. Pickwick

3. All of the following treated the Arthurian legends in poetry EXCEPT   3.____

    A. William Morris   B. Alfred Lord Tennyson
    C. Robert Browning   D. Algernon Charles Swinburne

4. Mr. Pickwick was imprisoned because he   4.____

    A. was tricked by Mr. Jingle
    B. lost a breach of promise suit
    C. was held responsible for Sam Weller's debts
    D. became involved in a duel

5. The author of *Ah, did you once see Shelley plain....* also wrote the line   5.____

    A. *Rafael made a century of sonnets*
    B. *My mind to me a kingdom is*
    C. *The poetry of earth is ceasing never*
    D. *Home they brought the warrior dead*

6. The poet who heard *the still sad music of humanity* was   6.____

    A. Matthew Arnold   B. John Keats
    C. William Wordsworth   D. Robert Browning

7. AVE ATQUE VALE by Swinburne is an elegy written in memory of   7.____

    A. William Morris   B. Charles Baudelaire
    C. Matthew Arnold   D. George Meredith

8. An important part of Walter Pater's philosophical outlook was to   8.____

    A. burn with a pure gemlike flame at the sight of beauty
    B. seek the answer to aesthetic problems by reverting to the principles of the painters who flourished before Raphael

C. aid others to live lives of moral earnestness
D. subscribe to the feeling of Matthew Arnold that certitude was possible

9. All of the following are characteristic of THE WAY OF ALL FLESH by Samuel Butler EXCEPT

   A. much autobiographical material
   B. unabashed realism
   C. preciousness of style
   D. the absence of a well-defined plot

10. PROMETHEUS UNBOUND by Shelley is a lyrical drama characterized by

    A. absence of personifications
    B. staccato dialogue
    C. frequent choruses
    D. extreme pessimism

11. The term *Cockney School* was applied to Hunt, Shelley, Keats, and others by

    A. Hazlitt   B. Lockhart   C. Butler   D. Lamb

12. Each of the following novels is correctly matched with the name of an important character EXCEPT

    A. TOM JONES - Squire Allworthy
    B. KENILWORTH - Amy Robsart
    C. THE MAYOR OF CASTERBRIDGE - Donald Farfrae
    D. JANE EYRE - Stephen Blackpool

13. *I read, before my eyelids dropt their shade,*
    "The Legend of Good Women", long ago
    Sung by the morning star of song, who made
    His music heard below.
    The lines that are quoted include a reference by

    A. Masefield to Shakespeare   B. Masefield to Chaucer
    C. Tennyson to Chaucer   D. Tennyson to Shakespeare

14. All of the following descriptions of style or manner are correctly matched with the author indicated EXCEPT

    A. Samuel Johnson: Latinized vocabulary, involved sentence structure, didacticism
    B. Walter Scott: subtlety of psychological analysis, multiplicity of incidents
    C. William Blake: mysticism, symbolism, simple diction
    D. Pery Bysshe Shelley: idealistic pantheism, richness of imagery

15. Charles Lamb's THE SUPERANNUATED MAN tells the story of his

    A. troubles with his relations
    B. hopes for marriage and family
    C. retirement
    D. devotion to his sister Mary

16. The end of each of the following novels is described correctly EXCEPT

   A. THE ORDEAL OF RICHARD FEVEREL: Lucy dies of shock when Richard is wounded in a duel
   B. VANITY FAIR: Becky Sharpe comes into a large sum of money from an insurance policy and spends the rest of her life in Europe
   C. GREAT EXPECTATIONS: Pip returns to Miss Havisham's mansion, only to find that Estella has died
   D. HENRY ESMOND: Henry marries the widow of Lord Castle-wood and migrates to America

17. *But now, since all is idle,*
    To this lost heart be kind,
    Ere to a town you journey
    Where friends are ill to find.
    In content, style, and manner, this passage MOST closely resembles the work of

   A. Stephen Spender   B. A.E. Housman
   C. Austin Dobson   D. William Butler Yeats

18. All of the following novels by H.G. Wells may be classified as science fiction EXCEPT

   A. TONO-BUNGAY   B. THE ISLAND OF DR. MOREAU
   C. THE TIME MACHINE   D. THE INVISIBLE MAN

19. Of the following characters from the works of George Bernard Shaw, the one who is matched CORRECTLY with his occupation or profession is

   A. Andrew Undershaft - shipbuilder
   B. James Morell - physician
   C. Cashel Byron - prizefighter
   D. Richard Dugeon - soldier

20. At the close of Synge's play RIDERS TO THE SEA,

   A. there is no idea of what is to be done about Maurya's sorrow
   B. the village decides never to send any of its men to sea again
   C. Maurya's final lament is a bitter deprecation of God
   D. Maurya's youngest son returns unexpectedly to comfort her

21. All of the following are true of H.H. Munro EXCEPT his(he)

   A. pen name is Saki
   B. is still living today
   C. is of Scottish origin
   D. is noted for humorous short stories and novels

22. All of the following have made important contributions to Shakespearean scholarship EXCEPT

   A. J. Dover Wilson   B. Ivor Brown
   C. Caroline Spurgeon   D. Marchette Chute

23. A PORTRAIT OF THE ARTIST AS A YOUNG MAN is the story of 23.____
    A. a young man's life told through the impressions which his personality makes upon those with whom he comes in contact
    B. the religious struggles and sexual problems of a young man whose environment is detrimental to his artistic development
    C. a painter who tires of his wife and wastes his youth pursuing other women
    D. a young man who leaves home because of his disgust with mechanized civilization, but finally returns and decides to devote his life to the laboring class

24. DEATH AND ENTRANCES is the title of a book of poems by 24.____
    A. Dylan Thomas   B. W.H. Auden
    C. William Butler Yeats   D. D.H. Lawrence

25. The small cabin of wattles was built by Yeats at 25.____
    A. Innisfree   B. Killarney
    C. Galway   D. Connaught

KEY (CORRECT ANSWERS)

1.	D		11.	B
2.	A		12.	D
3.	C		13.	C
4.	B		14.	B
5.	A		15.	C
6.	C		16.	C
7.	B		17.	B
8.	A		18.	A
9.	C		19.	C
10.	C		20.	A

21. B
22. B
23. B
24. A
25. A

TEST 3

DIRECTIONS: Each question or incomplete statement is followed by several suggested answers or completions. Select the one that BEST answers the question or completes the statement. *PRINT THE LETTER OF THE CORRECT ANSWER IN THE SPACE AT THE RIGHT.*

1. An Irish writer, with radical views, who has written a series of autobiographical works is   1._____

   A. James Joyce
   B. John Millington Synge
   C. Oliver St. John Gogarty
   D. Sean O'Casey

2. *Others may sing of the wine and the wealth and the mirth,*
   The portly presence of potentates goodly in girth -
   Mine be...
   ...the scum of the earth.
   The words omitted in the quoted passage are   2._____

   A. the dirt and the dross, the dust and
   B. the danger and care and the trouble
   C. the beaten, the lost, the neglected
   D. the scorned, the hemmed in, the rejected

3. Descendants of the characters in Trollope's CHRONICLES OF BARSETSHIRE appear in the present-day novels of   3._____

   A. J.B. Priestly
   B. Richard Aldington
   C. Angela Thirkell
   D. Henry Green

4. Christopher Fry has written all of the following plays EXCEPT   4._____

   A. THE BOY WITH THE CART
   B. A PHOENIX TOO FREQUENT
   C. THE LADY'S NOT FOR BURNING
   D. HOPE IS A THING WITH FEATHERS

5. *Let the Irish vessel lie*
   Emptied of its poetry...
   is from a poem by W.H. Auden praising the   5._____

   A. wit of Oscar Wilde
   B. dramas of J.M. Synge
   C. mind of George Bernard Shaw
   D. poetry of W.B. Yeats

6. An outstanding Shakespearean critic is   6._____

   A. I.A. Richards
   B. W.H. Gardner
   C. G. Wilson Knight
   D. T.E. Hulme

71

7. One of the horrible events described in WIELAND is the

   A. terrible revenge of Wieland on Carwin
   B. death of Clara in the fire set by Wieland
   C. torture inflicted on Wieland in the insane asylum
   D. murder by Wieland of his wife and children

8. SIR GAWAIN AND THE GREEN KNIGHT is

   A. an idyll in Tennyson's IDYLLS OF THE KING
   B. a book in THE FAERIE QUEENE
   C. one of the stories in Chaucer's CANTERBURY TALES
   D. a medieval metrical romance

9. The morality play EVERYMAN made use of

   A. abstract characters such as Knowledge and Good Deeds
   B. professional actors for the first time on the English stage
   C. humorous interludes to relieve the grimness of the plot
   D. stage techniques which were relatively new

10. Each of the following lines begins one of Shakespeare's sonnets EXCEPT

    A. *That time of year thou mayst in me behold*
    B. *When in disgrace with fortune and men's eyes,*
    C. *Shalt I compare thee to a Summer's day?*
    D. *Much have I travell'd in the realms of gold*

11. Faustus in Christopher Marlowe's play

    A. was redeemed because of his kind deeds
    B. faced his ultimate fate calmly
    C. repented too late to save himself
    D. outwitted Mephistopheles by a ruse

12. *His essays represent the man as he was - shrewd, incisive, epigrammatic and practical; and yet on occasion finely imaginative.*
    The writer described in the foregoing sentence is

    A. Francis Bacon   B. William Hazlitt
    C. Max Beerbohm   D. H.G. Wells

13. Of the following, the one who was a Cavalier Poet noted for his worldly, elegant verse is

    A. Thomas Gray   B. John Milton
    C. Alexander Pope   D. Richard Lovelace

14. All of the following works of John Milton are correctly matched with their description EXCEPT

    A. LYCIDAS: an elegy on the death of a friend
    B. IL PENSEROSO: a pastoral poem satirizing melancholy and contemplation
    C. AREOPAGITICA: a treatise in defense of freedom of the press
    D. COMUS: a masque attacking sensual pleasure and vice

15. All of the following are true of Robert Burns EXCEPT that 15.____

   A. his best poems were written in conventional English
   B. he exhibited many of the characteristics of romanticism
   C. he wrote a number of poems satirizing Calvinism
   D. he frequently used a six line stanza

16. A line that comes from Gray's ELEGY WRITTEN IN A COUNTRY CHURCHYARD is 16.____

   A. *Thoughts that do often lie too deep for tears*
   B. *And fools, who came to scoff, remained to pray*
   C. *The paths of glory lead but to the grave*
   D. *And we are here as on a darkling plain*

17. A MODEST PROPOSAL by Swift reveals his 17.____

   A. true gentle self beneath his forbidding exterior
   B. desire to join with Addison and Steele in their periodical work
   C. love for and offer to marry Stella
   D. disapproval of poverty in Ireland

18. Of the following writers, the one who is NOT matched with a correct description of style is 18.____

   A. Jane Austen: quiet satire, character revelation through action rather than analysis
   B. Charles Lamb: brisk and vigorous presentation of ideas; lack of sentiment
   C. Samuel Coleridge: intensity of imagination; evoking of supernatural atmosphere
   D. John Keats: sensuousness and love of beauty; luxurious imagery

19. The BEST statement of the attitude or conviction revealed in most of George Eliot's novels is that 19.____

   A. country people are usually good but dull
   B. life offers little that is amusing
   C. good people are foolish to expect happiness
   D. people are likely to have to reap what they sow

20. The statement LEAST applicable to Shelley is that 20.____

   A. his lyrics are intense, ardent, and rapturous
   B. most of his poetry contains an underlying note of pessimism
   C. his poems are often a succession of dazzling images
   D. he laments the death of Keats in the poem ADONAIS

21. The opening words of a famous sonnet by Wordsworth are 21.____

   A. *The world is too much with us*
   B. *The poetry of earth is never dead*
   C. *There was a time when meadow, grove, and stream*
   D. *I wandered lonely as a cloud*

22. Pictures of Renaissance life and people are characteristic of the poetry of 22.____

   A. Browning   B. Malory   C. Yeats   D. Pope

23. THE RETURN OF THE NATIVE shows men and women as 23.____
    A. emotional misfits in a modern world
    B. masters of their own destiny
    C. victims of circumstance and environment
    D. essentially immoral in character

24. Each of the following essayists is correctly matched with one of his important themes 24.____
    EXCEPT
    A. Carlyle: belief in strong, heroic leaders
    B. Macaulay: attack on Victorian political reforms
    C. Newman: support on the Oxford movement
    D. Ruskin: love of medieval art and architecture

25. Of the following poets, the one whose work is MOST marked by pessimism is 25.____
    A. Tennyson   B. Housman   C. Kipling   D. Browning

KEY (CORRECT ANSWERS)

1. D	11. C
2. A	12. A
3. C	13. D
4. D	14. B
5. D	15. A
6. C	16. C
7. D	17. D
8. D	18. B
9. A	19. D
10. D	20. B

21. A
22. A
23. C
24. B
25. B

TEST 4

DIRECTIONS: Each question or incomplete statement is followed by several suggested answers or completions. Select the one that BEST answers the question or completes the statement. *PRINT THE LETTER OF THE CORRECT ANSWER IN THE SPACE AT THE RIGHT.*

1. *He ran away from home and spent a number of years wandering about the world. For a time, he was in the United States, working as a bartender's assistant in New York and in a carpet factory in Yonkers. In 1930, he was made poet laureate of England.*
   The foregoing biographical sketch would apply to

   A. Alfred Noyes
   B. William Butler Yeats
   C. Siegfried Sassoon
   D. John Masefield

   1.____

2. *His dialogue, is so brilliant and his criticisms of established conventions so cogent that we have little time left to think or worry about the implausibility of his plots.*
   The writer MOST aptly described in the foregoing sentence is

   A. Noel Coward
   B. Oscar Wilde
   C. George Bernard Shaw
   D. John Galsworthy

   2.____

3. A pair of names NOT usually associated is that of

   A. Addison and Steele
   B. Kaufman and Connelly
   C. Tennyson and Kipling
   D. Wordsworth and Coleridge

   3.____

4. Two characters who do NOT appear in the same Dickens novel are

   A. Uriah Heep and Peggotty
   B. Oliver Twist and Fagin
   C. Charles Darnay and Madame Defarge
   D. Estella Havisham and Little Nell

   4.____

5. Maggie, in WHAT EVERY WOMAN KNOWS, made a success of her marriage because of her

   A. courage in facing poverty
   B. ability to substitute for her husband in making public speeches
   C. good sense and tact as a wife
   D. constant flattery of her husband

   5.____

6. LEPANTO is a poem about a

   A. fight with windmills
   B. donkey
   C. naval battle
   D. leper

   6.____

7. The lexicographer who sometimes used his dictionary as a vehicle for his own personal opinions was

   A. Daniel Webster
   B. Noah Webster
   C. James Boswell
   D. Samuel Johnson

   7.____

8. Lord Jim spent nearly all his life trying to   8.____

    A. find his real name
    B. atone for one act of cowardice
    C. become master of a ship
    D. discover the pirate's gold

9. An author who wrote much science fiction was   9.____

    A. Arnold Bennett   B. Hilaire Belloc
    C. H.G. Wells   D. G.K. Chesterton

10. The affairs of Miss Arabella Fermor figure prominently in a comic poem by   10.____

    A. Dryden   B. Johnson   C. Pope   D. Swift

11. Matthew Bramble is a character in   11.____

    A. JOSEPH ANDREWS   B. HUMPHREY CLINKER
    C. JONATHAN WILD   D. MOLL FLANDERS

12. The critic who used the term *metaphysical* to characterize the poetry of Donne, Cowley, and Vaughn was   12.____

    A. Arnold   B. Dryden   C. Swinburne   D. Johnson

13. William Morris, in his writings and lectures, spread those ideas which were also advocated by   13.____

    A. Thomas Carlyle   B. John Ruskin
    C. Matthew Arnold   D. Thomas Huxley

14. ...was a writer of varied interests. His love and knowledge of the stage, his study of painting, and his enthusiasm for Elizabethan literature enhanced his critical work and enlivened his informal essays. He was a pioneer in theatrical criticism, daring to say what he thought and able to say it forcibly.   14.____
Of the following writers, the one BEST characterized by this quotation is

    A. Charles Lamb   B. Thomas De Quincey
    C. Leigh Hunt   D. William Hazlitt

15. _____ 's plays reveal a devotion to classic ideals. His plays exemplify his solid learning, his keen sense of comedy, his biting satire, and his unqualified war on pretense and sham.   15.____
The writer referred to in this quotation is

    A. Christopher Marlowe   B. Ben Jonson
    C. Thomas Dekker   D. John Lyly

16. *Taking the picaresque tale as a basis, _____ built up a relatively unified story about one main character and aimed at a surface reality through careful amassing of detail.... His novels usually have the form of current memoirs with notes from a diary.*   16.____
The novelist referred to in this quotation is

    A. Fielding   B. Defoe   C. Smollett   D. Richardson

17. *His poetry was addressed to the intellect rather than to the emotions. He reflected in his poetry the questioning and doubt through which he was passing. Especially noticeable is the reflective and elegiac mood of his poems.*
    Of the following poets, the one BEST characterized by this quotation is

    A. Tennyson   B. Browning   C. Arnold   D. Swinburne

18. _____ *belongs with those who returned to nature, but his is not an idealized nature. His youth had been hards the world pitiless. Like a former preacher, he saw the "vanity of vanities" of nature and the world at large.*
    The poet referred to in this quotation is

    A. George Crabbe   B. William Cowper
    C. William Collins   D. Thomas Gray

19. *This early English poet was a leader in bringing to England the forms of Italian and French poetry. He translated Virgil into blank verse and is commonly given credit for first using blank verse in English. He was a contributor to TOTTEL'S MISCELLANY.*
    The poet characterized is

    A. Chaucer   B. Wyatt   C. Surrey   D. Campion

20. THE IDEA OF COMEDY AND THE USES OF THE COMIC SPIRIT was written by the author of

    A. DIANA OF THE CROSSWAYS
    B. HENRY ESMOND
    C. ADAM BEDE
    D. THE MAYOR OF CASTERBRIDGE

21. The Senecan formula for tragedy included all of the following characteristics EXCEPT

    A. comic relief   B. five acts
    C. unity of time   D. absence of stage action

22. The phrase *sweetness and light* appears in

    A. SARTOR RESARTUS   B. TRACTATE ON EDUCATION
    C. STONES OF VENICE   D. BATTLE OF THE BOOKS

23. All of the following writers held religious office EXCEPT

    A. John Donne   B. William Cowper
    C. Robert Herrick   D. Jonathan Swift

24. Of the following pairs of journals and writers, the one in which the items are INCORRECTLY paired is

    A. THE RAMBLER - Johnson   B. THE TATLER - Goldsmith
    C. THE EXAMINER - Swift   D. THE REVIEW - Defoe

25. Of the following writers, the one who was a poet, dramatist, translator, satirist, and critic is

    A. Lovelace   B. Dryden   C. Johnson   D. Addison

KEY (CORRECT ANSWERS)

1.	D	11.	B
2.	C	12.	D
3.	C	13.	B
4.	D	14.	D
5.	C	15.	B
6.	C	16.	B
7.	D	17.	C
8.	B	18.	A
9.	C	19.	C
10.	C	20.	A

21. A
22. D
23. B
24. B
25. B

TEST 5

DIRECTIONS: Each question or incomplete statement is followed by several suggested answers or completions. Select the one that BEST answers the question or completes the statement. *PRINT THE LETTER OF THE CORRECT ANSWER IN THE SPACE AT THE RIGHT.*

1. THE MEMOIRS OF MR. C.J. YELLOWPLUSH was a satire by 1.____
   A. Swift B. Wilde C. Thackeray D. Dickens

2. POOR SPLENDID WINGS by Frances Winwar contains a study of the life and poetry of 2.____
   A. Swinburne B. Shelley C. Keats D. Wilde

3. Of the following novels, the one in which the protagonist is the father of the medieval scholar, Desiderius Erasmus, is 3.____
   A. WESTWARD HO!
   B. THE RING AND THE BOOK
   C. THE CLOISTER AND THE HEARTH
   D. HYPATIA

4. Matthew Arnold wrote the threnody, THYRSIS, in memory of his friend, the poet, 4.____
   A. Arthur Hallam
   B. Arthur Hugh Clough
   C. Winthrop Praed
   D. Dante Gabriel Rossetti

5. PRAETERITA is the incomplete autobiography of 5.____
   A. Matthew Arnold
   B. Francis Thompson
   C. Cardinal Newman
   D. John Ruskin

6. The one of the following which Samuel Johnson wrote to defray the costs of his mother's funeral is 6.____
   A. RASSELAS
   B. VANITY OF HUMAN WISHES
   C. DICTIONARY
   D. LIVES OF THE POETS

7. Shelley's ODE TO THE WEST WIND was written in 7.____
   A. blank verse
   B. terza rima
   C. Spenserian stanza
   D. rhyme royal

8. Thomas Chatterton was termed *the marvelous boy* by 8.____
   A. Wordsworth
   B. Shelley
   C. Keats
   D. Coleridge

9. *Come one, come all! This rock shall fly from its firm base as soon as I!* was written by 9.____
   A. Byron B. Tennyson C. Campbell D. Scott

10. The characterization,
    A beautiful and ineffectual angel, beating in the void his luminous wings in vain,
    was written by

    A. Shelley about Coleridge
    B. Coleridge about Shelley
    C. Arnold about Shelley
    D. Shelley about Keats

11. The characterization, *No one else in English poetry, save Shakespeare, has in expression quite his fascinating felicity, his perfection of loveliness,* was written by

    A. Arnold about Keats
    B. Swinburne about Shelley
    C. Arnold about Shelley
    D. Leigh Hunt about Keats

12. Dotheboys Hall, a school for boys, is told about in

    A. OLIVER TWIST
    B. DAVID COPPERFIELD
    C. NICHOLAS NICKLEBY
    D. GREAT EXPECTATIONS

13. THE CHARACTERS OF SHAKESPEARE'S PLAYS is a critical work by

    A. Hazlitt   B. Lamb   C. Arnold   D. Johnson

14. Swinburne said, *...he had won for himself such a double crown of glory in verse and in prose as has been worn by no other Englishman but Milton,* about

    A. Wordsworth
    B. Southey
    C. Scott
    D. Landor

15. *God-gifted organ-voice of England* was said of

    A. Jonson by Dryden
    B. Milton by Tennyson
    C. Shakespeare by Milton
    D. Milton by Wordsworth

16. THE ESSAY OF DRAMATIC POESY was written by

    A. Sidney   B. Jonson   C. Dryden   D. Milton

17. Of the following, the poem that was NOT written in the Spenserian stanza is

    A. THE EVE OF ST. AGNES
    B. ADONAIS
    C. THE LOTOS-EATERS
    D. THE RING AND THE BOOK

18. Of the following pairs of characters and novels, the one in which the items are NOT properly matched is

    A. Uriah Keep - DAVID COPPERFIELD
    B. Widow Bardie - OLIVER TWIST
    C. Sairey Camp - MARTIN CHUZZLEWITT
    D. Mr. Squeers - NICHOLAS NICKLEBY

19. The description *A hooded eagle among blinking owls* was written by

    A. Arnold about Wordsworth
    B. Shelley about Coleridge
    C. Carlyle about Burns
    D. Arnold about Keats

20. Of the following pairs, the one in which the items are INCORRECTLY paired is

    A. Tom Jones - Parson Adams
    B. Jeanie Deans - Meg Wildfire
    C. Mr, Collins - Elizabeth Bennet
    D. Rev. Dr. Primrose - Squire Thornhill

21. The lines,
    Jenny kissed me when we met
    Jumping from the chair she sat in,
    was written by

    A. Hunt   B. Jonson   C. Shakespeare   D. Moore

22. STRAWBERRY HILL of Gothic fame was connected with the life and works of

    A. Samuel Johnson   B. Horace Walpole
    C. Thomas Hardy   D. William De Morgan

23. The one of the following who was NOT a dramatist of the Restoration period is

    A. William Wycherly   B. John Locke
    C. John Vanbrugh   D. George Farquhar

24. Of the following writers, the one who can BEST be described as a poet, novelist, essayist, and playwright is

    A. James M. Barrie   B. Henry Fielding
    C. Oliver Goldsmith   D. Walter Scott

25. In Shakespearean tragedy, the term *harmatia* refers to

    A. the theme of revenge
    B. a tragic flaw in the hero
    C. a moment of final suspense
    D. the progressive degeneration of a character

KEY (CORRECT ANSWERS)

1.	C	11.	A
2.	A	12.	C
3.	C	13.	A
4.	B	14.	D
5.	D	15.	B
6.	A	16.	C
7.	B	17.	D
8.	A	18.	B
9.	D	19.	B
10.	C	20.	A

21. A
22. B
23. B
24. C
25. B

EXAMINATION SECTION
TEST 1

DIRECTIONS: Each question or incomplete statement is followed by several suggested answers or completions. Select the one that BEST answers the question or completes the statement. *PRINT THE LETTER OF THE CORRECT ANSWER IN THE SPACE AT THE RIGHT.*

1. And still they gazed, and still the wonder grew,
   That one small head could carry all he knew
   are lines from

   A. ELEGY WRITTEN IN A COUNTRY CHURCHYARD by Gray
   B. ESSAY ON MAN by Pope
   C. DESERTED VILLAGE by Goldsmith
   D. ESSAY ON CRITICISM by Pope

2. God moves in a mysterious way. His wonders to perform;
   He plants his footsteps in the sea
   And rides upon the storm
   was written by

   A. Newman   B. Addison   C. Cowper   D. George Eliot

3. Though much is taken, much abides; and though
   We are not now that strength which in old days
   Moved earth and heaven, that which we are, we are,
   One equal temper of heroic hearts,
   Made weak by time and fate, but strong in will
   To strive, to seek, to find, and not to yield
   are lines from

   A. ULYSSES by Tennyson   B. RABBI BEN EZRA by Browning
   C. RUGBY CHAPEL by Arnold   D. IN MEMORIAM by Tennyson

4. And all men kill the thing they love,
   By all let this be heard
   Some do it with a bitter look,
   Some with a flattering word,
   The coward does it with a kiss,
   The brave man with a sword
   are lines by

   A. Kipling   B. Swinburne   C. Rossetti   D. Wilde

5. The lines,
   His life was gentle, and the elements
   so mixed in him, that nature might stand up,
   And say to all the world, 'This was a man!'
   were said of

   A. Brutus by Antony   B. Caesar by Brutus
   C. Hamlet's father by Hamlet   D. Othello by Iago

6. *Here was a man to hold against the world,*
    A man to match the mountains and the sea.
    These lines are by

    A. Edwin Markham   B. Matthew Arnold
    C. Edwin Arlington Robinson D. William Wordsworth

7. *I saw Eternity the other night*
    Like a great ring of pure and endless light.
    These lines are by

    A. Edna St. Vincent Millay   B. Percy Bysshe Shelley
    C. Henry Vaughan   D. John Donne

8. *She walks - the lady of my delight -*
    A Shepherdess of Sheep.
    These lines are by

    A. Shakespeare   B. Shelley   C. Meynell   D. Thomson

9. *And we are here as on a darkling plain*
    Swept with confused alarms of struggle and flight,
    Where ignorant armies clash by night
    are lines from

    A. LOCKSLEY HALL by Tennyson   B. DOVER BEACH by Arnold
    C. IN MEMORIAM by Tennyson   D. THYRSIS by Arnold

10. *Was it a vision or a waking dream?*
    Fled is that music; Do I wake or sleep?
    are lines from

    A. CHRISTABEL by Coleridge
    B. ODE TO A NIGHTINGALE by Keats
    C. THE BLESSED DAMOZEL by Rossetti
    D. ODE ON A GRECIAN URN by Keats

11. *I hold it true, whate'er befall;*
    I feel it when I sorrow most;
    'Tis better to have loved and lost,
    Than never to have loved at all
    are lines by

    A. Arnold   B. Byron   C. Browning   D. Tennyson

12. *Sigh no more ladies, sigh no more!*
    Men are deceivers ever
    are lines from a song by

    A. Shakespeare   B. Jonson   C. Beaumont   D. Marlowe

13. The lines
Theirs be the music, the color, the glory, the gold;
Mine be a handful of ashes, a mouthful of mold,
Of the maimed, of the halt and the blind in the rain and the cold-
Of these shall my songs be fashioned, my tales be told
were written by

    A. Kipling   B. Masefield   C. Lindsay   D. Sandburg

14. *Life is too strong for you –*
It takes life to love life
are lines by

    A. Edwin Arlington Robinson   B. Robert Frost
    C. Edgar Lee Masters   D. Carl Sandburg

15. In PICKWICK PAPERS, Mr. Pickwick is NOT

    A. sued for breach of promise
    B. served by Samuel Weller
    C. jealous of Mr. Stiggins
    D. a member of a club bearing his name

16. The influence of Petrarch on Elizabethan literature was LARGELY a result of his

    A. epic poetry   B. romantic sonnets
    C. literary criticism   D. plays in verse

17. The one of the following pairs of collaborators that does NOT belong with the others is

    A. Gilbert and Sullivan   B. Addison and Steele
    C. Beaumont and Fletcher   D. Wordsworth and Coleridge

18. Uncle Toby appears in the novel

    A. CLARISSA   B. RODERICK RANDOM
    C. TRISTRAM SHANDY   D. TOM JONES

19. OLD CHINA is an essay by

    A. Hazlitt   B. Lamb   C. Addison   D. Stevenson

20. The poem, CYNARA, was written by

    A. Francis Thompson   B. Alice Meynell
    C. Ernest Dowson   D. Walter De La Mare

21. DRAPIER'S LETTERS, by Jonathan Swift, were

    A. the published excerpts from his JOURNAL TO STELLA
    B. a series he wrote attacking the coining privilege
    C. his correspondence with people like Addison, Steele, Johnson, Reynolds
    D. his diary partly in cipher

22. Soames Forsyte is the central character in
    - A. THE MAN OF PROPERTY
    - B. LOYALTIES
    - C. FRATERNITY
    - D. ONE MORE RIVER

23. A definition of poetry as *the spontaneous overflow of powerful feelings; it takes its origin from emotion recollected in tranquility* was offered by
    - A. Arnold
    - B. Coleridge
    - C. Wordsworth
    - D. Poe

24. POLITICAL JUSTICE, a social tract, was written by
    - A. Percy Bysshe Shelley
    - B. William Wordsworth
    - C. John Locke
    - D. William Godwin

25. The traditional legend of Bishop Hatto who was devoured by a plague of mice is retold in a poem by
    - A. Southey
    - B. Byron
    - C. Browning
    - D. Leigh Hunt

KEY (CORRECT ANSWERS)

1. C
2. A
3. C
4. B
5. D

6. A
7. B
8. A
9. D
10. C

11. A
12. C
13. A
14. D
15. B

16. C
17. D
18. B
19. B
20. A

21. A
22. B
23. B
24. C
25. B

TEST 2

DIRECTIONS: Each question or incomplete statement is followed by several suggested answers or completions. Select the one that BEST answers the question or completes the statement. *PRINT THE LETTER OF THE CORRECT ANSWER IN THE SPACE AT THE RIGHT.*

1. The one of the following dramatists who did NOT write a play based on the story of Cleopatra is

    A. Shakespeare
    B. Dryden
    C. Shaw
    D. Congreve

    1._____

2. The English writer who took all knowledge from his province was

    A. Charles Dickens
    B. William Shakespeare
    C. Francis Bacon
    D. George Borrow

    2._____

3. CASTLE OF OTRANTO is a Gothic romance written by

    A. Jane Austen
    B. Monk Lewis
    C. William Beckford
    D. Horace Walpole

    3._____

4. Christy Mahon, as the *playboy*, gains a reputation for personal prowess by revealing the supposed

    A. murder of his father
    B. defeat of three attackers
    C. saving of a drowning girl
    D. stopping of a runaway horse

    4._____

5. Of the following, the poet who NEVER became poet laureate of England was

    A. Masefield B. Tennyson C. Wordsworth D. Browning

    5._____

6. Mrs. Malaprop is a character in

    A. THE RIVALS
    B. TONO BUNGAY
    C. THE DEVIL'S DISCIPLE
    D. SHE STOOPS TO CONQUER

    6._____

7. A man who deserts his family to paint in the South Seas is a character in

    A. A MODERN COMEDY
    B. ALMAYER'S FOLLY
    C. THE MOON AND SIXPENCE
    D. THE PLUMED SERPENT

    7._____

8. The writer whose treatment of country life was designed to dispel the idealized picture of THE DESERTED VILLAGE was

    A. Crabbe B. Cowper C. Burns D. Johnson

    8._____

9. A biography of the Brownings, THE IMMORTAL LOVERS, was written by

    A. Irving Stone
    B. Andre Maurois
    C. Frances Winwar
    D. Joyce Cary

    9._____

10. Donizetti's opera, LUCIA DI LAMMERMOOR, is based on a novel by

    A. Jane Austen
    B. Maria Edgeworth
    C. Matthew Lewis
    D. Sir Walter Scott

    10._____

11. Missolonghi is associated with

    A. Elizabeth Barrett Browning
    B. Lord Byron
    C. P. B. Shelley
    D. John Keats

11.___

12. The SAGE OF CHELSEA was

    A. Arnold   B. Carlyle   C. Dickens   D. Ruskin

12.___

13. The Bay of Spezzia is associated with

    A. Byron   B. Keats   C. Browning   D. Shelley

13.___

14. Tweedledum and Tweedledee appear in a work by

    A. G.B. Shaw   B. Lewis Carroll
    C. Willa Cather   D. T.B. Macaulay

14.___

15. Frankenstein is a character created by

    A. Mary Shelley   B. Byron
    C. Matthew Lewis   D. Ann Radcliffe

15.___

16. In A MIDSUMMER NIGHT'S DREAM, the play within the play deals with

    A. Pyramis and Thisbe   B. Palamon and Arcite
    C. Pelleas and Melisande   D. Oberon and Titania

16.___

17. The one of the following which does NOT belong with the others is

    A. THE WIFE OF USHER'S WELL
    B. LORD RANDALL
    C. SIR PATRICK SPENS
    D. THE HIND AND THE PANTHER

17.___

18. THE VISION OF PIERS THE PLOWMAN deals with

    A. pastoral pleasures
    B. agricultural improvements
    C. religious ecstasy
    D. corruption in church and state

18.___

19. Mulvaney, Ortheris, and Learoyd are the THREE MUSKETEERS in stories by

    A. Benet   B. Kipling   C. Dos Passos   D. Maugham

19.___

20. *This English poet and playwright is considered the greatest figure in the Elizabethan drama before Shakespeare. His contributions include the development of blank verse and the release of drama from the limitations of the Senecan tradition. His plays are concerned with the career and downfall of a single hero.*
    The playwright characterized is

    A. Chapman   B. Kyd   C. Lyly   D. Marlowe

20.___

21. Francis Jeffrey, Sydney Smith, and Henry Brougham were associated in the founding and conduct of

    A. QUARTERLY REVIEW
    B. EDINBURGH REVIEW
    C. BLACKWOOD'S MAGAZINE
    D. GENTLEMAN'S MAGAZINE

22. The great biography of Sir Walter Scott was written by

    A. Christopher North
    B. Francis Jeffrey
    C. John Lockhart
    D. Walter Savage Landor

23. NOSTROMO, by Joseph Conrad, deals with

    A. a silver mine in South America
    B. trading in the Pacific
    C. a typhoon
    D. conflict between Asiatics and Europeans

24. The *Five Towns* appear in the novels of

    A. John Galsworthy
    B. Arnold Bennett
    C. H.G. Wells
    D. Somerset Maugham

25. The Wessex country in England is associated with

    A. Siegfried Sassoon
    B. William Wordsworth
    C. Thomas Hardy
    D. Wilfred Owen

KEY (CORRECT ANSWERS)

1. D		11. B	
2. C		12. B	
3. D		13. D	
4. A		14. B	
5. D		15. A	
6. A		16. A	
7. C		17. D	
8. A		18. D	
9. C		19. B	
10. D		20. D	

21. B
22. C
23. A
24. B
25. C

TEST 3

DIRECTIONS: Each question or incomplete statement is followed by several suggested answers or completions. Select the one that BEST answers the question or completes the statement. *PRINT THE LETTER OF THE CORRECT ANSWER IN THE SPACE AT THE RIGHT.*

1. Byron's poetry has been criticized for all of the following weaknesses EXCEPT

   A. excessive preoccupation with form
   B. frequent lack of sincerity
   C. wearied self-sophistication
   D. affectation

2. The following poems elegize the persons indicated EXCEPT

   A. ADONAIS - Shelley
   B. IN MEMORIAM - Arthur Hallam
   C. THYRSIS - Arthur dough
   D. LYCIDAS - Edward King

3. The remark, *they were more desirous of being admired than understood,* was said of

   A. the Lake school of poets by Lockhart
   B. the Pre-Raphaelites by Ruskin
   C. the metaphysical poets by Samuel Johnson
   D. Byron and Shelley by Hazlitt

4. EVERYMAN is an example of a

   A. chronicle play   B. morality play
   C. masque   D. closet drama

5. A noble plea for freedom of the press may be found in

   A. AREOPAGITICA   B. TITHONUS
   C. TONO BUNGAY   D. THE DUNCIAD

6. Of the following, the one which is NOT a sonnet sequence is

   A. Venus and Adonis   B. Amoretti
   C. House of Life   D. Astrophel and Stella

7. Of the following quotations, the one which is a heroic couplet is

   A. Secret fates guide our states
      Both in mirth and mourning
   B. Here's a world of pomp and state,
      Buried in dust, once dead by fate
   C. Here we may reign secure; and, in my choice,
      To reign is worth ambition, though in hell
   D. True wit is nature to advantage dressed,
      What oft was thought, but ne'er so well expressed

8. A wicked plan is overheard by a boy hiding in an apple barrel in

   A. KIDNAPPED   B. TREASURE ISLAND
   C. WESTWARD HO!   D. QUENTIN DURWARD

9. Abbotsford is associated with

   A. the Brontes B. Scott
   C. Byron D. Tennyson

10. ON THE KNOCKING AT THE GATE IN MACBETH was written by

    A. Wilde B. DeQuincey C. Coleridge D. Hazlitt

11. Of the following writers, the one who achieved fame as a magistrate and as a novelist is

    A. Samuel Richardson B. Henry Fielding
    C. Tobias Smollet D. Laurence Sterne

12. The one of the following which does NOT belong with the others is

    A. NEW ATLANTIS B. BRAVE NEW WORLD
    C. EYELESS IN GAZA D. A TRAVELER FROM ALTRURIA

13. Hrothgar is a Danish king who appears in

    A. HAMLET B. BEOWULF
    C. HENRY V D. GIANTS IN THE EARTH

14. Of the following, the writer who did NOT translate Homer is

    A. Pope B. Cowper C. Johnson D. Chapman

15. *But trailing clouds of glory do we come*
    From God, who is our home;
    Heaven lies about us in our infancy
    is a quotation from a poem by

    A. Coleridge B. Wordsworth C. Byron D. Shelley

16. *No sadder proof can be given by a man of his own*
    littleness than disbelief in great men
    is a quotation from

    A. Lincoln B. Dickens C. Franklin D. Carlyle

17. *The old order changeth, yielding place to new,*
    And God fulfills himself in many ways,
    Lest one good custom should corrupt the world...
    are lines written by

    A. Crashaw B. Pope C. Tennyson D. Longfellow

18. *Men work together, I told him from the heart,*
    Whether they work together or apart
    are lines written by

    A. Thoreau B. Emerson C. Whitman D. Frost

19. *Heard melodies are sweet but those unheard are sweeter*
    is a line written by

    A. Dryden B. Keats C. Shakespeare D. Shelley

20. *Ill fares the land, to hastening ills a prey,*
    Where wealth accumulates and men decay...
    are lines from

    A. THE DESERTED VILLAGE
    B. ELEGY WRITTEN IN A COUNTRY CHURCHYARD
    C. ODE TO THE WEST WIND
    D. THE CASTLE OF INDOLENCE

21. *That to the height of this great argument*
    I may assert eternal providence
    And justify the ways of God to man
    are lines from

    A. THE FAERIE QUEENE   B. IDYLLS OF THE KIND
    C. PILGRIM'S PROGRESS   D. PARADISE LOST

22. The lines
    .... O Wind,
    If Winter comes, can Spring he far behind?
    were written by

    A. Shakespeare   B. Keats
    C. Shelley   D. Coleridge

23. All of the following are members of the Sitwell family EXCEPT

    A. Osbert   B. Edith   C. Elinor   D. Sacheverell

24. All of the following were connected with the Abbey Theater EXCEPT

    A. W.B. Yeats   B. Liam O'Flaherty
    C. John Synge   D. Lady Gregory

25. William Butler Yeats was associated with the _____ group.

    A. imagist   B. symbolist   C. dadaist   D. naturalist

KEY (CORRECT ANSWERS)

1.	A	11.	B
2.	A	12.	C
3.	C	13.	B
4.	B	14.	C
5.	A	15.	B
6.	A	16.	D
7.	D	17.	C
8.	B	18.	D
9.	B	19.	B
10.	B	20.	A

21. D
22. C
23. C
24. B
25. B

TEST 4

DIRECTIONS: Each question or incomplete statement is followed by several suggested answers or completions. Select the one that BEST answers the question or completes the statement. *PRINT THE LETTER OF THE CORRECT ANSWER IN THE SPACE AT THE RIGHT.*

1. A play in which the modern Don Juan is represented as the pursued, rather than the pursuer, was written by   1.____
    - A. Eugene O'Neill
    - B. Tennessee Williams
    - C. George Bernard Shaw
    - D. John van Druten

2. The novelist who began his professional life as an architect was   2.____
    - A. Walter Pater
    - B. William Morris
    - C. Thomas Hardy
    - D. George Eliot

3. The shirt of Nessus plays an important part in   3.____
    - A. OEDIPUS REX
    - B. MEDEA
    - C. ELECTRA
    - D. DAUGHTERS OF ATREUS

4. The title OUT OF THE NIGHT is from   4.____
    - A. Shakespeare
    - B. Henley
    - C. Dowson
    - D. Thompson

5. Of the following, the one famous as a novelist, dramatist, and poet is   5.____
    - A. Arnold Bennett
    - B. John Galsworthy
    - C. J.M. Barrie
    - D. Thomas Hardy

6. Hakluyt and Mandeville specialized in writing about   6.____
    - A. ecclesiastical theory
    - B. voyages
    - C. comparative linguistics
    - D. medieval drama

7. Stoke Poges is associated with   7.____
    - A. Landor
    - B. Milton
    - C. William Morris
    - D. Thomas Gray

8. Abbotsford is associated with   8.____
    - A. Burns
    - B. Scott
    - C. Ossian
    - D. Ruskin

9. Twickenham is associated with   9.____
    - A. Pope
    - B. Collins
    - C. Wordsworth
    - D. Coleridge

10. Of the following, the one who did NOT spend some time in prison was   10.____
    - A. John Bunyan
    - B. Oscar Wilde
    - C. Cervantes
    - D. Bernard Shaw

11. The origin of the word *bowdlerize* is associated with editions of   11.____
    - A. Scott
    - B. Pope
    - C. Shakespeare
    - D. Milton

12. Associated with the Lake District are

    A. Beaumont and Fletcher
    B. Shelley and Keats
    C. Coleridge and Wordsworth
    D. Gilbert and Sullivan

13. UTOPIA is NOT described in

    A. EREWHON
    B. LOOKING BACKWARD
    C. THE NEW ATLANTIS
    D. YOUTH

14. THE SOUL OF MAN UNDER SOCIALISM was written by

    A. William Morris
    B. Sydney Webb
    C. Bernard Shaw
    D. J. Ramsay Macdonald

15. THE PARLEMENT OF FOULES is a

    A. satire on representative government
    B. narrative poem in which birds are characters
    C. prose treatise on politicians
    D. translation from the Arabian Nights

16. A book of Shakespeare studies was written by

    A. John Livingston Lowes
    B. Kemp Malone
    C. Harley Granville Barker
    D. Fritz Klaeber

17. THE GERM was a literary organ of the

    A. Pre-Raphaelite Brotherhood
    B. Oxford Movement
    C. Saturday Club
    D. Mermaid Tavern

18. The framework of THE CANTERBURY TALES most closely resembles that of

    A. Balzac's DROLL STORIES
    B. Boccaccio's DECAMERON
    C. THE FORSYTE SAGA
    D. Dryden's FABLES

19. Of the following plays, the one NOT of the same period as the others is

    A. THE RIVALS
    B. THE SCHOOL FOR SCANDAL
    C. THE COUNTRY WIFE
    D. SHE STOOPS TO CONQUER

20. Teufelsdrockh appears in

    A. INLAND VOYAGE
    B. SARTOR RESARTUS
    C. SPECTRE BRIDEGROOM
    D. GULLIVER'S TRAVELS

21. Of the following, the one NOT a Shakespearean character is

    A. Albany   B. Enorbarbus   C. Hermione   D. Bobadill

22. Mr. Thornhill is a character in

    A. THE VICAR OF WAKEFIELD
    B. CRANFORD
    C. SANFORD AND MERTON
    D. JANE EYRE

23. Blifil is a character in
    - A. OLIVER TWIST
    - B. TOM JONES
    - C. BABBITT
    - D. BARCHESTER TOWERS

24. John Shand is a character in
    - A. WHAT EVERY WOMAN KNOWS
    - B. FORSYTE SAGA
    - C. LITTLE MINISTER
    - D. RETURN OF THE NATIVE

25. After experiences on the Continent as an art student, the hero retires at the end of the story to a country medical practice in
    - A. OF HUMAN BONDAGE
    - B. IN CHANCERY
    - C. ANTIC HAY
    - D. THE ROLL CALL

KEY (CORRECT ANSWERS)

1. C
2. C
3. B
4. B
5. D
6. B
7. D
8. B
9. A
10. D
11. C
12. C
13. D
14. B
15. B
16. D
17. A
18. B
19. C
20. B
21. D
22. A
23. B
24. A
25. A

TEST 5

DIRECTIONS: Each question or incomplete statement is followed by several suggested answers or completions. Select the one that BEST answers the question or completes the statement. *PRINT THE LETTER OF THE CORRECT ANSWER IN THE SPACE AT THE RIGHT.*

1. Democratic contempt is expressed for royal privilege and injustice in
   - A. PRINCE AND THE PAUPER
   - B. THE YEMASSEE
   - C. GENERALS DIE IN BED
   - D. A CONNECTICUT YANKEE

2. A vast epic drama based on the Napoleonic Wars is
   - A. VANITY FAIR
   - B. THE DYNASTS
   - C. LES MISERABLES
   - D. DANIEL DERONDA

3. The island of Capri, disguised under the name of Nepenthe, is the setting for
   - A. THE HOUNDS OF SPRING
   - B. BREAD AND WINE
   - C. SOUTH WIND
   - D. THE TEMPEST

4. Samuel Johnson was associated with each of the following EXCEPT
   - A. RASSELAS
   - B. LIVES OF THE POETS
   - C. RAMBLER
   - D. CITIZEN OF THE WORLD

5. Of the following, the one NOT noted as a writer on political or economic theory is
   - A. Jeremy Bentham
   - B. John Stuart Mill
   - C. Thomas Hardy
   - D. John Locke

6. Of the following, the one who did NOT write about professional pugilists is
   - A. George Bernard Shaw
   - B. Budd Schulberg
   - C. William Hazlitt
   - D. John Ruskin

7. Of the following quotations, the one which is a heroic couplet is:
   - A. *For of all the hardest things to bear and grin
     The hardest is being taken in.*
   - B. *Some praise at morning what they blame at night
     But always think the last opinion right.*
   - C. *Tis an old maxim in the schools,
     That flattery's the food of fools.*
   - D. *Nor less I deem that there are Powers
     Which of themselves our minds impress.*

8. The obtaining of a pardon for her half sister, whom she refused to save through perjury, is an important incident in a novel by
   - A. George Eliot
   - B. Virginia Woolf
   - C. George Meredith
   - D. Sir Walter Scott

9. The Romantic Period in English literature was marked by all of the following EXCEPT a(n)

    A. democratic attitude toward men
    B. return to nature
    C. elegance of diction
    D. return to the Middle Ages

10. The London printer who became a successful novelist was

    A. Samuel Richardson
    B. Arnold Bennett
    C. John Galsworthy
    D. Walter Pater

11. THE ARABIAN NIGHTS is similar in form and structure to all of the following works EXCEPT

    A. THE DECAMERON - Boccaccio
    B. TALES OF A WAYSIDE INN - Longfellow
    C. LAYS OF ANCIENT ROME - Macaulay
    D. THE CANTERBURY TALES - Chaucer

12. I. He was responsible for the translation from Anglo-Saxon into Latin of part of BEOWULF.
    II. He inspired, in part, work on THE ANGLO-SAXON CHRONICLE.
    III. He was responsible for a translation of THE CONSOLATION OF PHILOSOPHY.
    IV. He is the central figure in the Anglo-Saxon poem, THE WANDERER.

    With respect to the above statements, King Alfred's importance in the history of English literature is based on

    A. I, II   B. II, III   C. III, IV   D. I, III

13. I. It is in the framework of a dream-vision.
    II. It is written in alliterative verse.
    III. It treats of many personified virtues and vices.
    IV. It idealizes all strata of 14th century English society.

    Of the above statements, the ones generally accepted as CORRECT with respect to THE VISION CONCERNING PIERS PLOWMAN are

    A. I, III, IV
    B. I, II, III
    C. II, III, IV
    D. I, II, IV

14. Each of the following groups of names is properly associated within the framework of a literary work EXCEPT

    A. Patroclus, Chryseis, Agamemnon
    B. Scheherezade, Aladdin, Sinbad
    C. Panurge, Pantagruel, Friar John
    D. Roland, Count Oliver, Griselda

15. In THE DIVINE COMEDY, sentiment expressed in the line, *The greatest sorrow of all is remembrance of past happiness in present woe,* pertains to the episode of

    A. Paolo and Francesca
    B. Orpheus and Eurydice
    C. Petrarch and Laura
    D. Abelard and Heloise

16.
   I. His work was described in Bede's ECCLESIASTICAL HISTORY OF THE ENGLISH PEOPLE.
   II. He was taken into the service of the monastery at Whitby.
   III. Many fragments of his prose writings in the Northumbrian dialect have been found.
   IV. He wrote a description of the Battle of Maldon.

   The statements listed above generally accepted as CORRECT with respect to Caedmon are

   A. I, III   B. II, IV   C. I, II   D. III, IV

17. ANCRENE RIWLE was a

   A. prose work written for the guidance of certain English recluses
   B. forerunner of the medieval ballad
   C. verse paraphrase of the Psalms
   D. learned commentary on Genesis

18. Master Chaunticleer, Dame Pertelote, and Dan Russell, the Fox, all appear in Chaucer's _____ TALE.

   A. WIFE OF BATH'S   B. NUN'S PRIEST'S
   C. PARDONER'S   D. SQUIRE'S

19.
   I. Palmer
   II. Pardoner
   III. 'Pothecary
   IV. Pedlar
   V. 'Prentice
   VI. Peasant

   In John Heywood's THE FOUR P'S, the four P's, of those listed above, are

   A. II, III, IV, V   B. III, IV, V, VI
   C. I, II, III, IV   D. I, III, V, VI

20. John Skelton's COLYN CLOUTE, a satirical poem directed against ecclesiastical abuses, specifically attacks

   A. Thomas a Becket   B. Thomas More
   C. Cardinal Wolsey   D. Archbishop Laud

21. In 1698, the license and obscenity of the English drama were attacked in a work entitled SHORT VIEW OF THE IMMORALITY AND PROFANENESS OF THE ENGLISH STAGE written by

   A. Sir William D'Avenant B. Sir Robert Walpole
   C. Jeremy Collier   D. Jeremy Taylor

22.
   I. THE ADVANCEMENT OF LEARNING
   II. THE NEW ATLANTIS
   III. NOVUM ORGANUM
   IV. DE AUGUMENTIS

   Of the above literary works, Francis Bacon is the author of

   A. I   B. II   C. III   D. IV

23. Shakespeare's heroines and the masculine names they assumed when disguised are correctly paired in all of the following EXCEPT

    A. Portia - Balthazar   B. Viola - Cesario
    C. Rosalind - Ganymede   D. Helena - Demetrius

24. Navarre and Illyria are the locales, respectively, of

    A. LOVE'S LABOR LOST and TWELFTH NIGHT
    B. THE TAMING OF THE SHREW and THE MERRY WIVES OF WINDSOR
    C. CYMBELINE and A WINTER'S TALE
    D. AS YOU LIKE IT and A MIDSUMMER NIGHT'S DREAM

25.
    I. EPICENE
    II. THE GULL'S HORNBOOK
    III. BARTHOLOMEW FAIR
    IV. THE MALCONTENT

Of the above, the two comedies by Ben Jonson are

    A. I, II   B. III, IV   C. I, III   D. II, IV

KEY (CORRECT ANSWERS)

1. D
2. B
3. C
4. D
5. C

6. D
7. B
8. D
9. C
10. A

11. C
12. B
13. B
14. D
15. A

16. C
17. A
18. B
19. C
20. C

21. B
22. D
23. D
24. A
25. C

EXAMINATION SECTION
TEST 1

DIRECTIONS: Each question or incomplete statement is followed by several suggested answers or completions. Select the one that BEST answers the question or completes the statement. *PRINT THE LETTER OF THE CORRECT ANSWER IN THE SPACE AT THE RIGHT.*

1. *So I will, turn her virtue into pitch,*
   And out of her own goodness make the net
   That shall enmesh them all.
   Which character in the tragedy of Othello speaks the above lines?

   A. Emilia B. Iago C. Othello D. Brabantio

2. The lines in the above question imply mainly which of the following?

   A. Most people try to be good
   B. Most people will choose evil over good
   C. Those who are innocent are vulnerable to the manipulations of those who are evil
   D. Goodness is often overcome by evil

3. *To Mrs. Saville, England.*
   *St. Petersburg. December 11th, 17_*

   You will rejoice to hear that no disaster has accompanied the commencement of an enterprise which you have regarded with such evil forebodings. I arrived here yesterday; and my first task is to assure my dear sister of my welfare, and increasing confidence in the success of my undertaking.
   The above lines open which of the following novels?

   A. ROBINSON CRUSOE   B. FRANKENSTEIN
   C. MIDDLEMARCH   D. GULLIVER'S TRAVELS

4. Considered Rudyard Kipling's masterpiece, this novel follows the life and adventures of a young boy in India.
   The sentence above describes

   A. THE MAN WHO WOULD BE KING
   B. A PORTRAIT OF THE ARTIST AS A YOUNG MAN
   C. KIM
   D. HEART OF DARKNESS

5. Which of the following novels focuses on the lives and love affairs of two sisters, Ursula and Gudrun Brangwen?

   A. A ROOM WITH A VIEW   B. TO THE LIGHTHOUSE
   C. DUBLINERS   D. WOMEN IN LOVE

6. His philosophy, expressed in such essays as THE EVERLASTING NO, CAUSE AND EFFECT, and DEMOCRACY, influenced many of the best artists and intellectuals of his generation.
   The lines above describe

   A. Thomas Carlyle   B. John Henry Cardinal Newman
   C. William Tyndale   D. T.S. Eliot

101

7. When two or more words contain identical vowel and consonant sounds, the poet has created

   A. a poem
   B. assonance
   C. a rhyme
   D. alliteration

8. Which of the following poems provides a satirical examination of sexual politics during the 18th century?

   A. THE RAPE OF THE LOCK
   B. A VALEDICTION: FORBIDDING MOURNING
   C. TO HIS COY MISTRESS
   D. TO THE VIRGINS, TO MAKE MUCH OF TIME

9. Which of the following works was written by the Venerable Bede and tells the story of the Anglo-Saxon conquest of England?

   A. THE ECCLESIASTICAL HISTORY OF THE ENGLISH PEOPLE
   B. BEOWULF
   C. THE WIFE'S LAMENT
   D. THE BATTLE OF MALDON

Questions 10-12.

DIRECTIONS: Questions 10 through 12 are to be answered on the basis of the following poem.

> *Even such is time, which takes in trust*
> *Our youth, our joys, and all we have,*
> *And pays us but with age and dust;*
> *Who in the dark and silent grave,*
> *When we have wandered all our ways,*
> *Shuts up the story of our days:*
> *And from which earth, and grave, and dust*
> *The Lord shall raise me up, I trust.*

10. In the above lines, time is being compared to a

    A. book
    B. faithless companion
    C. violent storm
    D. deceitful lover

11. The author's tone at the end of the poem is best described as

    A. joyous
    B. despairing
    C. cynical
    D. hopeful

12. Which of the following identifies the poet's rhyme scheme in the poem above?

    A. abab cc dd
    B. abab cdcd
    C. aa bb cc dd
    D. aa bb cdcd

13. In the play OTHELLO, the characters of Iago and Desdemona function as 13._____

    A. doubles
    B. reflective opposites
    C. an example of pure love
    D. an example of pure evil

Questions 14-17.

DIRECTIONS: Questions 14 through 17 are to be answered on the basis of the following passage.

Men in great place are thrice servants: servants of the sovereign or state, servants of fame, and servants of business.(1) So as they have no freedom, neither in their persons, nor in their actions, nor in their times. (2) It is a strange desire, to seek power and to lose liberty, or to seek power over others and to lose power over a man's self.(3) The rising unto place is laborious, and by pains men come to greater pains; and it is sometimes base, and by indignities men come to dignities.(4)

14. The lines above open which of the following essays by Francis Bacon? 14._____

    A. OF SUPERSTITION
    B. OF TRUTH
    C. OF GREAT PLACE
    D. OF MARRIAGE AND SINGLE LIFE

15. The passage above mainly implies which of the following? 15._____

    A. Freedom is less desirable than power.
    B. There is no dignity in obscurity.
    C. Dignity is the result of working hard to achieve your goals.
    D. The climb to greatness requires a loss of freedom.

16. The phrase from line 3, *by pains men come to greater pains,* mainly implies that work 16._____

    A. leads to more work
    B. leads to happiness
    C. leads to unhappiness
    D. is unavoidable

17. In line 4, the word *base* most nearly means 17._____

    A. basic   B. immoral   C. necessary   D. frivolous

18. Who wrote RASSELAS and THE LIVES OF THE POETS? 18._____

    A. John Locke
    B. Francis Bacon
    C. Alexander Pope
    D. Samuel Johnson

19. *Nothing is* 19._____
    But what is not.
    The lines above, taken from MACBETH, are best summarized by which of the following?

    A. We are obsessed by what we cannot or should not have.
    B. Life is based on imagination.
    C. Security is illusory.
    D. Life is often richer than we imagine it to be.

20. Which of the following tells the story of a young shepherd who entered a monastery and founded a school of Christian poetry?

    A. THE CANTERBURY TALES
    B. THE ECCLESIASTICAL HISTORY OF THE ENGLISH PEOPLE
    C. CAEDMON'S HYMN
    D. BEOWULF

21. Which of the following is a literary form which often utilizes animals or characters in order to present, or dramatize, a clear moral?

    A. Epic   B. Fable   C. Myth   D. Tale

22. James Joyce and Virginia Woolf are considered the modern pioneers of this writing style which is meant to imitate, or mirror, the flow of an individual's emotional life from moment to moment.

    A. Realism
    C. Open verse
    B. Blank verse
    D. Stream-of-consciousness

23. A poetic line containing five stresses is written in

    A. terza rima
    C. iambic pentameter
    B. blank verse
    D. iambic hexameter

24. The main character of this play lusts after the power of forbidden knowledge and makes a deal with Lucifer to gain it.
    The sentence above describes

    A. DR. FAUSTUS
    C. KING LEAR
    B. PARADISE LOST
    D. THE FAERIE QUEENE

25. In KING LEAR, Regan and Goneril battle for the love of

    A. France   B. Albany   C. Gloucester   D. Edmund

26. In this novel, Miss Havisham cruelly intervenes in the course of young love, and represents the destructive force of unrequited love.
    The sentence above describes

    A. JANE EYRE
    C. PRIDE AND PREJUDICE
    B. GREAT EXPECTATIONS
    D. A TALE OF TWO CITIES

27. *Wherefore is light given to him that is in misery, and life unto the bitter in soul?*
    These are the final words from which of the following protagonists?

    A. David (from DAVID COPPERFIELD)
    B. Stephan (from A PORTRAIT OF THE ARTIST AS A YOUNG MAN)
    C. Jude (from JUDE THE OBSCURE)
    D. Dorothea Brooke (from MIDDLEMARCH)

28. Which of the following works was written earliest, or first?

    A. PARADISE LOST
    C. PRIDE AND PREJUDICE
    B. KING LEAR
    D. WOMEN IN LOVE

29. 'Tis here, but yet confused
Knavery's plain face is never seen till used
The lines above are best summarized by which of the following?

    A. Duplicity only works on ignorant people.
    B. Dishonest people are often ugly.
    C. Duplicity is often the result of stupidity.
    D. Duplicity often goes unnoticed until it is too late.

30. The story of King Arthur was first recorded in which of the following?

    A. LE MORTE D'ARTHUR (THE DEATH OF ARTHUR)
    B. HISTORY OF THE KINGS OF BRITAIN
    C. LE ROMAN DE BRUT (THE ROMAN CHALLENGE)
    D. BRUT (CHALLENGE)

31. Which of the following writers played a central role in developing the English essay?

    A. Francis Bacon   B. John Donne
    C. John Webster   D. Ben Jonson

32. Who wrote the SONGS OF INNOCENCE and the SONGS OF EXPERIENCE?

    A. William Wordsworth   B. John Milton
    C. William Blake   D. Alexander Pope

Questions 33-37.

DIRECTIONS: Questions 33 through 37 are to be answered on the basis of the following poem.

Turning and turning in the widening gyre
The falcon cannot hear the falconer;
Things fall apart; the center cannot hold;
Mere anarchy is loosed upon the world,
The blood-dimmed tide is loosed, and everywhere
The ceremony of innocence is drowned;
The best lack of all conviction, while the worst
Are full of passionate intensity.

33. The lines above are from a poem written by

    A. T.S. Eliot   B. John Keats
    C. William Shakespeare   D. William Butler Yeats

34. In this poem, the poet predicts the coming of

    A. the anti-Christ   B. Christ
    C. Armageddon   D. revolution

35. Lines 1-2 of the poem above are meant to represent

    A. the redemptive powers of nature   B. the innocence of wildlife
    C. the breakdown of order   D. absolute destruction

36. In line 1, *gyre* most nearly means

    A. wind   B. circle   C. darkness   D. storm

37. Lines 7-8 most mainly imply which of the following?

    A. Those who should be leaders remain passive when they are most needed.
    B. Indifference will cause the downfall of society.
    C. Immoral people always have more power than moral people.
    D. Morality is not for lazy people.

38. In the opening act of OTHELLO, the city of Venice represents

    A. the tempering influence of civilization
    B. wilderness
    C. the hypocrisy of civilized manners and behavior
    D. the danger of primal human emotion

Questions 39-41.

DIRECTIONS: Questions 39 through 41 are to be answered on the basis of the following passage.

The Dream of the Rood

Listen, I will speak of the best of dreams, of what I dreamed at midnight when men and their voices were at rest.(1) It seemed to me that I saw a most rare tree reach high aloft, wound in light, brightest of beams. (2) All the beacon was covered with gold; gems stood fair where it met the ground, five were above the crosspiece.(3) Many hosts of angels gazed on it, fair in the form created for them. (4) This was surely no felon's gallows, but holy spirits beheld it there, men upon earth, and all this glorious creation. (5) Wonderful was the triumph-tree, and I stained with sins, wounded with wrongdoings.(6) I saw the tree of glory shine splendidly, adorned with garments, decked with gold: jewels had worthily covered the Lord's tree.(7)

39. The tree is compared metaphorically to a

    A. king
    B. beggar
    C. beautifully dressed person
    D. beautiful woman

40. In sentence 3, the word *fair* most nearly means

    A. temperate   B. beautiful
    C. balanced   D. holy

41. The imagery of this excerpt mainly suggests

    A. triumph   B. regret
    C. damnation   D. redemption

42. *Men must endure*
    Their going hence, even as their coming hither:
    Ripeness is all.
    Which of the following is the best summary of the lines above?

    A. Death is as difficult as birth, and each journey depends upon proper preparation.
    B. Death is easier than birth, since we are prepared for it.
    C. Death and birth are both events to be celebrated and appreciated.
    D. Birth is easier than death, since we do not anticipate it.

Questions 43-46.

DIRECTIONS: Questions 43 through 46 are to be answered on the basis of the following poem.

The Tyger

Tyger! Tyger! burning bright
In the forests of the night,
What immortal hand or eye
Could frame thy fearful symmetry?

In what distant deeps or skies
Burnt the fire of thine eyes?
On what wings dare he aspire?
What the hand dare seize the fire?

43. This poem was written by

    A. William Wordsworth   B. William Blake
    C. John Milton   D. Alexander Pope

44. In line 4, the word *symmetry* refers to the tiger's

    A. perfection   B. ferociousness
    C. indifference   D. speed

45. The speaker's attitude toward the tiger is best described as

    A. desolate   B. angry
    C. fearful awe   D. enthusiastic

46. The last line of the poem asks the question:

    A. Who dared to create you?
    B. Why is God brutal?
    C. Why is God indifferent?
    D. Who created the universe?

47. THE WIFE OF BATH, THE NUN'S PRIEST'S TALE, and THE MILLER'S TALE all appear in which of the following?

    A. UTOPIA   B. PILGRIM'S PROGRESS
    C. THE CANTERBURY TALES   D. PIERS PLOWMAN

48. April is the cruellest month, breeding
    Lilacs out of the dead land, mixing
    Memory and desire, stirring
    Dull roots with spring rain.
    The lines excerpt above begins which of the following poems?

    A. THE LOVE SONG OF J. ALFRED PRUFROCK
    B. LAPUS LAZULI
    C. BYZANTIUM
    D. THE WASTE LAND

49. Winston Smith's doomed struggle against a totalitarian state in many ways embodies the modernist fear of the loss of individuality in the face of government and cultural authority. The sentence above describes which of the following novels?

    A. 1984
    B. ANIMAL FARM
    C. ULYSSES
    D. SONS AND LOVERS

50. Which of the following is the opening line to a poem by William Butler Yeats?

    A. When I have fears that I may cease to be
    B. Tyger! Tyger! burning bright
    C. I will arise and go now, and go to Innisfree
    D. Let us go then, you and I

KEY (CORRECT ANSWERS)

1. B	11. D	21. B	31. A	41. D
2. C	12. A	22. D	32. C	42. A
3. B	13. B	23. C	33. D	43. B
4. C	14. C	24. A	34. A	44. A
5. D	15. D	25. D	35. C	45. C
6. A	16. A	26. B	36. B	46. A
7. C	17. B	27. C	37. A	47. C
8. A	18. D	28. B	38. A	48. D
9. A	19. A	29. D	39. C	49. A
10. B	20. C	30. B	40. B	50. C

TEST 2

DIRECTIONS: Each question or incomplete statement is followed by several suggested answers or completions. Select the one that BEST answers the question or completes the statement. *PRINT THE LETTER OF THE CORRECT ANSWER IN THE SPACE AT THE RIGHT.*

Questions 1-3.

DIRECTIONS: Questions 1 through 3 are to be answered on the basis of the following passage.

Two households both alike in dignity,
In fair Verona, where we lay our scene,
From ancient grudge break to new mutiny,
Where civil blood makes civil hands unclean.

1. The lines above open which of the following plays?

   A. THE DUCHESS OF MALFI B. ROMEO AND JULIET
   C. THE CANTERBURY TALES D. OTHELLO

2. In the passage above, the phrase *both alike in dignity* refers to

   A. social standing B. political influence
   C. manners D. power

3. In the passage above, line 3 mainly implies

   A. a recent feud
   B. a long, ongoing feud
   C. an ancient feud, long dead
   D. impending war

4. In this novel, E.M. Forester explores English society in colonial India, dramatizing the prejudices and misunderstandings that lead to political and personal tragedy.
   The sentence above describes

   A. A ROOM WITH A VIEW B. HEART OF DARKNESS
   C. KIM D. A PASSAGE TO INDIA

5. BEOWULF is considered a(n)

   A. epic poem B. sonnet
   C. tragic couplet D. heroic elegy

6. William Shakespeare, Henry Howard, Earl of Surrey, and Christopher Marlowe all relied primarily on which of the following forms for their sonnets?

   A. Petrarchan B. English
   C. Villanelle D. Heroic couplet

Questions 7-8.

DIRECTIONS: Questions 7 and 8 are to be answered on the basis of the following passage.

The Nymph's Reply to the Shepherd

*If all the world and love were young,
And truth in every shepherd's tongue,
These pretty pleasures might me move
To live with thee and be thy love.*

7. The lines above are best summarized by which of the following?

   A. Though the world is flawed, our love is ideal.
   B. Since you are a liar, I will not be your lover and companion.
   C. If the world were ideal, I would be your lover and companion.
   D. Our love is ideal, and I will live with you and be your companion.

8. The second line from the poem above mainly implies which of the following? The speaker

   A. questions the shepherd's honesty
   B. questions the honesty of all men
   C. does not believe in honesty
   D. is honest

9. Who wrote THE FAERIE QUEENE?

   A. William Shakespeare
   B. John Donne
   C. John Milton
   D. Edmund Spenser

Questions 10-14.

DIRECTIONS: Questions 10 through 14 are to be answered on the basis of the following passage.

1   *It is the cause, it is the cause, my soul.
    Let me not name it to you, you chaste stars.
    It is the cause. Yet I'll not shed her blood,
    Nor soar that whiter skin of hers than snow,*
5   *And smooth as monumental alabaster.
    Yet she must die, else she'll betray more men.
    Put out the light, and then put out the light.
    If I quench thee, thou flaming minister,
    I can again thy former light restore,*
10   *Should I repent me; but once put out thy light,
    Thou cunning'st pattern of excelling nature,
    I know not where is that Promethean heat
    That can thy light relume. When I have plucked the rose,
    I cannot give it vital growth again;*
15   *It needs must whither.*

10. The soliloquy above is delivered by which of the following characters? 10._____

    A. Othello   B. King Lear
    C. Hamlet   D. Macbeth

11. In lines 8-9 *(If I quench thee, thou flaming minister/ I can again thy former light restore)*, 11._____
    what light is the speaker referring to?
    The light

    A. of the sun   B. of the moon
    C. or spark, of life D. he carries in his hand

12. In line 10, the phrase *Should I repent me* implies which of the following? 12._____

    A. If he decides to confess his deed
    B. In the event he asked for forgiveness
    C. In the event he changed his mind
    D. If he is overcome with shame

13. In lines 10-13 *(but once put out thy light/Thou cunning'st pattern of excelling nature/I 13._____
    know not where is that Promethean heat/That can thy light relume)*, what light is the
    speaker referring to?
    The light

    A. of the sun   B. of the moon
    C. or spark, of life D. he carries in his hand

14. The speaker in the lines above intends to 14._____

    A. commit adultery   B. commit murder
    C. escape from prison D. betray his friend

15. In the novel, TO THE LIGHTHOUSE, the final image of the painting by Lily Driscoe is 15._____
    meant to represent

    A. chaos   B. form amidst chaos
    C. emotional restraint D. emotional communion

16. In HEART OF DARKNESS, the Thames is compared to the Congo for the purpose of 16._____

    A. proving that the Congo is a more powerful river
    B. contrasting European and African values
    C. illuminating the Congo's barbarity, and the Thames civility
    D. illuminating the constancy of human barbarity

Questions 17-18.

DIRECTIONS: Questions 17 and 18 are to be answered on the basis of the following passage.

To An Athlete Dying Young

The time you won your town the race
We chaired you through the market-place;
Man and boy stood cheering by,
And home we brought you shoulder-high.

Today, the road all runners come,
Shoulder-high we bring you home,
And set you at your threshold down,
Townsman of a stiller town.

17. The poem above was written by

    A. A.E. Housman
    B. T.S. Eliot
    C. William Butler Yeats
    D. John Keats

18. The two stanzas contrast a victory parade and a

    A. graveyard
    B. funeral procession
    C. defeated return
    D. graduation procession

19. In which of the following plays does the character of Ophelia appear?

    A. MACBETH
    B. HAMLET
    C. KING LEAR
    D. OTHELLO

Questions 20-22.

DIRECTIONS: Questions 20 through 22 are to be answered on the basis of the following passage.

The Wanderer

Therefore I cannot think why the thoughts of my heart should not grow dark when I consider all the life of men through this world -- with what terrible swiftness they forgo the hall-floor, bold young retainers.(1) So this middle-earth each day fails and falls. (2) No man may indeed become wise before he has had his share of winters in the world's kingdom. (3) The wise man must be patient, must never be too hot-hearted, nor too hasty of speech, nor too fearful, nor too glad, nor too greedy for wealth, nor ever too eager to boast before he has thought clearly.(4) A man must wait, when he speaks in boast, until he knows clearly, sure-minded, where the thoughts of his heart may turn.(5)

20. Sentence 3 mainly implies that

    A. the winter season accelerates aging
    B. suffering leads to wisdom
    C. wisdom is gained through travel and experience
    D. the world's kingdoms are numerous and strange

21. In sentence 4, the phrase, *nor too hasty of speech*, mainly implies that one should

    A. speak slowly and clearly
    B. speak before acting

C. think before speaking
D. consult others before speaking

22. The main purpose of this paragraph is to

    A. convey a sense of despair
    B. create a sense of hopelessness
    C. deliver a warning
    D. offer advice

23. In KING LEAR, Gloucester's folly in placing his illegitimate son, Edmund, before his legitimate son, Edgar, is symbolized by

    A. Kent's imprisonment
    B. Gloucester's blinding
    C. Gloucester's imprisonment
    D. the presence of the Fool

24. This masterfully plotted novel, which focuses on provincial values and courtship, features a spirited and intelligent heroine who at first matches wits with Fitzwilliam Darcy and then later marries him.
    The lines above describe

    A. PRIDE AND PREJUDICE   B. EMMA
    C. SENSE AND SENSIBILITY   D. JANE EYRE

25. 'Twas brillig, and the slithy toves
      Did gyre and gimble in the wabe:
    All mimsy were the borogoves,
    And the mome raths outgrabe.
    The lines above begin

    A. THE CHARGE OF THE LIGHT BRIGADE
    B. THE RIME OF THE ANCIENT MARINER
    C. JABBERWOCKY
    D. KUBLA KHAN

26. In HEART OF DARKNESS, when Kurtz cries out to Marlow, *The horror, the horror,* Kurtz is referring to

    A. his own savagery
    B. the savagery of the natives
    C. the pain of isolation
    D. the horrors of the jungle

27. This novel, told in 3 sections and written in the stream-of-consciousness style for which this author was famous, tells the story of Mrs. Ramsay and the lasting influence she had on her family and friends.
    The sentence above describes

    A. WOMEN IN LOVE   B. A ROOM WITH A VIEW
    C. TO THE LIGHTHOUSE   D. ULYSSES

28. This work makes brilliant and satirical use of the double entendre in a name and identity which the hero, Jack Worthing, devises for himself in order to hide his double-life.
    The sentence above describes

    A. DAVID COPPERFIELD
    B. THE IMPORTANCE OF BEING EARNEST
    C. VANITY FAIR
    D. THE TAMING OF THE SHREW

29. *Whether I shall turn out to be the hero of my own life, or whether that station will be held by anyone else, these pages must show.*
    The sentence above begins

    A. GREAT EXPECTATIONS
    B. PRIDE AND PREJUDICE
    C. A PORTRAIT OF THE ARTIST AS A YOUNG MAN
    D. DAVID COPPERFIELD

30. On this play, the enactment of The Mouse Trap, a play-within-a-play, provides one of the great dramatic mirrors in literature.
    The lines above describe which of the following plays?

    A. ROMEO AND JULIET   B. MACBETH
    C. HAMLET   D. OTHELLO

31. In this Canterbury Tale, a woman defends her gender against the anti-feminist teachings of the Church.
    The sentence above describes the

    A. WIFE OF BATH'S TALE   B. NUN'S PRIEST'S TALE
    C. PARDONER'S TALE   D. MILLER'S TALE

32. *In a summer season when soft was the sun*
    The line above relies mainly upon

    A. simile   B. metaphor
    C. rhyme   D. alliteration

33. Who is the anchoress whose spiritual visions are explained and clarified in A BOOK OF SHOWINGS?

    A. Marie De France   B. Julian of Norwich
    C. Anne Askew   D. Margery Kempe

34. Among other achievements, this novel is masterful in the way it shifts through time and place to tell the story of the doomed love affair between Heathcliff and Catherine.

    A. WUTHERING HEIGHTS   B. JANE EYRE
    C. MIDDLEMARCH   D. PRIDE AND PREJUDICE

35. Who wrote the essays OF TRUTH; OF MARRIAGE AND SINGLE LIFE; and OF GREAT PLACE?

    A. Sir Walter Raleigh   B. William Tyndale
    C. Francis Bacon   D. John Calvin

Questions 36-39.

DIRECTIONS: Questions 36 through 39 are to be answered on the basis of the following passage.

1   My heart leaps up when I behold
       A rainbow in the sky;
       So was it when my life began;
4   So is it now I am a man;
       So be it when I shall grow old,
       Or let me die!
       The Child is the father of the Man;
8   And I could wish my days to be
       Bound to each by natural piety.

36. The poem above was written by

    A. William Wordsworth   B. William Blake
    C. Alexander Pope   D. T.S. Eliot

37. The ideas, images, and rhythms of this poem are most indicative of the

    A. Medieval period   B. Restoration
    C. Romantic period   D. Victorian period

38. In line 7, the sentence *The Child is the father of the Man* mainly implies that childhood is

    A. a time of pure joy
    B. a time of pain and powerlessness
    C. shaped by indifferent adults
    D. shaped by childhood experiences

39. The last words of the poem, *natural piety,* refer to

    A. traditional religious worship
    B. the worship of God through nature
    C. the pagan belief in many gods
    D. quiet prayer

40. The term *lay* refers to which of the following? A(n)

    A. short narrative poem in verse
    B. epic poem in verse
    C. type of villanelle
    D. type of heroic couplet

41. In which of the following plays does the character of the Fool appear, acting as an alter-ego during the hero's fall from power?

    A. OTHELLO   B. MACBETH
    C. HAMLET   D. KING LEAR

Questions 42-44.

DIRECTIONS: Questions 42 through 44 are to be answered on the basis of the following passage.

```
1    But at my back I always hear
     Time's winged chariot hurrying near;
     And yonder all before us lie
4    Deserts of vast eternity.
     Thy beauty shall no more be found,
     Nor, in thy marble vault, shall sound
     My echoing song; then worms shall try
8    That long-preserved virginity,
     And your quaint honor turn to dust,
     And into ashes all my lust:
     The grave's a fine and private place,
12   But none, I think, do there embrace
```

42. The tone of this poem is best described as

    A. angry   B. chiding   C. ironic   D. desolate

43. In line 6, the *marble vault* refers to

    A. a statue   B. history
    C. a funeral crypt   D. eternity

44. In this poem, the speaker is warning his mistress against

    A. marrying the wrong man
    B. marrying too young
    C. taking lovers before marriage
    D. waiting too long to consummate their relationship

45. Which of the following is an epic poem whose settings include heaven, hell, Eden, and chaos?

    A. THE FAERIE QUEENE   B. PARADISE LOST
    C. THE TEMPEST   D. THE CANTERBURY TALES

46. Which of the following novels contains the line, *Reader, I married him?*

    A. JANE EYRE   B. WUTHERING HEIGHTS
    C. MIDDLEMARCH   D. TO THE LIGHTHOUSE

Questions 47-48.

DIRECTIONS: Questions 47 and 48 are to be answered on the basis of the following passage.

I would not do such a thing for a joint-ring, nor for measures of lawn, nor for gowns, petticoats, nor caps, nor any petty exhibition, but for all the whole world? Why, who would not make her husband a cuckold to make him a monarch? I should venture purgatory for't.

47. The lines above are spoken by which of the following characters from the tragedy of OTHELLO?   47._____

    A. Othello
    C. Iago
    B. Desdemona
    D. Emilia

48. What is the speaker talking about in the excerpt from OTHELLO?   48._____

    A. Murder
    C. Robbery
    B. Adultery
    D. Political assassination

49. *A man proud, moody, cynical, with defiance on his brow, and misery in his heart, a scorner of his kind, implacable in revenge, yet capable of deep and strong affection.*   49._____
    The lines above describe a _____ hero.

    A. Byronic   B. classical   C. epic   D. Miltonian

50. Who wrote the poems NATURE THAT WASHED HER HANDS IN MILK; FAREWELL, FALSE LOVE; and THE NYMPH'S REPLY TO THE SHEPHERD?   50._____

    A. Sir Walter Raleigh
    C. Christopher Marlowe
    B. Edmund Spenser
    D. Alexander Pope

KEY (CORRECT ANSWERS)

1. B	11. D	21. C	31. A	41. D
2. A	12. C	22. D	32. D	42. B
3. B	13. C	23. B	33. B	43. C
4. D	14. B	24. A	34. A	44. D
5. A	15. B	25. C	35. C	45. B
6. B	16. D	26. A	36. A	46. A
7. C	17. A	27. C	37. C	47. D
8. A	18. B	28. B	38. D	48. B
9. D	19. B	29. D	39. B	49. A
10. A	20. B	30. C	40. A	50. A

TEST 3

DIRECTIONS: Each question or incomplete statement is followed by several suggested answers or completions. Select the one that BEST answers the question or completes the statement. *PRINT THE LETTER OF THE CORRECT ANSWER IN THE SPACE AT THE RIGHT.*

Questions 1-5.

DIRECTIONS: Questions 1 through 5 are to be answered on the basis of the following passage.

1   So. The Spear-Danes in days gone by
    and the kings who ruled them had courage and greatness.
    We have heard of those princes' heroic campaigns.
        There was Shield Sheafson, scourge of many tribes,
5   a wrecker of mead-benches, rampaging among foes.
    This terror of the hall-troops had come far.
    A foundling to start with, he would flourish later on
    as his powers waxed and his worth was proved.
10 In the end each clan on the outlying coasts
    beyond the whale-road had to yield to him
    and begin to pay tribute. That was one good king.

1. The language and ideas in this excerpt are most characteristic of which of the following periods?

   A. Middle Ages   B. Restoration
   C. Romantic Period   D. Victorian Period

2. In line 4, *scourge* most nearly means

   A. criminal   B. ally   C. terror   D. leader

3. In line 7, *foundling* most nearly means

   A. orphan   B. baby
   C. step-child   D. foster child

4. Lines 7 and 8 *(he would flourish later on/as his powers waxed)* mainly imply that he

   A. lost influence due to his weakness
   B. gained influence through his weakness
   C. grew weaker with age
   D. grew stronger with age

5. Lines 9-11 mainly imply that Sheafson _____ these areas.

   A. was beloved by the people in
   B. terrorized the people in
   C. conquered
   D. committed crimes in

Questions 6-11.

DIRECTIONS: Questions 6 through 11 are to be answered on the basis of the following passage.

1   Let me not to the marriage of true minds
    Admit impediments; love is not love
    Which alters when it alteration finds,
4   Or bends with the remover to remove:
    O, no, it is an ever-fixed mark,
    That looks on tempests and is never shaken;
    It is the star to every wand'ring bark,
8   Whose worth's unknown, although his highth be taken.
    Love's not Time's fool, though rosy lips and cheeks
    Within his bending sickle's compass come;
    Love alters not with his brief hours and weeks,
12 But bears it out even to the edge of doom.
        If this be error and upon me proved,
14   I never writ, nor no man ever loved.

6. The author of this sonnet is

   A. John Donne
   B. Christopher Marlowe
   C. Ben Jonson
   D. William Shakespeare

7. The rhyme scheme of the sonnet above is

   A. abcd efef ghgh ii
   B. abab cdcd efef gh
   C. abab cdcd efef gg
   D. aabb ccdd eeff gg

8. Lines 1 through 4 of the sonnet are best summarized by which of the following?

   A. Love does not change as circumstances change.
   B. Love changes with time and circumstance.
   C. Love is often altered by jealousy.
   D. True love is not possible between mere humans.

9. In line 6, the word *tempests* most nearly means

   A. storms
   B. death
   C. difficulties
   D. arguments

10. Lines 9 through 12 of the sonnet are best summarized by which of the following?

    A. Both love and youth are altered by time.
    B. Though youth is altered by time, love is not.
    C. Youth and beauty are altered by time.
    D. Time destroys all human connection.

11. The last two lines of the stanza mainly imply that the poet

    A. stakes his life and reputation upon this truth
    B. has never experienced true love
    C. stakes his life and reputation upon the honesty of his lover
    D. does not trust his lover

12. A medieval poem which contains allegorical characters named Lady Holy Church, Lady   12._____
    Meed, and three gentlemen named False, Conscience, and Reason.
    The sentence above describes

    A. THE CANTERBURY TALES
    B. THE VISIONS OF PIERS PLOWMAN
    C. PILGRIM'S PROGRESS
    D. THE FAERIE QUEENE

13. This play, which focuses on the contrast between innocence (as embodied in the charac-   13._____
    ter of Desdemona) and the primal human emotions of jealousy, greed, and suspicion (as
    embodied in the character of Iago) is one of Shakespeare's most haunting examinations
    of a hero's downfall.
    The lines above describe which of the following plays?

    A. MACBETH   B. HAMLET   C. OTHELLO   D. KING LEAR

14. Which of the following poems by Percy Bysse Shelley centers upon the image of the bust   14._____
    of a great and arrogant king, wrecked in the sands of time?

    A. OZYMANDIAS   B. PROMETHESUS UNBOUND
    C. MASK OF ANARCHY   D. ODE TO THE WEST WIND

15. Thomas Hobbes wrote which of the following?   15._____

    A. THE FAERIE QUEENE   B. THE DUCHESS OF MALFI
    C. LE MORTE D'ARTHUR   D. LEVIATHAN

Questions 16-19.

DIRECTIONS: Questions 16 through 19 are to be answered on the basis of the following pas-
             sage.

```
1    Nay, but this dotage of our general's
     O'erflows the measure. Those his goodly eyes,
     That o'er the files and musters of the war
     Have glow'd like plated Mars, now bend, now turn
5    The office and devotion of their view
     Upon a tawny front; his captain's heart,
     Which in the scuffles of great fights hath burst
     The buckles on his breast, reneges all temper,
     And is become the bellows and the fan
10   To cool a gipsy's lust.
```

16. The lines above begin which of the following plays?   16._____

    A. HAMLET   B. PARADISE LOST
    C. ANTONY AND CLEOPATRA   D. ROMEO AND JULIET

17. In line 1, the word *dotage* most nearly means   17._____

    A. old age   B. loving attention
    C. indifference   D. anger

18. The implication of lines 2-6 is best summarized by which of the following? 18._____

    A. His war-hardened eyes have grown soft in the presence of a woman.
    B. His war-hardened eyes have grown blind.
    C. His eyes have seen too much war and death.
    D. The hope has gone out of his eyes.

19. The main implication of the passage above is that the general 19._____

    A. has grown harsher through heartbreak
    B. is indifferent to lust
    C. is despairing
    D. has been mellowed by love

20. In OTHELLO, what is Desdemona falsely accused of? 20._____

    A. Murder   B. Adultery   C. Duplicity   D. Robbery

Questions 21-24.

DIRECTIONS: Questions 21 through 24 are to be answered on the basis of the following passage.

Lanval

1   *Another lay to you I'll tell,*
    Of the adventure that befell
    A noble vassal whom they call
    In the Breton tongue Lanval.
5   *Arthur, the brave and courtly king,*
    At Carlisle was sojourning
    Because the Scots and Picts allied
    Were ravaging the countryside;
    Of Logres they had crossed the border
10 *Where often they caused great disorder.*

21. The lines above are written in 21._____

    A. blank verse   B. couplets
    C. iambic pentameter   D. terza rima

22. In line 2, *befell* most nearly means 22._____

    A. afflicted   B. surprised
    C. struck down   D. happened to

23. In line 6, *sojourning* most nearly means 23._____

    A. resting   B. traveling
    C. celebrating   D. hiding

24. The principal character in this poem is 24._____

    A. King Arthur   B. Breton
    C. Lanval   D. Carlisle

25. Who wrote the poems THE TEMPLE; THE ALTAR; AFFLICTION; and PRAYER? 25.___

   A. George Herbert B. Francis Bacon
   C. John Webster D. William Shakespeare

26. In which of Shakespeare's plays does a young noblewoman named Viola transform herself into a young man named Cesario? 26.___

   A. THE TAMING OF THE SHREW
   B. AS YOU LIKE IT
   C. TWELFTH NIGHT
   D. A MIDSUMMER NIGHT'S DREAM

27. Which of the following writers claimed that life is *solitary, poor, nasty, brutish, and short*? 27.___

   A. William Tyndale B. Thomas Hobbes
   C. John Milton D. Francis Bacon

28. The use of nature to reflect human emotion and psychology is most characteristic of which literary period? 28.___

   A. Romantic B. Restoration
   C. Victorian D. Modern

29. Who wrote THE DEFENSE OF POESY, an argument for the worth of imaginative literature? 29.___

   A. John Calvin B. Sir Philip Sydney
   C. Sir Walter Raleigh D. John Donne

Questions 30-32.

   DIRECTIONS: Questions 30 through 32 are to be answered on the basis of the following passage.

1   *Experience, though noon auctoritee*
    Were in this world, is right ynough for me
    To speke of wo that is in mariage:
4   *For lordinges, sith I twelf yeer was of age - gentlemen*
    Thanked be God that is eterne on live -
    Housbondes at chirche dore I have had five
    (If I so ofte mighte han wedded be),
8   *And ale were worthy men in hir degree.*

30. The lines above serve as the opening to THE _____ TALE. 30.___

   A. MILLER'S B. PARDONER'S
   C. NUN'S PRIEST'S D. WIFE OF BATH'S

31. In the lines above, the speaker admits that she has 31.___

   A. five illegitimate children
   B. been married five times
   C. five legitimate children
   D. been engaged five times, but never married

32. Which of the following summarizes the last four lines of the excerpt above? The speaker

   A. was first married when she was twelve years old
   B. was first engaged when she was twelve years old
   C. had her first child at twelve
   D. was first baptized when she was twelve years old

32._____

Questions 33-36.

DIRECTIONS: Questions 33 through 36 are to be answered on the basis of the following passage.

Of the eternal election, whereby God hath predestinate some to salvations and other some to destruction.

But now whereas the covenant of life is not equally preached to all men, and with then to whom it is preached it doth not either equally or continually find like place; in this diversity the wondrous depth of the judgment of God appeareth.

33. In the first line of the excerpt, the word *whereas* most nearly means

   A. so   B. therefore   C. however   D. because

33._____

34. The meaning of this excerpt is best summarized by which of the following?

   A. The story of Christ, and the possibility for redemption, is not revealed to all men.
   B. The story of Christ, and the possibility for redemption, is revealed to all men.
   C. God makes himself known to all men, but in different ways.
   D. Once a man knows God, he will be saved.

34._____

35. The lines above are taken from an essay written by

   A. Anne Askew
   B. Sir Thomas Wyatt the Elder
   C. William Tyndale
   D. John Calvin

35._____

36. This excerpt introduces the idea of Christian

   A. sinfulness   B. predestination
   C. redemption   D. grace

36._____

37. Who wrote THE MORTE D'ARTHUR?

   A. Sir Thomas Wyatt the Elder
   B. Geoffrey Chaucer
   C. Sir Thomas Malory
   D. William Langland

37._____

38. Epic poem which focuses on the activities in and around the court of Gloriana, who rules over the fairy kingdom. The sentence above describes

   A. DR. FAUSTUS   B. THE TEMPEST
   C. PARADISE LOST   D. THE FAERIE QUEENE

38._____

39. When that April with <u>his</u> showers <u>soote</u>   its/fresh   39.____
    The droughte of March hath perced to the roote
    The lines above provide an example of

    A. alliteration   B. iambic pentameter
    C. metaphor   D. allegory

Questions 40-45.

DIRECTIONS: Questions 40 through 45 are to be answered on the basis of the following passage.

> My mistress' eyes are nothing like the sun,   1
> Coral is far more red than her lips' red;
> If snow be white, why then her breasts are dun;
> If hairs be wires, black wires grow on her head.   4
> I have seen roses <u>damasked</u>, red and white,   variegated
> But no such roses see I in her cheeks;
> And in some perfumes is there more delight
> Than in the breath that from my mistress reeks.   8
> I love to hear her speak, yet well I know
> That music hath a far more pleasing sound;
> I grant I never saw a goddess go;
> My mistress, when she walks, treads on the ground.   12
>   And yet, by heaven, I think my love as <u>rare</u>   extraordinary
>   As any she belied with false compare.

40. The poem above is an example of which type of sonnet?   40.____

    A. Villanelle   B. Petrarchan
    C. Shakespearean   D. Renaissance

41. In lines 1 through 3 of the poem above, the speaker compares his mistress to these   41.____
    things in order to make the point that

    A. she is ugly
    B. her beauty is not heavenly or divine, but human
    C. her beauty lies outside the bounds of human beauty
    D. he (the speaker) does not care about her beauty

42. In line 11, the word *go* most nearly means   42.____

    A. walk   B. die   C. visit   D. retreat

43. The speaker's feelings for his mistress are best described as   43.____

    A. joyous   B. despairing
    C. disgusted   D. loving

44. In line 14, the word *belied* most nearly means   44.____

    A. destroyed   B. defeated
    C. misrepresented   D. outshone

45. The main point of this sonnet is best summarized by which of the following?

    A. True beauty does not require false comparisons to reveal its worth.
    B. True beauty outshines the most beautiful elements of nature.
    C. Beauty is in the eye of the beholder.
    D. Beauty is fleeting, and women use it to snare men.

46. In the opening act of KING LEAR, how does Lear test his daughters' love for him? He

    A. tells Cordelia he loves her more than he loves her sisters
    B. tries to marry his youngest daughter, Cordelia, to a man she does not love
    C. requires each one to confess her love for him before granting their inheritance
    D. divides his kingdom unequally

Questions 47-48.

DIRECTIONS: Questions 47 and 48 are to be answered on the basis of the following passage.

Or, a Vision in a Dream. A Fragment.

In Xanadu did Kubla Khan
A stately pleasure-dome decree:
Where Alph, the sacred river, ran
Through caverns measureless to man
Down to a sunless sea.

47. The lines above were written by

    A. William Wordsworth   B. Samuel Taylor Coleridge
    C. William Blake   D. Alexander Pope

48. The lines above are most indicative of which literary period?

    A. Victorian   B. Restoration
    C. Romantic   D. Medieval

49. *My heart aches, and a drowsy numbness pains*
    My sense, as though of hemlock I had drunk.
    The lines above begin which of the following poems by John Keats?

    A. LA BELLE DAME SANS MERCI   B. ODE ON A GRECIAN URN
    C. ODE TO PSYCHE   D. ODE TO A NIGHTINGALE

50. Who wrote the poems TO THE VIRGINS; TO MAKE MUCH OF TIME; and UPON THE LOSS OF HIS MISTRESSES?

    A. Richard Lovelace   B. Andrew Marvell
    C. Robert Herrick   D. George Herbert

KEY (CORRECT ANSWERS)

1. A	11. A	21. B	31. B	41. B
2. C	12. B	22. D	32. A	42. A
3. B	13. C	23. A	33. D	43. D
4. D	14. A	24. C	34. A	44. C
5. C	15. D	25. A	35. D	45. A
6. D	16. C	26. C	36. B	46. C
7. C	17. B	27. B	37. C	47. B
8. A	18. A	28. A	38. D	48. C
9. C	19. D	29. B	39. B	49. D
10. B	20. B	30. D	40. C	50. C

TEST 4

DIRECTIONS: Each question or incomplete statement is followed by several suggested answers or completions. Select the one that BEST answers the question or completes the statement. *PRINT THE LETTER OF THE CORRECT ANSWER IN THE SPACE AT THE RIGHT.*

Questions 1-2.

DIRECTIONS: Questions 1 and 2 are to be answered on the basis of the following passage.

Full of grief, I make this poem about myself, my own fate.(1) I have the right to say what miseries I have endured since I grew up, new or old – never greater than now.(2) Endlessly I have suffered the wretchedness of exile. (3)

First my lord went away from his people here across the storm-tossed sea.(4) At daybreak I worried in what land my lord might be. (5) Then I set out – a friendless exile – to seek a household to shelter me against wretched need. (6) Hiding their thoughts, the man's kinfolk hatched a plot to separate us so that we two should live most unhappy and farthest from one another in this wide world.(7) And I felt longing. (8)

1. In sentence 3, *exile* most nearly means

    A. religious banishment
    B. economic hardship
    C. loneliness
    D. social ostracism

1._____

2. The tone of this passage is best described as a(n)

    A. lamentation
    B. elegy
    C. diatribe
    D. plea

2._____

Questions 3-7.

DIRECTIONS: Questions 3 through 7 are to be answered on the basis of the following passage.

```
1      Come, let's away to prison:
       We two alone will sing like birds i' th' cage:
       When thou dost ask me blessing, I'll kneel down
4      And ask of thee forgiveness: so we'll live,
       And pray, and sing, and tell old tales, and laugh
       At gilded butterfles, and hear poor rogues
       Talk of court news; and we'll talk with them too,
8      Who loses and who wins, who's in, who's out;
       And take upon's the mystery of things,
       As if we were God's spies: and we'll wear out,
       In a walled prison, packs and sects of great ones
12     That ebb and flow by th' moon.
```

3. In the excerpt above, King Lear is speaking to

    A. Gloucester   B. Regan
    C. Goneril   D. Cordelia

4. In line 6, the phrase *gilded butterflies* refers to

    A. people who occupy themselves with fashion and gossip
    B. prison guards
    C. the study of wildlife
    D. people who come to spy upon them

5. The last two lines of this excerpt mainly refer to people

    A. whose power and influence is transitory
    B. whose power and influence is eternal
    C. whose lives are lived beyond the walls of prison
    D. opposed King Lear

6. In the excerpt above, the speaker's intention is to

    A. spy on his enemies until he escapes from prison
    B. escape from prison
    C. renounce the world beyond prison
    D. embrace the world beyond prison

7. The speaker's tone is best described as

    A. cynical   B. ironic
    C. reproachful   D. earnest and loving

8. *Half a league, half a league.*
    Half a league onward,
All in the valley of Death
    Rode the six hundred.
The lines above begin which of the following poems?

    A. THE CHARGE OF THE LIGHT BRIGADE
    B. THE LADY OF SHALOTT
    C. THE RIME OF THE ANCIENT MARINER
    D. ULYSSES

9. Allegorical novel in which the hero, named Christian, must confront characters named Pagan and Pope on his path to spiritual enlightenment.
The sentence above describes

    A. SIR GAWAIN AND THE GREEN KNIGHT
    B. GULLIVER'S TRAVELS
    C. PILGRIM'S PROGRESS
    D. THE CANTERBURY TALES

Questions 10-14.

DIRECTIONS: Questions 10 through 14 are to be answered on the basis of the following passage.

The Flea

*Mark but this flea,, and mark in this,
How little that which thou deniest me is;
Me it sucked first, and now sucks thee,
And in this flea our two blood mingled be;
Thou know'st that this cannot be said
A sin, or shame, or loss of maidenhead,
    Yet this enjoys before it woo,
    And pampered swells with one blood made of two,
    And this, alas, is more than we would do.*

10. The poem above was written by

    A. John Donne
    B. William Shakespeare
    C. Ben Jonson
    D. Geoffrey Chaucer

11. The tone of this poem is

    A. despairing
    B. angry
    C. lighthearted
    D. foreboding

12. The flea is a symbol of

    A. death
    B. sexual intercourse
    C. love
    D. birth

13. The phrase *loss of maidenhead* refers to the loss of

    A. honor
    B. status
    C. childhood
    D. virginity

14. The image of the blood comingling in the flea suggests

    A. pregnancy
    B. death
    C. eternity
    D. salvation

15. Hamlet's downfall is caused by the fact that he hesitates to enact revenge for which of the following crimes?

    A. The murder of his father
    B. The murder of his mother
    C. His mother's adultery
    D. His uncle's adultery with Hamlet's mother

16. Who wrote the romance of TROILUS AND CRISEDE?

    A. William Langland
    B. Christopher Marlowe
    C. William Shakespeare
    D. Geoffrey Chaucer

17. A disturbing satire about human and societal greed which, although set in Venice, was intended to reflect 17th century London.
    The lines above describe which of the following plays?

    A. THE CANTERBURY TALES, by Geoffrey Chaucer
    B. VOLPONE, by Ben Johnson
    C. PARADISE LOST, by John Milton
    D. OTHELLO, by William Shakespeare

18. *To see a world in a grain of sand*
    And a heaven in a wild flower,
    Hold infinity in the palm of your hand
    And eternity in an hour
    Each line of the poem above contains a(n)

    A. allegory   B. simile
    C. alliteration   D. metaphor

19. The imagery surrounding the character of Bertha Mason, locked in the dark attic because of her insanity, parallels the imagery surrounding the heroine, and it is this similarity that lends this novel much of its psychological depth and complexity.
    The lines above describe

    A. WUTHERING HEIGHTS   B. JANE EYRE
    C. THE MILL ON THE FLOSS   D. TO THE LIGHTHOUSE

20. The epic poem which relates a battle between a group of Vikings and Englishmen, and which contains characters named Birhtnoth, earl of Essex and Birhtwold.
    The lines above describe

    A. BEOWULF   B. THE BATTLE OF MALDON
    C. THE WIFE'S LAMENT   D. THE WANDERER

Questions 21-22.

DIRECTIONS: Questions 21 and 22 are to be answered on the basis of the following passage.

What is our life? a play of passion;
Our mirth the music of division;
Our mother's wombs the tiring-houses be
Where we are dressed for this short comedy.

21. In line 2, the word *mirth* most nearly means

    A. humor   B. sadness   C. hope   D. deceit

22. In the excerpt above, life is being compared to a

    A. tragedy   B. poem
    C. performance   D. factory job

23. Critics have said of this play, set in Scotland, that it is Shakespeare's greatest expression of the power of evil at work in civilization and the hearts of men and women.

    A. HAMLET
    B. MACBETH
    C. KING LEAR
    D. ROMEO AND JULIET

Questions 24-28.

DIRECTIONS: Questions 24 through 28 are to be answered on the basis of the following passage.

Nature (the art whereby God hath made and governs the world) is by the art of man, as in many other things, so in this also imitated, that it can make an artificial animal. (1) For seeing life is but a motion of limbs, the beginning whereof is in some principal part within why may we not say that all automata (engines that move themselves by springs and wheels as doth a watch) have an artificial life?(2)

24. The lines above begin which of the following works?

    A. THE WAY OF THE WORLD
    B. AN ESSAY CONCERNING HUMAN UNDERSTANDING
    C. OF SUPERSTITUTION
    D. LEVIATHAN

25. The lines above mainly imply that

    A. humans operate much like machines
    B. God is a machine
    C. Life is no more mysterious than the workings of a clock
    D. that which cannot be seen does not exist

26. Which of the following best summarizes the author's ideas about nature? It

    A. is a well-designed machine
    B. represents the artistic expression of God
    C. represents the goodness of God
    D. is as cold and indifferent to humanity as a machine

27. In sentence 1, the phrase *artificial animal* mainly means

    A. robotic beings
    B. all things living
    C. an object created through artistic means
    D. anything that is not alive

28. This excerpt from sentence 2, *the beginning whereof is in some principal part within,* mainly implies that

    A. the spark of life is mysterious
    B. the spark of life is no more surprising than the workings of a clock
    C. life is predictable
    D. the mechanism that sets life in motion is concrete and discoverable

29. A drama about an upper class heroine who defies her brothers and society by marrying for love, and is destroyed by the greed and pride of her family.
    The lines above describe

    A. PARADISE LOST B. ROMEO AND JULIET
    C. THE DUCHESS OF MALFI D. OTHELLO

30. In KING LEAR, what is the fate of Goneril and Regan?

    A. Their jealousy causes their deaths.
    B. They are killed by Cordelia's army.
    C. They are killed by their father.
    D. They kill Lear and Cordelia and rule over the kingdom.

31. Medieval poet who wrote THE LAIS, THE FABLES, and ST. PATRICK'S PURGATORY, and whose work was characterized by elements of magic and mystery.
    The lines above describe which of the following poets?

    A. Margery Kempe B. Anne Askew
    C. Isabella Whitney D. Marie de France

32. In the play OTHELLO, why does Desdemona's father oppose her marriage?

    A. It was conducted in secret.
    B. Because Othello is a Moor.
    C. She is too young to be married.
    D. She was betrothed to someone else.

33. Which of the following is a religious allegory whose characters include Messenger, God, Good Deeds, Five-Wits, and Knowledge?

    A. EVERYMAN
    B. PILGRIM'S PROGRESS
    C. THE VISION OF PIERS PLOWMAN
    D. UTOPIA

Questions 34-35.

DIRECTIONS: Questions 34 and 35 are to be answered on the basis of the following passage.

*Witch 1: When shall we three meet again?
In thunder, ligtning, or in rain?*

*Witch 2: When the hurly-burly's done,
When the battle's lost and won*

Witch 3: That will be ere the set of sun.

34. The lines above begin which of the following plays?

    A. PARADISE LOST B. HAMLET
    C. MACBETH D. THE DUCHESS OF MALFI

35. In the excerpt above, the word *ere* most nearly means 35.____

    A. soon B. after C. during D. before

36. For its narrative structure, this poem relies upon a religious pilgrimage and the stories the pilgrims tell one another during the course of their journey. 36.____
    The sentence above describes

    A. PIERS PLOWMAN B. THE CANTERBURY TALES
    C. PILGRIM'S PROGRESS D. GULLIVER'S TRAVELS

37. *From the oval-shaped flower bed there rose perhaps a hundred stalks spreading into heart-shaped or tongue-shaped leaves half way up and unfurling at the tip red or blue or yellow petals marked with spots of colour raised upon the surface; and from the red, blue, or yellow gloom of the throat emerged a straight bar, rough with gold dust and slightly clubbed at the end. The petals were voluminous enough to be stirred by the summer breeze, and when they moved, the red, blue, and yellow lights passed one over the other, staining an inch of the brown earth with a spot of the most intricate colour.* 37.____
    The excerpt above opens the short story

    A. THE GARDEN PARTY B. ARABY
    C. KEW GARDENS D. THE DEAD

38. This novel, written by Jean Rhys and set in Jamaica, provides a political and cultural subtext for JANE EYRE by dramatizing the story of the marriage between Mr. Rochester and Antoinette Bertha Cosway, from Bertha's point of view. 38.____
    The sentence above describes

    A. WIDE SARGASSO SEA
    B. A PASSAGE TO INDIA
    C. THE DAUGHTERS OF THE LATE COLONEL
    D. THINGS FALL APART

Questions 39-41.

DIRECTIONS: Questions 39 through 41 are to be answered on the basis of the following passage.

Troilus's Song

1	If no love is, O God, what feele I so?	
	And if love, is, what thing and which is he?	
	If love be good, from whennes cometh my wo?	
4	If it be <u>wikke</u>, a wonder <u>thinketh</u> me,	miserable/it seems to
	Whan every torment and adversitee	
	That cometh of him may to me <u>savory thinke</u>,	pleasant/seem
	For <u>ay</u> thurste I, the more that <u>ich</u> drinke.	always/I

39. In line 3, in the phrase, *from whennes cometh my wo*, the speaker is asking 39.____

    A. whether love is real
    B. whether he deserves such happiness
    C. why he feels so happy
    D. why he suffers

40. The last line of this excerpt is best summarized by which of the following?

    A. The more I suffer, the more I pursue love.
    B. The more I love, the happier I feel.
    C. My soul thirsts for love.
    D. Though I thirst for love, I will not drink.

41. In this excerpt, love is compared to

    A. nectar
    B. poison
    C. an irresistible drink
    D. a rainstorm

Questions 42-43.

DIRECTIONS: Questions 42 and 43 are to be answered on the basis of the following passage.

> *If it were done, when 'tis done, then 'twere well*
> *It were done quickly.*

42. The lines above are spoken by which character in the play MACBETH?

    A. Macduff
    B. Duncan
    C. Lady Macbeth
    D. Macbeth

43. In the excerpt above, what is the speaker talking about?

    A. Betrayal   B. Murder   C. Adultery   D. Robbery

Questions 44-46.

DIRECTIONS: Questions 44 through 46 are to be answered on the basis of the following passage.

A wide plan, where the broadening Floss hurries on between its green banks to the sea, and the loving tide, rushing to meet it, checks its passage with an impetuous embrace.(1) On this mighty tide the black ships – laden with the fresh-scented fir-planks, with rounded sacks of oil-bearing seed, or with the dark glitter of coal – are borne along to the town of St. Ogg's.(2)

44. The lines above begin which of the following novels?

    A. JANE EYRE
    B. VILLETTE
    C. MIDDLEMARCH
    D. THE MILL ON THE FLOSS

45. In the first sentence, the word *checks* most nearly means

    A. slows
    B. stops
    C. crashes against
    D. joins

46. The first sentence depends primarily upon

    A. irony   B. allegory   C. metaphor   D. simile

47. This satire examines the mores of society through the lives of two women, Rebecca Sharp and Amelia Sedley, who meet as children at Miss Pinkerton's Academy for Young Ladies.
The sentence above describes

    A. GREAT EXPECTATIONS   B. VANITY FAIR
    C. SENSE AND SENSIBILITY   D. MIDDLEMARCH

48. Who wrote ALICE IN WONDERLAND?

    A. T.S. Eliot   B. James Joyce
    C. Charles Dickens   D. Lewis Carroll

49. BEOWULF, CAEDMON'S HYMN, and THE BATTLE OF MALDON were written during which of the following periods?

    A. Middle Ages   B. Restoration
    C. Victorian   D. Romantic

50. In which of the following does Virginia Woolf explore the financial limitations placed on women and outline the conditions that will have to exist before women will be truly independent?

    A. A SKETCH OF THE PAST   B. MOMENTS OF BEING
    C. A ROOM OF ONE'S OWN   D. TO ROOM 19

KEY (CORRECT ANSWERS)

1. D	11. C	21. A	31. D	41. C
2. A	12. B	22. C	32. B	42. D
3. D	13. D	23. B	33. A	43. B
4. A	14. A	24. D	34. C	44. D
5. B	15. A	25. A	35. D	45. A
6. C	16. D	26. B	36. B	46. C
7. D	17. B	27. C	37. C	47. B
8. A	18. D	28. A	38. A	48. D
9. C	19. B	29. C	39. D	49. A
10. A	20. B	30. A	40. A	50. C

EXAMINATION SECTION
TEST 1

DIRECTIONS: Each question or incomplete statement is followed by several suggested answers or completions. Select the one that BEST answers the question or completes the statement. *PRINT THE LETTER OF THE CORRECT ANSWER IN THE SPACE AT THE RIGHT.*

Questions 1-7.

DIRECTIONS: Questions 1 through 7 are to be answered on the basis of the following passage.

> 1 But where the greater malady is fixed,
> The lesser is scarce felt. Thou'dst shun a bear;
> But if thy flight lay toward the roaring sea,
> 4 Thou'dst meet the bear i' th' mouth. When the mind's free,
> The body's delicate. The tempest in my mind
> Doth from my senses take all feeling else,
> Save what beats there. Filial ingratitude,
> 8 Is it not as this mouth should tear this hand
> For lifting food to't? But I will punish home.
> No, I will weep no more. In such a night
> To shut me out! Pour on, I will endure.

1. These lines are spoken by which of the following characters?

   A. Romeo   B. Othello   C. King Lear   D. Macbeth

2. Lines 1 and 2 of this excerpt mainly imply which of the following?

   A. The speaker has only one problem to deal with.
   B. Some problems are permanent and intractable.
   C. The speaker has so many difficulties that he feels nothing.
   D. Greater difficulties overshadow the pains of smaller ones.

3. In line 1, the word *fixed* most nearly means

   A. lodged   B. solved   C. overcome   D. endured

4. The line, *When the mind's free/the body's delicate,* is best summarized by which of the following?

   A. Spiritual and physical health are inextricable.
   B. When the mind is healthy, the lesser problems of body emerge and can be attended to.
   C. Spiritual problems lead to physical problems.
   D. When the body suffers, the mind is at peace.

5. The phrase *filial ingratitude* in line 7 refers to

   A. a friend who has betrayed him
   B. an unfaithful wife

C. unappreciative children
D. unappreciative siblings

6. The sentence, in lines 8 and 9, *Is it not as this mouth should tear this hand/For lifting food to't,* mainly refers to which of the following?
The

   A. speaker's ideas about friendship
   B. speaker's feelings about marriage
   C. closeness that should exist between siblings
   D. closeness that should exist between parents and children

7. In line 11, the phrase *pour on* refers to the

   A. storm outside
   B. speaker's companions
   C. speaker's children
   D. gods

Questions 8-9.

DIRECTIONS: Questions 8 and 9 are to be answered on the basis of the following passage.

Lordinges – quod he – in chirches whan I preche,
I paine me to han an hautein speeche,
And ringe it out as pound as gooth a belle,
for I can al by rote that I telle.

8. The style of the above lines is most characteristic of which of the following periods?

   A. Middle Ages
   B. Restoration
   C. Romantic
   D. Victorian

9. The lines above are best summarized by which of the following?

   A. In church, it is important to speak clearly.
   B. I speak haughtily in church, since I know the bible by heart.
   C. I have preached within every church in the country.
   D. I speak as loudly as I can in churches since I know my sermons by heart.

10. In which of the following poems by W.H. Auden does the poet examine the isolated nature of human suffering by analyzing the painting ICARUS created by the artist Brueghel?

    A. MUSEE DES BEAUX ARTS
    B. THE SHIELD OF ACHILLES
    C. PETITION
    D. IN MEMORY OF W.B. YEATS

11. Who wrote the poems MONT BLANC and PROMETHESUS UNBOUND?

    A. Percy Bysshe Shelley
    B. William Shakespeare
    C. Geoffrey Chaucer
    D. John Milton

12. Who wrote the epic poem PARADISE LOST?

    A. John Donne
    B. John Milton
    C. William Shakespeare
    D. Geoffrey Chaucer

13. Her novels, set in South Africa, dramatize the cultural and political turmoil of life in that country during the reign of apartheid.
    The sentence above describes

    A. Edna O'Brien
    B. Doris Lessing
    C. Nadine Gordimer
    D. Jean Rhys

Questions 14-19.

DIRECTIONS: Questions 14 through 19 are to be answered on the basis of the following passage.

> 1 Thus do I ever make my fool my purse;
>   For I mine own gained knowledge should profane
>   If I would time expend with such snipe
> 4 But for my sport and profit. I hate the Moor,
>   And it is thought abroad that 'twixt my sheets
>   H'as done my office. I know not if't be true,
>   But I, for mere suspicion in that kind,
> 8 Will do, as if for surety. He holds me well;
>   The better shall my purpose work on him.

14. The excerpt above appears in OTHELLO. The speaker is

    A. Emilia
    B. Desdemona
    C. Roderigo
    D. Iago

15. The first line of the excerpt is best summarized by which of the following?
    The speaker

    A. manipulates people for fun
    B. manipulates people in order to make money
    C. makes money off those s/he deceives
    D. gives money to those s/he deceives

16. Lines 4-6 mainly imply that Othello has

    A. committed adultery with the speaker's wife
    B. demoted or insulted the speaker
    C. told others that the speaker is incompetent
    D. spread rumors about the speaker abroad

17. In line 6, the word *H'as* most nearly means

    A. has   B. he has   C. desires to   D. will

18. In line 8, the phrase, *He holds me well,* most nearly means which of the following?
    He

    A. thinks he knows me, but he does not
    B. thinks ill of me
    C. holds me in check
    D. holds me in high esteem

19. In line 8, the word *surety* most nearly means

   A. suspicion
   B. uncertainty
   C. certainty
   D. a bond

20. Who wrote THE MASQUE OF BLACKNESS?

   A. Ben Jonson
   B. William Shakespeare
   C. John Milton
   D. Edmund Spenser

Questions 21-25.

DIRECTIONS: Questions 21 through 25 are to be answered on the basis of the following passage.

```
1   I tell you, hopeless grief is passionless;
       That only men incredulous of despair,
       Half-taught in anguish, through the midnight air
4   Beat upward to God's throne in loud access.
       Of shrieking and reproach. Full desertness
       In souls as countries, lieth silent-bare
       Under the blanching, vertical eye-glare
8   Of the absolute Heavens.
```

21. The poem above was written by

   A. Samuel Taylor Coleridge
   B. Elizabeth Barrett Browning
   C. William Butler Yeats
   D. Geoffrey Chaucer

22. In line 2, the phrase, *incredulous of despair,* mainly implies which of the following?

   A. Surprised by sorrow
   B. Overwhelmed by sorrow
   C. Untouched by sorrow
   D. Anger toward God

23. The meaning of lines 1-4 are best summarized by which of the following?

   A. Death leads to more suffering.
   B. Death is a release from suffering.
   C. Grief and suffering are most often borne silently.
   D. Grief and suffering are most often borne loudly.

24. Lines 5-8 rely primarily on

   A. allegory
   B. metaphor
   C. irony
   D. the juxtaposition of images

25. The poem above is an example of a(n)

   A. sonnet
   B. villanelle
   C. couplet
   D. open-verse poem

26. Which of the following is an opening line to a poem by Alfred Lord Tennyson?

   A. When I have fears that I may cease to be
   B. That time of year thou mayest in my behold
   C. In Xanadu did Kubla Khan
   D. Dark house by which once more I stand

27. The poem LEDA AND THE SWAN by William Butler Yeats tells the story of the

   A. birth of Helen of Troy and her sister, Clytemnestra
   B. rape of Leda by the god Zeus
   C. romance between Lancelot and the Lady of Shalott
   D. destruction of Troy

28. *Chapter One: The Early Married Life of the Morels*
   "The Bottoms" succeeded to "Hell Row." Hell Row was a block of thatched, bulging cottages that stood by the brook-side on Greenhill Lane.
   The excerpt above begins the novel

   A. SONS AND LOVERS   B. TO THE LIGHTHOUSE
   C. ULYSSES   D. GREAT EXPECTATIONS

29. This poem, written in five sections subtitled BURIAL OF THE DEAD, A GAME OF CHESS, THE FIRE SERMON, DEATH BY WATER, and WHAT THE THUNDER SAID, is considered a masterpiece of modern poetry.
   The sentence above describes

   A. THE SECOND COMING   B. ULYSSES
   C. THE WASTE LAND   D. OZYMANDIAS

30. The Arthurian Romance in which a young knight's chivalry undergoes a series of supernatural tests.
   The sentence above describes

   A. LE ROMAN DE BRUT
   B. LE MORTE D'ARTHUR
   C. THE CANTERBURY TALES
   D. SIR GAWAIN AND THE GREEN KNIGHT

31. In Mary Shelley's FRANKENSTEIN, Dr. Frankenstein's creation represents his own

   A. love for Elizabeth   B. subconscious
   C. hatred of his father D. fear of failure

Questions 32-34.

DIRECTIONS: Questions 32 through 34 are to be answered on the basis of the following passage.

   On either side the river lie
   Long fields of barley and of rye,
   That clothe the wold and meet the sky;
   And thro' the field the road runs by
   *   To many-towered Camelot;*

32. The lines above begin which of the following poems?

    A. LA BELLE DAME SANS MERCI
    B. THE LADY OF SHALOTT
    C. PROMETHEUS UNBOUND
    D. THE RIME OF THE ANCIENT MARINER

33. The opening line of the poem above relies primarily upon

    A. simile   B. end rhyme   C. alliteration   D. assonance

34. In line 3, the word *clothe* most nearly means

    A. cover   B. obscure   C. overwhelm   D. destroy

35. Which of the following poems by Robert Browning tells the story of a Duke who murdered his wife out of jealousy?

    A. LOVE AMONG THE RUINS
    B. THE BISHOP ORDERS HIS TOMB AT SAINT PRAXED'S CHURCH
    C. MY LAST DUCHESS
    D. SOLILOQUOY OF THE SPANISH CLOISTER

36. *Miss Brooke had that kind of beauty which seems to be thrown into relief by poor dress.* The sentence above begins which of the following novels?

    A. MIDDLEMARCH   B. JANE EYRE
    C. EMMA   D. PRIDE AND PREJUDICE

Questions 37-39.

DIRECTIONS: Questions 37 through 39 are to be answered on the basis of the following passage.

The sea-reach of the Thames stretched before us like the beginning of an interminable waterway. (1) In the offing the sea and the sky were welded together without a joint, and in the luminous space the tanned sails of the barges drifting up with the tide seemed to stand still in red clusters of canvas sharply peaked, with gleams of varnished sprits. (2) A haze rested on the low shores that ran out to sea in vanishing flatness. (3) The air was dark above Gravesend, and farther back still seemed condensed into a mournful gloom, brooding motionless over the biggest, and the greatest, town on earth.(4)

37. The lines above are taken from

    A. THE MAN WHO WOULD BE KING
    B. MIDDLEMARCH
    C. GREAT EXPECTATIONS
    D. HEART OF DARKNESS

38. In sentence 4, the *greatest town on Earth* refers to

    A. New York   B. London   C. Los Angeles   D. Venice

39. The mood of these lines is best described as

    A. despairing   B. foreboding   C. optimistic   D. joyful

Questions 40-43.

DIRECTIONS: Questions 40 through 43 are to be answered on the basis of the following passage.

She walks in beauty, like the night
Of cloudless climes and starry skies;
And all that's best of dark and bright
Meet in her aspect and her eyes:
Thus mellowed to that tender light
Which heaven to gaudy day denies

40. The poem above was written by

   A. William Shakespeare
   B. Lord Byron
   C. John Keats
   D. Geoffrey Chaucer

41. In line 4, the *word aspect* most nearly means

   A. style   B. voice   C. posture   D. soul

42. The last line of the excerpt above mainly implies that the woman's beauty

   A. does not exist
   B. is brighter than the sun
   C. is subtle and sublime
   D. outshines the heavens

43. In the excerpt above, the author's tone is best described as

   A. loving   B. desperate   C. grieving   D. angry

44. *There was no possibility of taking a walk that day. We had been wandering, indeed, in the leafless shrubbery an hour in the morning; but since dinner (Mrs. Reed, when there was no company, dined early) the cold weather had brought with it clouds so sombre, and a rain so penetrating, that further outdoor exercise was now out of the question.*
    The lines above begin which of the following novels?

   A. PRIDE AND PREJUDICE
   B. MIDDLEMARCH
   C. JANE EYRE
   D. TO THE LIGHTHOUSE

45. Who wrote THE IMPORTANCE OF BEING EARNEST and AN IDEAL HUSBAND?

   A. William Thackeray
   B. James Joyce
   C. William Shakespeare
   D. Oscar Wilde

46. The heroine for which this novel is named is betrayed twice in the course of her life: first by the abandonment of her hypocritical husband and then by his return, which begins the sequence of events that leads to her execution for killing him.
    The sentence above describes

   A. TESS OF THE D'URBERVILLES
   B. EMMA
   C. JUDE THE OBSCURE
   D. JANE EYRE

47. In this satirical allegory, a group of animals grows agitated when a fellow creature, the horse, is taken to a glue factory to be killed, and this agitation leads to a revolution.

    A. ROBINSON CRUSOE B. THE WASTE LAND
    C. ANIMAL FARM D. 1984

Questions 48-49.

DIRECTIONS: Questions 48 and 49 are to be answered on the basis of the following passage.

The Unknown Citizen
(To JS/07/M/378
This Marble Monument
Is Erected by the State)

He was found by the Bureau of Statistics to be
One against whom there was no official complaint,
And all the reports on his conduct agree
That, in the modern sense of an old-fashioned word, he was a saint,
For in everything he did he served the Greater Community.

48. The poem above was written by

    A. W. H. Auden B. William Butler Yeats
    C. Dylan Thomas D. Thom Gunn

49. The tone of the poem above is best described as

    A. allegorical B. hopeful
    C. despairing D. ironic

50. Which of the following poets died before completing his epic poem HYPERION?

    A. William Butler Yeats B. John Keats
    C. Wilfred Owen D. T. S. Eliot

KEY (CORRECT ANSWERS)

1. C	11. A	21. B	31. B	41. D
2. D	12. B	22. A	32. B	42. C
3. A	13. C	23. C	33. D	43. A
4. B	14. D	24. B	34. A	44. C
5. C	15. C	25. A	35. C	45. D
6. D	16. A	26. D	36. A	46. A
7. A	17. B	27. B	37. D	47. C
8. A	18. D	28. A	38. B	48. A
9. D	19. C	29. C	39. B	49. D
10. A	20. A	30. D	40. B	50. B

TEST 2

DIRECTIONS: Each question or incomplete statement is followed by several suggested answers or completions. Select the one that BEST answers the question or completes the statement. *PRINT THE LETTER OF THE CORRECT ANSWER IN THE SPACE AT THE RIGHT.*

Questions 1-4.

DIRECTIONS: Questions 1 through 4 are to be answered on the basis of the following passage.

> 1 We have this hour a constant hour to publish
> Our daughters several dowers, that future strife
> May be prevented now. The Princes, France and Burgundy,
> 4 Great rivals in our youngest daughter's love,
> Long in our court have made their amorous sojourn,
> And here are to be answered. Tell me, my daughters
> (Since now we will divest us both of rule,
> 8 Interest of territory, cares of state),
> Which of you shall we say doth love us most,
> That we our largest bounty may extend
> Where nature doth with merit challenge.

1. In the excerpt above, King Lear is

   A. speaking at his daughter's wedding
   B. reclaiming his kingdom
   C. dividing his kingdom
   D. disinheriting Cordelia

2. In line 5, the phrase *amorous sojourn* refers to

   A. Lear's infidelity
   B. Cordelia's infidelity
   C. Cordelia's banishment
   D. the courting of Cordelia

3. In line 7, the word *divest* most nearly means

   A. withdraw
   B. turn over responsibility
   C. lay claim
   D. assert

4. The last 3 lines of this excerpt are best summarized by which of the following?

   A. She who expresses the greatest degree of love will receive the largest inheritance.
   B. Each daughter will receive an equal share of the kingdom.
   C. She who expresses the greatest degree of love will win the King's favor.
   D. She who expresses the greatest degree of love will marry either France or Burgundy.

5. In the opening act of OTHELLO, how is the quarrel between Othello and Desdemona's father settled?

   A. Othello and Desdemona escape to Turkey
   B. Through the intervention of Iago

1.____

2.____

3.____

4.____

5.____

145

C. Through a duel in the streets of Venice
D. By members of the Venetian Senate

6. In which of the following does Chauntecleer the Rooster appear as a character? 6.____

   A. ROBINSON CRUSOE B. GULLIVER'S TRAVELS
   C. THE CANTERBURY TALES D. PILGRIM'S PROGRESS

Questions 7-9.

DIRECTIONS: Questions 7 through 9 are to be answered on the basis of the following passage.

Generous tears filled Gabriel's eyes.(1) He had never felt like that himself towards any woman but he knew that such a feeling must be love. (2) The tears gathered more thickly in his eyes and in the partial darkness he imagined he saw the form of a young man standing under a dripping tree. (3) Other forms were near. (4) His soul had approached that region where dwell the vast hosts of the dead. (5) He was conscious of, but could not apprehend, their wayward and flickering existence. (6) His own identity was fading out into a grey impalpable world: the solid world itself which these dead had one time reared and lived in was dissolving and dwindling. (7)

7. The lines above are taken from 7.____

   A. THE DEAD B. KEW GARDENS
   C. TO ROOM 19 D. ARABY

8. The moment of revelation described above is referred to as a(n) 8.____

   A. insight B. climax
   C. epiphany D. denouement

9. In sentence 7, the word *reared* most nearly means 9.____

   A. fled B. created C. resisted D. destroyed

10. A medieval allegory which includes a history of Christianity and whose theme is the redemption of the soul. 10.____
    The sentence above describes

    A. HISTORY OF THE KINGS OF BRITAIN
    B. BEOWULF
    C. THE CANTERBURY TALES
    D. THE VISIONS OF PIERS PLOWMAN

11. This novel, written in the author's signature stream-of-consciousness style, focuses on a single day in the life of its protagonist. 11.____
    The sentence above describes

    A. THE DEAD B. MRS. DALLOWAY
    C. TO THE LIGHTHOUSE D. ULYSSES

12. Sir Guyan, Gloriana, and the female knight Britomart all appear in the epic poem 12.____

    A. LE MORTE D'ARTHUR B. PARADISE LOST
    C. THE TEMPEST D. THE FAERIE QUEENE

13. Which verse form is most commonly found in Old English poems?

    A. Single line
    B. Couplet
    C. Iambic pentameter
    D. Villanelle

14. *The Best State of a Commonwealth*
    A Discourse by the Extraordinary
    Raphael Hythloday, as Recorded by
    The Noted Thomas More,
    Citizen and Sheriff
    of the Famous
    City of Britain, London
    The lines above serve as the opening to

    A. PILGRIM'S PROGRESS
    B. DOCTOR FAUSTUS
    C. ROBINSON CRUSOE
    D. EVERYMAN

15. The Weird Sisters act as temptresses in this tragedy, with no direct power over human will, but only the ability to perceive each man's greatest desire and tempt him with it. The lines above describe which of the following plays?

    A. HAMLET
    B. MACBETH
    C. JULIUS CAESAR
    D. KING LEAR

16. The friendship of these two poets shaped the philosophy of Romanticism.

    A. Alexander Pope and Samuel Taylor Coleridge
    B. William Blake and Alexander Pope
    C. William Wordsworth and Samuel Taylor Coleridge
    D. William Wordsworth and William Blake z

17. The characters of Gloucester and his two sons, Edgar and Edmund, serve as a brilliant subplot which both reflects ana foreshadows plot of the main story.
    The lines above describe which of the following plays?

    A. OTHELLO
    B. ROMEO AND JULIET
    C. KING LEAR
    D. MACBETH

18. William Shakespeare, John Donne, and John Webster are considered by literary historians to be

    A. Jacobeans
    B. Romantics
    C. Victorians
    D. Renaissance writers

19. Author of THINGS FALL APART, a novel which is set in Nigeria and which explores the destructive impact of European colonization on a small village.

    A. Alan Paton
    B. Chinua Achebe
    C. Nadine Gordimer
    D. Doris Lessing

20. Othello's tragic flaw is best summarized as

    A. jealousy   B. inaction   C. pride   D. greed

21. The characters of Hrothgar, Halfdane, and Aeschee appear in which of the following?

    A. THE ODYSSEY
    B. BEOWULF
    C. THE CANTERBURY TALES
    D. THE BATTLE OF MALDON

22. Who wrote THE OBEDIENCE OF A CHRISTIAN MAN?

    A. John Calvin
    B. Queen Elizabeth
    C. William Tyndale
    D. Sir Thomas More

23. Which of the following details the mythic story of King Arthur's birth, reign, and death, including the affair between Lancelot and Guinevere and the chivalric adventures of the Knights of the Round Table?

    A. EVERYMAN
    B. LE MORTE D'ARTHUR
    C. SIR GAWAIN AND THE GREEN KNIGHT
    D. BRUT

24. Which of the following is an opening line to a poem by Dylan Thomas?

    A. Five summer days, five summer nights
    B. Sir, no man's enemy, forgiving all
    C. The force that through the green fuse drives the flower
    D. April is the cruellest month, breeding

25. This story, by Doris Lessing, examines the alienation and suicide of Susan Rawlings, a young, intelligent, and successful wife and mother.

    A. KEW GARDENS
    B. THE GARDEN PARTY
    C. THE DEAD
    D. TO ROOM NINETEEN

26. In this novel, V.S. Naipaul chronicles the life of a man from birth to death, dramatizing the destruction of a traditional way of life at the hands of colonial pressures and incursions. The sentence above describes

    A. A HOUSE FOR MR. BISWAS
    B. THE BURGER'S DAUGHTER
    C. THINGS FALL APART
    D. WIDE SARGASSO SEA

27. *It was the best of times, it was the worst of times, it was the age of wisdom, it was the age of foolishness...*
    The line above begins which of the following novels?

    A. VANITY FAIR
    B. JANE EYRE
    C. A TALE OF TWO CITIES
    D. GREAT EXPECTATIONS

28. *"Yes, of course, if it's fine tomorrow," said Mrs. Ramsay. "But you'll have to be up with the lark," she added. To her son these words conveyed an extraordinary joy, as if it were settled the expedition were bound to take place, and the wonder to which he had looked forward, for years and years it seemed, was, after a night's darkness and a day's sail, within touch.*
    The excerpt above begins the novel

    A. ULYSSES
    B. TO THE LIGHTHOUSE
    C. A PASSAGE TO INDIA
    D. MRS. DALLOWAY

29. The story of a hero who fights an evil monster named Grendel in order to save his people.
    The work described above is

    A. THE ODYSSEY
    B. BEOWULF
    C. THE CANTERBURY TALES
    D. THE BATTLE OF MALDON

30. Plays which dramatize the prophecies of the Old Testament and the redemption of the New Testament are called

    A. epics
    B. morality plays
    C. tragedies
    D. mystery plays

31. Who wrote DR. FAUSTUS?

    A. Christopher Marlowe
    B. William Shakespeare
    C. John Milton
    D. John Donne

32. *But jealous souls will not be answered so;*
    They are not ever jealous for the cause,
    But jealous for they're jealous. It is a monster
    Begot upon itself, born on itself.
    The lines above are best summarized by which of the following?

    A. Jealous people are monstrous.
    B. The roots of jealousy are too numerous to count.
    C. Jealousy needs no reason; it feeds upon itself.
    D. Jealousy has no cure.

Questions 33-41.

DIRECTIONS: Questions 33 through 41 are to be answered on the basis of the following passage.

Redemption
1 *Having been tenant long to a rich lord,*
   Not thriving, I resolved to be bold,
   And make a suit unto him, to afford
4 *A new small-rented lease, and cancel th' old.*

   In heaven at his manor I him sought:
   They told me there that he was lately gone
   About some land which he had dearly bought
8 *Long since on earth, to take possession.*

   I straight returned, and knowing his great birth,
   Sought him accordingly in great resorts -
   In cities, theaters, gardens, parks, and courts;
12 *At length I heard a ragged noise and mirth*

   Of thieves and murderers; there I him espied,
14 *Who straight, "Your suit is granted," said, and died.*

33. The poem above was written by

    A. Ben Jonson
    B. George Herbert
    C. Thomas Hobbes
    D. Alexander Pope

34. The rhyme scheme of this poem is

    A. abab cdcd effe gg
    B. abab cdcd efef gg
    C. abba cddc effe gg
    D. abba cddc effe fg

35. The poem above is a(n)

    A. epic   B. couplet   C. sonnet   D. villanelle

36. Who is the *rich lord* of the first line?

    A. The speaker's wife
    B. The landlord
    C. God of the New Testament
    D. God of the Old Testament

37. The central metaphor of the poem above compares

    A. God/Christ to a beggar
    B. God/Christ to a just king
    C. God/Christ to a landlord
    D. a landlord to a king

38. In line 3, the word *suit* most nearly means

    A. plea   B. lawsuit   C. appearance   D. gift

39. In line 4, the phrase *cancel th' old* refers metaphorically to the

    A. New Testament
    B. Old Testament
    C. land-lease agreement
    D. feudal relationship

40. The main implication of lines 9-11 is that

    A. the man the speaker sought could not be found
    B. the man the speaker sought was not fulfilling his duties
    C. despite his noble birth, the man the speaker sought was not to be found in the houses of power
    D. despite his noble birth, the man the speaker sought had lost all of his money and influence and could no longer frequent the houses of power

41. The last two lines of the poem refer metaphorically to

    A. the French revolution
    B. the English revolution
    C. the birth of Christ
    D. Christ's crucifixion

42. His plays, which include TAMBURLAINE and THE JEW OF MALTA, include heroes whose ambition for power inevitably leads them to tragedy.
    The lines above describe

    A. William Shakespeare
    B. Christopher Marlowe
    C. Ben Jonson
    D. John Milton

43. Which of the following is a political satire whose chief narrative device is the sea voyage of a doctor and his encounters with the inhabitants of several kingdoms, including the Houyhnhnms and the Brobdingnag?

    A. GULLIVER'S TRAVELS
    B. ROBINSON CRUSOE
    C. PILGRIM'S PROGRESS
    D. ULYSSES

Questions 44-50.

DIRECTIONS: Questions 44 through 50 are to be answered on the basis of the following passage.

1   Gather ye rosebuds while ye may,
     Old time is still a-flyings;
     And this same flower that smiles today,
4   Tomorrow will be dying.

     The glorious lamps of heaven, the sun,
     The higher he's a-getting,
     The sooner will his race be run,
8   And nearer he's to setting.

     That age is best which is the first,
     When youth and blood are warmer;
     But being spent, the worse, and worst
12 Times still succeed the former.

     Then be not coy, but use your time,
     And while ye may, go marry;
     For having lost but once your prime,
16 You may forever tarry.

44. The poem above is entitled

    A. A VALEDICTION: FORBIDDING MOURNING
    B. TO THE VIRGINS, TO MAKE MUCH OF TIME
    C. TO HIS COY MISTRESS
    D. THE RAPE OF THE LOCK

44.____

45. The main implication of this poem is best summarized by which of the following?

    A. Youth is fleeting, so make the most of it.
    B. A youth spent foolishly leads to an unhappy old age.
    C. Young people do not understand the gravity of life.
    D. Life is not worth living once youth has passed.

45.____

46. The metaphor of the flower in the first stanza is meant to symbolize

    A. the permanence of youth
    B. eternity
    C. the transitory nature of youth
    D. death

46.____

47. Lines 10-11 mainly imply that

    A. youth is a state of mind
    B. youth is the most difficult time of life for some people
    C. old age is more rewarding than youth
    D. age, and the grief it brings, always follows youth

47.____

48. In line 13, the word *coy* most nearly means

   A. kind   B. cruel   C. teasing   D. deceitful

49. The last two lines of the poem mainly imply that

   A. the potential of youth should not be wasted on games
   B. the potential of old age should not be wasted on games
   C. old age offers more satisfactions than youth
   D. youth should be spent on wild and dangerous pursuits

50. The tone of this poem is best described as

   A. angry
   B. cautionary
   C. warning
   D. ironic

KEY (CORRECT ANSWERS)

1. C	11. B	21. B	31. A	41. D
2. D	12. D	22. C	32. C	42. B
3. B	13. A	23. B	33. B	43. A
4. A	14. D	24. C	34. A	44. B
5. D	15. B	25. D	35. C	45. A
6. C	16. C	26. A	36. D	46. C
7. A	17. C	27. C	37. C	47. D
8. C	18. A	28. B	38. A	48. C
9. B	19. B	29. B	39. B	49. A
10. D	20. A	30. D	40. C	50. B

TEST 3

DIRECTIONS: Each question or incomplete statement is followed by several suggested answers or completions. Select the one that BEST answers the question or completes the statement. *PRINT THE LETTER OF THE CORRECT ANSWER IN THE SPACE AT THE RIGHT.*

1. *From this World to That Which Is to Come: Delivered under the Similitude of a Dream*

   [Christian sets out for the Celestial City]

   As I walked through the wilderness of this world, I lighted on a certain place where there was a Den, and I laid me down in that place to sleep; and as I slept I dreamed a dream.
   The excerpt above begins which of the following?

   A. GULLIVER'S TRAVELS
   B. ROBINSON CRUSOE
   C. PARADISE LOST
   D. PILGRIM'S PROGRESS

   1.____

2. Which of the following was originally written in Medieval English?

   A. ROBINSON CRUSOE
   B. HAMLET
   C. BEOWULF
   D. All of the above

   2.____

3. Who wrote the poems SHALL I COMPARE THEE TO A SUMMER'S DAY; TH' EXPENSE OF SPIRIT IN A WASTE OF SHAME; and MY LOVE IS AS A FEVER, LONGING STILL?

   A. John Milton
   B. Sir Walter Raleigh
   C. Christopher Marlowe
   D. William Shakespeare

   3.____

4. Which of the following poets is best known for his exploration of the separation between physical lust and spiritual love, body, and soul, and sin and grace?

   A. Andrew Marvell
   B. Ben Jonson
   C. William Shakespeare
   D. Alexander Pope

   4.____

Questions 5-9.

DIRECTIONS: Questions 5 through 9 are to be answered on the basis of the following passage.

   1 *Do not go gentle into that good night,*
   Old age should burn and rave at close of day;
   Rage, rage against the dying of the light.

   4 *Though wise men at their end know dark is right,*
   Because their words had forked no lightning they
   Do not go gentle into that good night.

   Good men, the last wave by, crying how bright
   8 *Their frail deeds might have danced in a green bay,*
   Rage, rage against the dying of the light.

153

> Wild men who caught and sang the sun in flight,
> And learn, too late, they grieved it on its way,
> 12 Do not go gentle into that good night.
>
> Grave men, near death, who see with blinding sight
> Blind eyes could blaze like meteors and be gay,
> Rage, rage against the dying of the light.
>
> 16 And you, my father, there on the sad height,
> Curse, bless, me now with your fierce tears, I pray.
> Do not go gentle into that good night.
> Rage, rage against the dying of the light.

5. The poem above was written by

   A. Charles Causley
   B. W.B. Yeats
   C. Dylan Thomas
   D. W.H. Auden

6. The poem is an example of a(n)

   A. villanelle
   B. Shakespearean sonnet
   C. Petrarchan sonnet
   D. epic

7. The phrase *dying of the light* refers to

   A. despair   B. death   C. old age   D. fury

8. In line 13, the word *grave* most nearly means

   A. elderly
   B. despairing
   C. ill
   D. serious

9. In the final stanza of the poem, the speaker beseeches his father to

   A. resist the infirmity of his old age
   B. accept his old age peacefully
   C. accept his death peacefully
   D. fight against dying

Questions 10-13.

DIRECTIONS: Questions 10 through 13 are to be answered on the basis of the following passage.

From, *Ancrene Riwle*

This king is Jesus, Son of God, who in just this way wooed our soul, which devils had besieged. (1) And he, like a noble suitor, after numerous messengers and many acts of kindness came to prove his love, and showed by feats of arms that he was worthy of love, as was the custom of knights once upon a time.(2) Be entered the tournament and, like a bold knight, had his shield pierced through and through in battle for love of his lady.(3) His shield, which hid his divinity, was his dear body, which was stretched out on the cross: broad as a shield above in his extended arms, narrow below, where the one foot (as many people think) was fixed above the other.

10. In line 1, *besieged* most nearly means   10.____

    A. conquered   B. surrounded   C. stolen   D. destroyed

11. This passage relies primarily upon an elaborate   11.____

    A. ruse   B. allegory   C. metaphor   D. simile

12. Christ is compared to a(n)   12.____

    A. desperate suitor   B. innocent lover
    C. dutiful soldier   D. chivalric knight

13. The divinity of Christ is compared to a   13.____

    A. shield   B. spear   C. tournament   D. human body

14. *Bifel* that in that seson on a day   It happened   14.____
    In Southwerk at the Tabard as I lay
    The lines above provide an example of

    A. a sonnet   B. alliteration   C. a couplet   D. a villanelle

Questions 15-18.

DIRECTIONS: Questions 15 through 18 are to be answered on the basis of the following passage.

Containing
The Legende of the
Knight of the Red Crosse
or
Of Holinesse

1 Lo I the man, whose Muse whilome did maske,
     As time hey taught, in lowly Shepheards weeds,
3 Am now enforst a far unfitter taske,
     For trumpets sterne to chaunge mine Oaten reeds,
     And sing of Knights and Ladies <u>gentle</u> deedes;   noble
6 Whose prayses having slept in silence long,
     Me, aii too <u>meane</u>, the sacred Muse <u>areeds</u>   low/counsels
     To <u>blazon</u> broad emongst her learned throng:
9 Fierce wares and faithful loves shall moralize my song.

15. The excerpt above serves as the opening to   15.____

    A. THE CANTERBURY TALES   B. THE TEMPEST
    C. THE FAERIE QUEENE   D. PARADISE LOST

16. Line 3 is best summarized by which of the following?   16.____

    A. I must undertake a more difficult task.
    B. I am not qualified for this task.
    C. This task has been forced upon me.
    D. I have agreed to this task against my better judgment.

17. Lines 4 and 5 are best summarized by which of the following? The poet

    A. hates heroic poetry
    B. hates pastoral poetry
    C. is leaving heroic poetry to write pastoral poetry
    D. is leaving pastoral poetry to write heroic poetry

18. The main purpose of these opening lines is for the poet to

    A. ask for the reader's attention
    B. introduce himself and his subject to the reader
    C. prepare the reader for the difficult material to come
    D. warn the reader

19. In KING LEAR, the storm into which Lear is banished by his daughters Goneril and Regan symbolizes

    A. Lear's madness
    B. Lear's anger
    C. the insanity of Lear's daughters
    D. Lear's despair

20. THE CANTERBURY TALES was written by

    A. Geoffrey of Monmouth   B. Geoffrey Chaucer
    C. Sir Thomas Malory   D. Christopher Marlowe

21. A poetic line containing six stresses is written in

    A. iambic hexameter   B. iambic pentameter
    C. blank verse   D. terza rima

22. One of the most brilliant and haunting characters ever created by Shakespeare, Iago's silence about his motiva-tions in destroying so many innocent lives casts a pall over the play and underscores the idea that evil cannot be explained.
    The lines above describe which of the following plays?

    A. MACBETH   B. OTHELLO
    C. HAMLET   D. ROMEO AND JULIET

23. Who was the first English woman writer to compose and sign her own plays?

    A. Margaret Cavendish   B. Katherine Phillips
    C. Aphra Behn   D. Anne Finch

24. In which of the following essays does the author attack the educational and cultural limitations placed on women in the 18th century?

    A. THE ANGEL IN THE HOUSE
    B. A ROOM OF ONE'S OWN
    C. THE POOR SINGING DAME
    D. A VINDICATION OF THE RIGHTS OF WOMEN

25. Who wrote THE INSTITUTION OF CHRISTIAN RELIGION?   25._____

    A. John Foxe   B. William Tyndale
    C. Anne Askew   D. John Calvin

26. A fourteen line poem written in pentameter rhythm with an alternating rhyme scheme is   26._____
    called a(n)

    A. sonnet   B. villanelle   C. epic   D. couplet

27. Which of the following writers emphasized the belief that all elements of life, including   27._____
    spiritual and religious considerations, consisted of matter and anything that could not be
    seen did not exist?

    A. Alexander Pope   B. William Tyndale
    C. John Locke   D. Thomas Hobbes

28. *Of man's first disobedience, and the fruit*   28._____
    Of that forbidden tree, whose mortal taste
    Brought death into the world, and all our woe.
    The lines above begin

    A. THE CANTERBURY TALES   B. THE FAERIE QUEENE
    C. PARADISE LOST   D. THE TEMPEST

29. In the play MACBETH, what is the fate of Lady Macbeth?   29._____

    A. Madness   B. Banishment
    C. Madness and death   D. Death

30. Religious allegories which dramatize God's plan in the lifespan of a single representative   30._____
    character are called

    A. morality plays   B. mystery plays
    C. allegories   D. tales

Questions 31-35.

DIRECTIONS: Questions 31 through 35 are to be answered on the basis of the following passage.

```
 1    What guyle is this, that those her golden tresses,
          She doth attyre under a net of gold:
          And with sly skill so cunningly them dresses,            clever
          That which is gold or heare, may scarse be told?         hair
 5    Is it that mens frayle eyes, which gaze too bold,
          She may entangle in that golden snare:
          And being caught may craftily enfold
          Theyr weaker harts, which are not wel aware?
      Take heed therefore, myne eyes, how y doe stare
10        henceforth too rashly on that guile full net,
          In which if ever ye entrapped are,
          Out of her bands ye by no means shall get.
      Fondnesse it were for any being free,                        foolishness
          To covet fetters, though they golden bee.
```

31. In the poem above, hair is being compared to a

　　A. beam of moonlight　　　　B. tree
　　C. snare　　　　　　　　　　D. rainshower

32. In line 3, the phrase *sly skill* mainly implies

　　A. danger　　　　　　　　　B. cunning
　　C. hard work　　　　　　　　D. forthrightness

33. Lines 7 and 8 are best summarized by which of the following?

　　A. Men are skilled at separating physical beauty from spiritual beauty.
　　B. Attracted by her inner beauty, a man will be unable to escape her honesty and charm.
　　C. She uses her beauty to attract and kill men.
　　D. Once attracted by her physical beauty, an unwitting man will be unable to escape her influence.

34. Lines 10 and 11 function as a

　　A. warning the poet provides himself
　　B. warning to all men and women
　　C. warning to god
　　D. plea for love

35. This sonnet is best summarized by which of the following? A(n)

　　A. plea for love
　　B. warning against love based on financial considerations
　　C. warning against love based on appearances
　　D. illustration of true spiritual love

36. 　　　Then poor Cordelia!
　　And yet, not so, since I am sure my love's
　　More ponderous than my tongue.
　　The lines above mainly imply which of the following?

　　A. Her love is deceitful.
　　B. Her love is more substantial than her words can express.
　　C. Her love is so substantial that she will have no trouble articulating it.
　　D. She feels no love, and therefore cannot articulate it.

37. In her novel WUTHERING HEIGHTS, Emily Bronte primarily utilizes elements of which two literary periods?

　　A. Victorian and Modern　　　　B. Victorian and Restoration
　　C. Romantic and Gothic　　　　　D. Romantic and Victorian

38. This novel's focus on the independent and imaginative Dorothea Brooke, who must choose between her own integrity and the values of the narrow-minded and materialistic society, is one of its greatest achievements.
　　The lines above describe

　　A. MIDDLEMARCH　　　　　　B. JANE EYRE
　　C. THE MILL ON THE FLOSS　　D. TO THE LIGHTHOUSE

39. One of the tragic ironies of this play is that the one character who is truly pure, truly chaste, is the character who is undone by a false accusation of adultery leveled by the corrupt characters around her.
    The lines above describe which of the following plays?

    A. OTHELLO
    B. THE DUCHESS OF MALFI
    C. PARADISE LOST
    D. ROMEO AND JULIET

40. Who wrote the poems A VALEDICTION: OF WEEPING and A VALEDICTION: FORBIDDING MOURNING?

    A. Ben Jonson
    B. William Shakespeare
    C. John Milton
    D. John Donne

Questions 41-45.

DIRECTIONS: Questions 41 through 45 are to be answered on the basis of the following passage.

```
 1  The long love that in my thought doth, harbor
    And in mine heart doth keep his residence,
    Into my face presseth with bold pretense
 4  And therein campeth spreading his banner.
    She that me learneth to love and suffer
    And will that my trust and lust's negligence
    Be reined by reason, shame, and reverence,
 8  With his hardiness taketh displeasure.
    Wherewithal unto the heart's forest he fleeth,
    Leaving his enterprise with pain and cry,
    And there him hideth, and not appeareth.
12  What may I do, when my master feareth,
    But in the field with him to live and die?
    For good is the life ending faithfully.
```

41. In the poem above, love is being compared to a

    A. woodsman   B. warrior   C. ship   D. king

42. In line 3, the phrase *with bold pretense* most nearly means

    A. making a bold claim
    B. making a rude gesture
    C. with cunning and bravery
    D. an arrogant gesture

43. Line 4 most nearly means

    A. retreating from the challenge ahead
    B. resting after his victory
    C. taking forceful possession
    D. announcing his love

44. Line 5 is best summarized by which of the following?

    A. She who changes herself for me
    B. She who teaches me to love and suffer
    C. The woman who accepts me despite my faults
    D. The woman who merely endures my presence

45. In line 7, the word *shame* most nearly means

    A. modesty   B. disgrace   C. horror   D. sinfulness

46. Considered by many literary historians to be the first novel, this tale of self-sufficiency focuses on a man shipwrecked on a desert island.
    The lines above describe which of the following novels?

    A. ROBINSON CRUSOE   B. GULLIVER'S TRAVELS
    C. FRANKENSTEIN   D. MIDDLEMARCH

47. THE MERRY WIVES OF WINDSOR; A COMEDY OF ERRORS; and MEASURE FOR MEASURE were all written by

    A. John Milton   B. John Donne
    C. William Shakespeare   D. Geoffrey Chaucer

48. In this novel, Jane Austen examines the contrasting effects of passion and restraint in the characters of two sisters, Marianne and Elinor.
    The novel described above is

    A. PRIDE AND PREJUDICE   B. SENSE AND SENSIBILITY
    C. EMMA   D. MANSFIELD PARK

49. When the child, nicknamed *Old Father Time,* kills himself and his siblings in order to spare their parents the hardship of providing for them, the life of the novel's hero is brought to a symbolic and spiritual end.
    The sentence above describes

    A. ULYSSES   B. TO THE LIGHTHOUSE
    C. MIDDLEMARCH   D. JUDE THE OBSCURE

50. *Okonkwo was well known throughout the villages and even beyond. His fame rested on solid personal achievements. As a young man of eighteen he had brought honor to his village by throwing Amalinze the Cat. Amalinze was the great wrestler who for seven years was unbeaten, from Umuofia to Mbaino.*
    The lines above begin which of the following novels?

    A. CRY, THE BELOVED COUNTRY
    B. A HOUSE FOR MR. BISWAS
    C. THINGS FALL APART
    D. THE BURGHER'S DAUGHTER

KEY (CORRECT ANSWERS)

1. D	11. C	21. A	31. C	41. B
2. C	12. D	22. B	32. B	42. A
3. D	13. A	23. C	33. D	43. D
4. A	14. C	24. D	34. A	44. C
5. C	15. C	25. D	35. C	45. A
6. A	16. A	26. A	36. B	46. A
7. B	17. D	27. D	37. C	47. C
8. D	18. B	28. C	38. A	48. B
9. C	19. A	29. C	39. A	49. D
10. B	20. B	30. A	40. D	50. C

ENGLISH LITERATURE
MAJOR WRITERS AND THEIR WORKS

CONTENTS

THE EARLY NINETEENTH CENTURY

William Wordsworth	1
Samuel Taylor Coleridge	1
Sir Walter Scott	1
George Gordon, Lord Byron	2
Percy Bysshe Shelley	2
John Keats	2
Walter Savage Landor	2
Charles Lamb	3
William Hazlitt	3
Thomas DeQuincey	3
Samuel Rogers	3
James Hogg	3
Robert Southey	3
Thomas Campbell	3
Thomas Moore	3
Allan Cunningham	3
James Henry Leigh Hunt	3
Thomas Love Peacock	3
Charles Wolfe	4
William Motherwell	4
Thomas Hood	4
Thomas Lovell Beddoes	4

THE LATER NINETEENTH CENTURY

Thomas Carlyle	4
Thomas Babington Macaulay	4
John Henry Newman	4
John Stuart Mil	4
Alfred, Lord Tennyson	4
Robert Browning	5
John Ruskin	5
Matthew Arnold	5
Thomas Henry Huxley	5
Elizabeth Barrett Browning	5
Edward Fitzgerald	6
Dante Gabriel Rossetti	6
Emily Bonte	6
Arthur Hugh Clough	6
Christina Georgina Rossetti	6
William Morris	6
James Thomson	7
Algernon Charles Swinburne	7
Walter Pater	7
William Ernest Henley	7
Robert Louis Stevenson	7
Oscar Wilde	7
Francis Thompson	7
George Meredith	7
Thomas Hardy	7
Rudyard Kipling	8
Alfred Edward Housman	8
John Masefield	8
William Butler Yeats	8
John Millington Synge	8

ENGLISH LITERATURE
MAJOR WRITERS AND THEIR WORKS

THE EARLY NINETEENTH CENTURY

WILLIAM WORDSWORTH (1770-1850)
- Lines Written in Early Spring
- Expostulation and Reply
- The Tables Turned
- Lines Composed a Few Miles Above Tintern Abbey
- Lucy
- Lucy Gray
- The Simplon Pass
- Michael
- My Heart Leaps Up
- To the Cuckoo
- Resolution and Independence
- Composed upon Westminster Bridge, September 3, 1802
- Composed by the Seaside near Calais, August, 1802
- It is a Beauteous Evening, Calm and Free
- On the Extinction of the Venetian Republic
- To Toussaint L'Ouverture
- She was a Phantom of Delight
- I Wandered Lonely as a Cloud
- Elegiac Stanzas
- Ode to Duty
- To a Skylark
- Character of the Happy Warrior
- Ode on Intimations of Immortality from Recollections of Early Childhood
- Preface to Lyrical Ballads
- *From* The Prelude:
   - Book First: Childhood and School-Time
   - Book Fourth: Summer Vacation
   - Book Eighth: Retrospect
   - Book Ninth: Residence in France
   - Book Tenth: Residence in France
   - Book Eleventh: France (concluded)
   - Book Twelth: Imagination and Taste
   - Book Thirteenth: Imagination and Taste (concluded)
- Near Dover, September 1802
- Written in London, 1802
- London, 1802
- To the Daisy
- When I Have Borne in Memory
- At the Grave of Burns, 1803
- The Solitary Reaper
- The World is Too Much With us
- Song at the Feast of Brougham Castle
- Laodamia
- Composed Upon an Evening of Extraordinary Splendor and Beauty
- Mutability
- Inside of King's College Chapel, Cambridge
- The Trosachs

SAMUEL TAYLOR COLERIDGE (1772-1834)
- Kubla Khan; or, A Vision in a Dream
- The Rime of the Ancient Mariner
- Frost at Midnight
- Christabel
- Dejection: An Ode
- Youth and Age
- Work Without Hope
- Biographic Literaria

SIR WALTER SCOTT (1771-1832)
- Lochinvar, *From* Marmion, Canto v, Lady Heron's Song
- The Lady of the Lake
- Soldier, Rest! Thy Warfare O'er. *From* The Lady of the Lake, Canto I
- Jock of Hazeldean
- Boat Song. *From* The Lady of the Lake, Canto II
- Coronach. *From* The Lady of the Lake, Canto III
- Brignall Banks. *From* Rokeby, Canto III
- Pibroch of Donald Dhu

SIR WALTER SCOTT (1771-1832)
- Clarion. *From* Old Mortality
- Lullaby of an Infant Chief
- Proud Maisie. *From* The Heart of Midlothian

(cont'd)
- County Guy. *From* Quentin Durward
- Bonny Dundee
- Here's a Health to King Charles. *From* Woodstock

GEORGE GORDON, LORD BYRON (1788-1824)
- When We Two Parted
- Maid of Athens, Ere We Part
- She Walks in Beauty
- The Destruction of Sennacherib
- Stanzas for Music
- Mazeppa
- Stanzas
- The Prisoner of Chillon
- *From* Childe Harold's Pilgrimage. Canto the Third
- Sonnet on Chillon
- To Thomas Moore
- So We'll Go No More A Roving
- Don Juan
- On This Day I Complete My Thirty-Sixth Year

PERCY BYSSHE SHELLEY (1792-1822)
- Hymn to Intellectual Beauty
- Ozymandias
- Stanzas Written in Dejection near Naples
- The Masque of Anarchy
- Ode to the West Wind
- The Indian Serenade
- Prometheus Unbound
- The Cloud
- A Defense of Poetry
- To a Skylark
- To Night
- Time
- Mutability
- Adonais
- The Final Chorus from Hellas
- To-----
- Lines: When the Lamp is Shattered
- A Dirge

JOHN KEATS (1795-1821)
- Sonnet: On First Looking into Chapman's Homer
- To My Brothers
- Endymion
- When I Have Fears That I May Cease to Be
- On Seeing the Elgin Marbles
- Robin Hood Ode on Indolence
- Ode on a Grecian Urn
- Ode to a Nightingale
- Ode on Melancholy
- To Autumn
- La Belle Dame Sans Merci
- Stanzas: In a Drear-Nighted December
- On the Grasshopper and Cricket
- To Leight Hunt, Esq.
- Lines on the Mermaid Tavern
- Fancy
- The Eve of St. Agnes
- Ode
- Two Sonnets on Fame
- To Sleep
- Sonnet: To a Young Lady Who Sent Me a Laurel Crown
- Lamia
- Sonnet

WALTER SAVAGE LANDOR (1775-1864)
- Iphigenia and Agamemnon
- Rose Aylmer
- A Fiesolan Idyl
- Various the Roads of Life
- Why Do Our Joys Depart
- On His Seventy-Fifth Birthday
- Imaginary Conversations
- Marcellus and Hannibal
- Leofric and Godiva
- Henry VIII and Anne Boleyn
- Bossuet and the Duchess de Fontages The Empress Catharine and Princess Dashk of

3

CHARLES LAMB (1775-1834)
  The Old Familiar Faces
  Essays of Elia
    Christ's Hospital Five and
      Thirty Years Ago
    Mrs. Battle's Opinions on
      Whist
    Imperfect Sympathies

Essays of Elia (cont'd)
  Witches and Other Night-Fears
  Dream Children: A Reverie
  In Praise of Chimney-Sweepers
  A Dissertation Upon Roast Pig
  Poor Relations
  A Character of the Late Elia

———

WILLIAM HAZLITT (1778-1830)
  My First Acquaintance With Poets
  On Going a Journey

The Fight
A Farewell to Essay-Writing

———

THOMAS DE QUINCEY (1785-1859)
  From Suspiria De Profundis:
  Levana and Our Ladies of
    Sorrow

The English Mail Coach

———

SAMUEL ROGERS (1763-1855)
  A Wish

———

JAMES HOGG (1770-1835)
  The Skylark

A Boy's Song

———

ROBERT SOUTHEY (1774-1843)
  The Battle of Blenheim
  The Cataract of Lodore

The Inchcape Rock
The Legend of Bishop Hatto

———

THOMAS CAMPBELL (1777-1844)
  Ye Mariners of England
  Hohenlinden

Lord Ullin's Daughter

———

THOMAS MOORE (1779-1852)
  The Harp That Once Through
    Tara's Halls
  Believe Me, If All Those En
    dearing Young Charms

The Minstrel Boy
The Light of Other Days
The Last Rose of Summer

———

ALLAN CUNNINGHAM (1734-1842)
  A Wet Sheet and a Flowing Sea

Cupid Drowned

JAMES HENRY LEIGHT HUNT (1784-1859
  Abou Ben Adhem and the Angel
    Rondeau

———

THOMAS LOVE PEACOCK (1785-1866)
  Love and Age

———

CHARLES WOLFE (1791-1823)
    The Burial of Sir John Moore at Coruiia

WILLIAM MOTHERWELL (1797-1835)
    Jeanie Morrison

THOMAS HOOD (1799-1845)
    I Remember, I Remember   The Death Bed
    The Bridge of Sighs   Morning Meditations
    The Song of the Shirt

THOMAS LOVELL BEDDOES (1803-1849)
    Dream-Pedlary

THE LATER NINETEENTH CENTURY

THOMAS CARLYLE (1795-1881)
    Sartor Resartus   The French Revolution
    Past and Present   Life of John Sterling

THOMAS BABINGTON MACAULAY (1800-1859)
    Milton   Francis Bacon

JOHN HENRY NEWMAN (1801-1890)
    England   The Idea of a University
    The Pillar of the Cloud   The Definition of a Gentleman
    Apologia Pro Vita Sua

JOHN STUART MILL (1806-1873)
    Autobiography   On Liberty

ALFRED, LORD TENNYSON (1809-1892)
    The Poet   The Charge of the Light Brigade
    The Lady of Shalott   Maud
    (Enone   The Brook
    The Palace of Art   The Voyage
    The Lotos-Eaters   Milton
    The Epic   Northern Farmer, Old Style
    Morte d'Arthur   Northern Farmer, New Style
    Ulysses   In the Valley of Cauteretz
    Locksley Hall   The Flower
    Sir Galahad   Wages
    Break, Break, Break   The Higher Pantheism
    The Princess   The Revenge
    In Memoriam A.H.H.   Rizpah
    Ode on the Death of the Duke   Locksley Hall Sixty Years After
      of Wellington   Merlin and the Gleam
    Crossing the Bar

ROBERT BROWNING (1812-1889)
- Pippa's Song
- Cavalier Tunes
  - Marching Along
  - Give a Rouse
  - Boot and Saddle
- How They Brought the Good News from Ghent to Aix
- My Last Duchess
- Soliloquy of the Spanish Cloister
- The Lost Leader
- Meeting at Night
- Parting at Morning
- Home-Thoughts, from Abroad
- Pictor Ignotus
- The Bishop Orders His Tomb at Saint Praxed's Church
- A Woman's Last Word
- Evelyn Hope
- Love Among the Ruins
- Up at a Villa-Down in the City
- A Toccata of Galuppi's
- De Gustibus ....
- My Star
- Two in the Campagna
- One Way of Love
- Respectability
- The Guardian-Angel
- Memorabilia
- The Last Ride Together
- A Grammarian's Funeral
- The Statue and the Bust
- Childe Roland to the Dark Tower Came
- Fra Lippo Lippi
- Andrea del Sarto
- One Word More
- Abt Vogler
- Rabbi Ben Ezra
- Prospice
- Epilogue

JOHN RUSKIN (1819-1900)
- Modern Painters
- The Stones of Venice
- Unto This Last
- Fors Clavigera

MATTHEW ARNOLD (1822-1888)
- Quiet Work
- Shakespeare
- The Forsaken Merman
- Empodocles on Etna
- Self-Dependence
- Morality
- The Buried Life
- Lines Written in Kensington Gardens
- The Future
- Requiescat
- The Scholar-Gypsy
- Thyrsis
- Isolation
- Dover Beach
- Rugby Chapel
- Essays in Criticism
- The Function of Criticism at the Present Time
- Sweetness and Light
- Literature and Science

THOMAS HENRY HUXLEY (1825-1895)
- Autobiography
- On the Advisableness of Improving Natural Knowledge
- A Liberal Education; and Where to Find It
- On the Physical Basis of Life
- Science and Culture

ELIZABETH BARRETT BROWNING (1806-1861)
- Sonnets from the Portuguese
  1. I thought once how Theocritus had sung
  2. Unlike are we, unlike, O princely Heart!

ELIZABETH BARRETT BROWNING (1806-1861) (cont'd)
    4. Thou hast thy calling to some palace floor
  14. If thou must love me, let it for for nought
  22. When out two souls stand up erect and strong
  35. If I leave all for thee, wilt thou exchange
  43. How do I love thee? Let me count the ways.

To George Sand	The Cry of the Children

EDWARD FITZGERALD (1809-1883)
    Rubáiyát of Omar Khayyám of Naishápúr

DANTE GABRIEL ROSSETTI (1828-1882)

The House of Life	The Blessed Damozel
The Sonnet	Sister Helen
Love-Sight	Francois Villon
Silent Noon	Troy Town
The Choice	The Cloud Confines
Vain Virtues	
Lost Days	
A Superscription	
The One Hope	

EMILY BRONTË (1818-1848)

The Philosopher	Shall Earth No More Inspire Thee?
Remembrance	Self-Interrogation
That Wind, I Used to Hear	The Wanderer from the Fold
The Night is Darkening	Stanzas
Fall, Leaves	The Old Stoic
The Weary Task	Last Lines

ARTHUR HUGH CLOUGH (1819-1861)

Say Not the Struggle Nought Availeth	Qui Laborat, Orat
	Ite Domum Saturae, Venit
Dipsychus	Hesperus
Qua Cursum Ventus	Life is Struggle
The Latest Decalogue	In a London Square
Hope Evermore and Believe	All is Well

CHRISTINA GEORGINA ROSSETTI (1830-1894)

Song: When I am Dead, My Dearest	Goblin Market
Looking Forward	Sleeping at Last
The Heart Knoweth its Own Bitterness	

WILLIAM MORRIS (1834-1896)

The Defence of Guenevere	The Earthly Paradise
The Eve of Crecy	An Apology
The Haystack in the Floods	L'Envoi
Art, Wealth, and Riches	

7

JAMES THOMSON (1834-1882)
    Mater Tenebrarum   The City of Dreadful Night
    Sunday at Hampstead

ALGERNON CHARLES SWINBURNE (1837-1909)
- Atalanta in Calydon
- Hymn to Proserpine
- A Match
- A Ballad of Burdens
- The Garden of Proserpine
- Hertha
- To Walt Whitman in America
- A Ballad of Francois Villon
- On the Deaths of Thomas Carlyle and George Eliot
- Hope and Fear
- A Child's Future

WALTER PATER (1839-1894)
- Studies in the History of the Renaissance
- Plato and Platonism
- Wordsworth
- The Child in the House
- Marius the Epicurean Sandro Botticelli

WILLIAM ERNEST HENLEY (1849-1903)
From In Hospital
    1. Enter Patient
    2. Waiting
    4. Before
    23. Music
    28. Discharged

- Invictus
- Margaritae Sorori
- On the Way to Kew
- London Voluntaries
- Rhymes and Rhythms

ROBERT LOUIS STEVENSON (1850-1894)
- A Gossip on Romance
- The Lantern-Bearers
- Pulvis et Umbra
- A Christmas Sermon

OSCAR WILDE (1856-1900)
- The Ballad of Reading Gaol
- Lady Windermere's Fan

FRANCIS THOMPSON (1859-1907)
- The Poppy
- The Hound of Heaven
- Little Jesus
- The Kingdom of God
- Envoy

GEORGE MEREDITH (1828-1909)
- Modern Love
- Love in the Valley
- The Spirit of Shakespeare
- Lucifer in Starlight
- A Certain People
- The Woods of Westermain
- The Thrush in February
- Hard Weather
- A Stave of Roving Tim

THOMAS HARDY (1840-1928)
- At Casterbridge Fair
- The Ballad-Singer
- Former Beauties
- After the Club Dance
- Her Dilemma
- Revulsion
- Her Initials
- Rome

The Market-Girl
The Inquiry
A Wife Waits
After the Fair
The Darkling Thrush
To Life

Lausanne
An August Midnight
Embarcation
A Christmas Ghost-Story
I Said to Love

RUDYARD KIPLING (1865-1936)
  A Ballad of East and West
  Fuzzy-Wuzzy
  Gunga Din

  L'Envoi
  Recessional

ALFRED EDWARD HOUSMAN (1859-1936)
  From A Shropshire Lad
    1. 1887
    2. Loveliest of trees, the cherry now
    18. Oh, when I was in love with you
    19. To an Athlete Dying Young
    36. White in the moon the long road lies
    40. Into my heart an air that kills
    47. The Carpenter's Son
    49. Think no more, lad; laugh, be jolly
    54. With rue my heart is laden
    58. When I came last to Ludlow
    62. Terence, this is stupid stuff
  From Last Poems
    10. Could man be drunk forever
    12. The laws of God, the laws of man
  From More Poems
    They say my verse is sad: no wonder
    27. To stand up straight and tread the turning mill

JOHN MASEFIELD (1878-1967)
  A Consecration
  Cargoes
  Roadways
  The West Wind

  On Malvern Hill
  London Town
  Laugh and Be Merry
  On Growing Old Sea-Fever

WILLIAM BUTLER YEATS (1865-1939)
  From Meditations in Time of
    Civil War
    11. My House
  The Fisherman

  When You are Old
  The Voice
  The Song of the Happy Shepherd
  The Falling of the Leaves

JOHN MILLINGTON SYNGE (1871-1909)
  The Playboy of the Western World

BRIEF SYNOPSES OF SHAKESPEARE'S PLAYS

TABLE OF CONTENTS

	Page
COMEDIES (14)	
All's Well That Ends Well	1
As You Like It	1
Comedy of Errors, The	2
Love's Labour's Lost	2
Measure for Measure	3
Merchant of Venice, The	3
Merry Wives of Windsor, The	4
Midsummer Night's Dream, A	5
Much Ado About Nothing	5
Taming of the Shrew, The	6
Tempest, The	6
Twelfth Night	7
Two Gentlemen of Verona, The	7
Winter's Tale, The	8
HISTORIES (10)	
King Henry IV, Part I	8
King Henry IV, Part II	8
King Henry V	9
King Henry VI, Part I	9
King Henry VI, Part II	10
King Henry VI, Part III	10
King Henry VIII	11
King John	11
King Richard II	12
King Richard III	12
TRAGEDIES	
Antony and Cleopatra	13
Coriolanus	13
Cymbeline	14
Hamlet, Prince of Denmark	14
Julius Caesar	15
King Lear	15
Macbeth	16
Othello	16
Pericles, Prince of Tyre	17
Romeo and Juliet	17
Timon of Athens	18
Titus Andronicus	18
Troilus and Cressida	19

BRIEF SYNOPSES OF SHAKESPEARE'S PLAYS
COMEDIES

ALL'S WELL THAT ENDS WELL
He needs must go that the devil drives.
         Act I, Scene 3

BERTRAM, Count of Rousillon, is about to leave home to enter the service of the King of France. In his mother's household is an orphan, HELENA, whose father was a physician. She is in love with BERTRAM, but he scarcely notices her, regarding her as far below his station in life. HELENA learns that the King is desperately ill of a malady his physicians cannot cure, and that it is one for which her father had a remedy, the secret of which is now in her possession. She decides to go to Paris, partly to cure the King, and partly because BERTRAM is there.

HELENA'S treatment is a success, and in his gratitude at his recovery the King tells HELENA she may choose a husband from among all his knights. Though many are willing to espouse her, it is BERTRAM she chooses. He declines to marry her, until he is ordered to do so by the King. He is leaving for the war in Italy, however, and immediately after the ceremony sends HELENA back to Rousillon.

Here HELENA receives a message from her husband saying that he will have nothing to do with her until she shows him a certain ring she must take from his finger, and also a child she has begotten by him. In pilgrim's garb she sets out for Florence.

BERTRAM becomes enamored by a certain DIANA, daughter of a Florentine widow, and tries to seduce her. HELENA persuades the girl to pretend to consent, and then let HELENA herself take her place under cover of darkness. In this way she persuades BERTRAM to trade rings with her, and begets a child.

Again in France, BERTRAM is confronted with an accusation of seduction by DIANA, and when he is relieved of his predicament by HELENA'S explanation of what actually transpired, he has the good grace to admit his cruelty, and really seems to have fallen in love with his wife at last.

AS YOU LIKE IT
Sweet are the uses of adversity,
Which, like the toad, ugly and venomous,
Wears yet a precious jewel in his head.
         Act 2, Scene 1

FREDERICK has usurped the power of his elder brother who retires to the Forest of Arden. ROSALIND, the daughter of the rightful Duke, remains at FREDERICK'S court as companion to her cousin, CELIA.

FREDERICK is gracious to ORLANDO, who is a skilled wrestler, but when he finds that ORLANDO is the son of a friend of the banished Duke, his favor cools. ROSALIND, however, falls in love with ORLANDO. She, too, is banished because of her popularity and CELIA accompanies her.

ROSALIND dons male clothing and goes to Arden with CELIA. There they meet ORLANDO who has been forced to flee from his brother, OLIVER ROSALIND now tests ORLANDO'S professed love for her.

ORLANDO, in saving his brother OLIVER from wild beasts, is wounded. This leads to their reconciliation.

When OLIVER and CELIA meet, they fall in love. ROSALIND finds her father, the Duke, and both pairs of lovers are married. At the same time, TOUCHSTONE, the court clown, takes a wife.

Duke FREDERICK is converted by a hermit and restores his brother to his rightful position.

THE COMEDY OF ERRORS
The pleasing punishment that women bear.
Act I, Scene I

It is quite impossible to tell the story of this comedy, since it is what today would be called "slapstick." It is a comedy of twins identical in appearance, and not merely of one pair of twins, but two. Only the background of the farce can be related coherently.

The time is between two and three centuries B.C. AEGEON, a merchant of Ephesus, was presented by his wife with twins while they were away from home, he on a business trip. In the same inn a poor woman at the same time also gave birth to twins, and the merchant brought them to be servants to his own. The couple started home on a ship, a storm arose, the ship was wrecked, and AEGEON with one of his own children and one of the other twins drifted one way and his wife with the other half of the quartet in another.

Years passed, AEGEON had no word of his wife, but his son and the servant twin insisted that the merchant go searching for the remainder of the household. He finally reached Ephesus, his funds depleted, and becoming separated from his son and their attendant was arrested because of a feud between Ephesus and his own city of Syracuse. So bitter was this rivalry that any man of Syracuse found in Ephesus was automatically sentenced to pay a large fine or be executed. AEGEON could not pay the fine. The Duke listened to his story and was quite sympathetic, but insisted that the law must be obeyed, and unless the Syracusan could raise the money for his fine, he would have to die.

With this, the farce begins, its action being based upon repeated incidents of mistaken identity involving the two pairs of twins. It may be as well here to relieve all suspense by promising that the unfortunate merchant will not be executed

LOVE'S LABOUR'S LOST
A jest's prosperity lies in the ear
Of him that hears it, never in the tongue
Of him that makes it.
Act 5, Scene 2

FERDINAND, King of Navarre, has decided to go into academic retirement for three years, to see no woman, and to live very simply and spend the time in study. He is accompanied by three lords, BIRON, LONGAVILLE and DUMAIN. The enterprise is barely launched when they receive word that the King of France is sending his daughter to Navarre to attend to the settlement of a claim involving title to Aquitaine. FERDINAND'S modest court is also haunted by a curious Spaniard, ARMADO, whose doings, together with those of various country folk, provide comedy scenes paralleling the main story.

FERDINAND meets the Princess, who is accompanied by three ladies, ROSALINE, MARIA and KATHARINE, but excuses himself for not inviting the party to his court, explaining the vow which he and his three companions have taken. It appears, however, that the resolution of the four recluses has been weakened by the presence of the lovely ladies.

The Princess and her party are entertained in the King's park, and FERDINAND and his friends are finally compelled to admit to one another that love has caused them to lose interest in scholarly pursuits. They make little progress in the good graces of the ladies, however. This merry war, and masquerades, comprise the greater part of the play.

News arrives that the Princess' father is dead, and she must return home. To the proposals of marriage by the King and the three lords, the ladies reply that they will give the men a twelve-month to prove themselves worthy. BIRON complains that this is not the way a play should end, and to the King's observation that it is only a year they have to wait, replies "That's too long for a play." And there it ends.

MEASURE FOR MEASURE
*O, it is excellent
To have a giant's strength; but it is tyrannous
To use it like a giant!*
Act 2, Scene 2

VINCENTIO, Duke of Vienna, absenting himself for a time from his official duties, leaves the severe and upright ANGELO as his deputy. One of ANGELO's first acts is to condemn to death CLAUDIO, a young man who has seduced his sweetheart, JULIET, whom he is unable to marry because of financial difficulties. CLAUDIO's sister, ISABELLA, is persuaded to make a personal appeal to ANGELO on her brother's behalf.

ANGELO replies to all ISABELLA'S arguments with a stern refusal to interfere with the course of the law, but promises to see her again the following day. When she has left, he muses upon the temptation he feels coming upon him. At their next meeting he offers to save her brother, at the price of her own chastity. Confident that CLAUDIO would prefer his own death to her dishonor, ISABELLA scornfully rejects the offer and goes to visit her brother.

ISABELLA finds that CLAUDIO has not the moral stamina she expected, but she leaves the prison still determined not to submit herself to ANGELO. The Duke, masquerading as a friar, learns all the facts, and tells ISABELLA to pretend to accept ANGELO's proposal.

There is a woman, MARIANA, to whom ANGELO was betrothed, but whom he abandoned because she lost her dowry. The Duke arranges to substitute her for ISABELLA in ANGELO's house, under cover of darkness.

The Duke reappears in his own guise and resumes his position as ruler of the city. He tells ANGELO what has happened, and requires him to marry MARIANA. He himself makes ISABELLA his Dutchess, and CLAUDIO is freed, to make an honest woman of his JULIET.

THE MERCHANT OF VENICE
The quality of mercy is not strained.
Act 4, Scene 1

In order to assist his friend, BASSANIO, who is in love with PORTIA, ANTONIO, a merchant of Venice, borrows 3,000 ducats from SHYLOCK on condition that ANTONIO will forfeit a pound of flesh if he cannot repay the debt. SHYLOCK's hatred of ANTONIO is increased by the elopement of *JESSICA, SHYLOCK*'s daughter, with *LORENZO*, another friend of *ANTONIO*.

On being confronted by a choice among a gold, silver, and lead casket in accordance with a provision in the will of *PORTIA'S* father, *BASSANIO* selects the lead casket containing *PORTIA*'s portrait and he is accepted by her.

When *ANTONIO* fails to repay the debt, *SHYLOCK* requests a trial before the Duke of Venice. *PORTIA* disguises herself as a lawyer and defends *ANTONIO* successfully. *SHYLOCK* is forced to will his property to *JESSICA*.

At her request *PORTIA* receives, as the attorney's fee, a ring which she had given to *BASSANIO*. Her maid, *NERISSA*, married to *GRATIANO*, a friend of *BASSANIO*, also gets back from her husband her engagement ring. After pretending anger, *PORTIA* explains the situation to *BASSANIO* and all ends well.

THE MERRY WIVES OF WINDSOR
The world's mine oyster.
Act 2, Scene 2

SIR JOHN FALSTAFF is having difficulties with a country justice who accuses the knight and his three followers of all manner of misbehavior, including poaching. *PAGE*, a gentleman of the neighborhood, endeavoring to straighten the matter out, invites them both to dinner, and there *FALSTAFF* becomes enamored, in his heavy way, of both *MRS. PAGE* and her friend *MRS. FORD*. Later he sends one of his followers with two letters, expressing his feelings, one to each lady. While these incidents are occurring, it appears that three young men have cast longing eyes upon *PAGE'S* daughter, *ANNE*. These three are *SLENDER*, a country lout, *DR. CAIUS*, a peppery Frenchman, and *FENTON*, a likeable youth.

MRS. FORD and *MRS. PAGE* compare notes, and decide to trap the fat knight, *FALSTAFF*. They send him word to be at *MRS. FORD'S* house at a certain hour.

The trick works better than they had hoped, for the untimely arrival of the jealous husband, *FORD*, causes the escape of *FALSTAFF* in a hamper of dirty linen, to be more realistic than was intended. Meanwhile, *FENTON's* courtship of *ANNE PAGE* progresses.

FALSTAFF has hardly cleaned off the slime of the ditch into which he was thrown with the soiled clothes, when *MRS. PAGE* and *MRS. FORD* prepare another trap into which he falls with equal innocence. This time again his escape from *FORD* is real, but less successful. The merry wives dress the elephantine *FALSTAFF* as an old witch, and he gets a terrific beating, *FORD* having a special antipathy against witches. *FENTON's* love affair with *ANNE PAGE* is not prospering quite so well.

Still unsuspecting, *FALSTAFF* follows a third lure, and appears in Windsor Park at midnight, disguised as a deer, at least to the extent of wearing a buck's head. Here he is attached, pinched, buffeted, burned and otherwise tortured by a crowd dressed as fairies. In the confusion, two independent schemes, one to have *SLENDER* run off with *ANNE PAGE*, and the other to have her spirited away by *DR. CAIUS*, are frustrated by *FENTON*, who steals away with the girl himself.

A MIDSUMMER NIGHT'S DREAM
Lord, what fools these mortals be!
Act 3, Scene 2

When THESEUS, Duke of Athens, becomes engaged to HIPPOLYTA, Queen of the Amazons, BOTTOM, a weaver, and his friends prepare a play to be given at court. In the meantime HERMIA, daughter of EGEUS, is ordered by the Duke to marry DEMETRIUS, selected by EGEUS, or to enter a convent. HERMIA's plan to elope with LYSANDER is revealed to DEMETRIUS by HELENA in order to win his love.

PUCK, a sprite, is ordered by OBERON, King of the fairies, to pour a love-juice on the eyes of TITANIA, Queen of the fairies. When OBERON sees DEMETRIUS and HELENA quarreling, he orders PUCK to anoint the eyes of DEMETRIUS. However, PUCK, anoints the eyes of LYSANDER so that the latter falls in love with HELENA. When BOTTOM passes by, PUCK places an ass's head on him. On waking, TITANIA sees him and falls in love with him.

OBERON anoints the eyes of DEMETRIUS and a quarrel ensues among the four lovers. The problem is resolved by THESEUS who permits DEMETRIUS to marry HELENA and LYSANDER to marry HERMIA. OBERON removes the spell from TITANIA. BOTTOM, restored to his natural form, gathers his players and they perform "Pyramus and Thisbe" in honor of the triple marriage.

MUCH ADO ABOUT NOTHING
There was never yet philosopher
That could endure the toothache patiently.
Act 5, Scene 1

In the household of LEONATO, Governor of Messina, are his daughter, HERO, and his niece, BEATRICE. DON PEDRO, Prince of Arragon, visits the Governor on his way home from a victorious campaign, in which two of his retainers have especially distinguished themselves, CLAUDIO and BENEDICK. A less desirable member of his company is his ill-natured brother, DON JOHN, whose greatest happiness is in causing trouble. CLAUDIO falls in love immediately with HERO, and the Prince says he will arrange the match. BEATRICE and BENEDICK are old acquaintances however, and they have made such a constant game of biting repartee that each thinks the other is in earnest in the sarcasm and abuse.

DON JOHN arranges a plot with his servant BORACHIO to disgrace HERO, and break up the match with CLAUDIO. More benevolent schemes surround BENEDICK, for a conversation is staged purposely for him to hear, in which it is declared that BEATRICE is fairly ill for love of him. A similar trick is played upon BEATRICE, who believes her presence is unsuspected while HERO and a waiting woman discuss BENEDICK'S adoration of her.

The arrangements for CLAUDIO to marry HERO are completed when DON JOHN informs the Prince and CLAUDIO that HERO is a wanton. He takes them at night to the garden beneath HERO'S window, and there shows them BORACHIO making love to a woman who, they have every right to believe is HERO, but who is actually her waiting woman. CLAUDIO decides that HERO shall be disgraced publicly.

The marriage ceremony is about to take place, when CLAUDIO denounces HERO, and is supported by DON JOHN. Amazed and shocked, HERO falls, apparently dead. The scene changes to a prison, where DOGBERRY, an amusing constable, is questioning BORACHIO, who was heard telling about the trick that had been played on HERO and CLAUDIO.

LEONATO still believes his daughter was maligned, and in a quarrel with CLAUDIO they have reached the verge of deadly combat when BENEDICK interrupts. DOGBERRY arrives with his prisoner, and BORACHIO, whose master has fled from Messina, confesses the entire plot. CLAUDIO repents at the family tomb of LEONATO, and praises the innocent HERO. LEONATO has forgiven CLAUDIO, and has suggested that he marry BEATRICE. LEONATO learns, however, that his daughter is not dead, but has been secreted by the friar. A wedding in masks is arranged by LEONATO, at which it appears that CLAUDIO is marrying BEATRICE, to the great discomfiture of BENEDICK. The masked bride, however, turns out to be HERO, and BENEDICK gets his BEATRICE after all.

THE TAMING OF THE SHREW

He that is giddy thinks the world turns round.
                                              Act 5, Scene 2

BIANCA, daughter of BAPTISTA, may not marry until her elder sister, KATHARINA, is married. Because of KATHARINA's vile temper, BIANCA's suitors are at a loss until the arrival of PETRUCHIO who woos KATHARINA by overriding all of her objections. In order to win BIANCA, LUCENTIO trades identities with his servant, TRANIO.

After the wedding of PETRUCHIO and KATHARINA, the bride is forced to subordinate her own wishes to the unreasonable demands of her husband. After LUCENTIO wins BIANCA and the wedding is held, KATHARINA is shown to be the most submissive of all the wives present at the feast.

THE TEMPEST

We are such stuff
As dreams are made of, and our little life
Is rounded with a sleep.
                                              Act 4, Scene 1

PROSPERO, formerly Duke of Milan and ousted by his brother, ANTONIO, with the aid of ALONSO, King of Naples, is set adrift with his daughter, MIRANDA. Aided by GONZALO, they reach an island where they dwell for many years with only CALIBAN, a brutish slave, on the island.

PROSPERO, who had studied magic, raises a tempest, which wrecks a vessel containing ALONSO, his brother, SEBASTIAN, FERDINAND, the King's son, and ANTONIO, GONZALO, and several others. FERDINAND, separated from the others, is found by PROSPERO. On meeting MIRANDA, FERDINAND falls in love with her. PROSPERO, however, puts him to work at hard labor.

SEBASTIAN and ANTONIO plot to kill ALONSO, but their plan is foiled by ARIEL, the chief of PROSPERO's spirits. A plot by CALIBAN and two of the shipwrecked passengers to kill PROSPERO is also frustrated by ARIEL.

As the King and the others of his company wander around the island, ARIEL tantalizes them with visions of a banquet. Finally, ARIEL leads them to PROSPERO, who reveals his identity. ALONSO restores his dukedom to him and all set sail for Naples to celebrate the marriage of FERDINAND and MIRANDA.

TWELFTH NIGHT
Some are born great, others achieve greatness, others have greatness thrust upon them.
Act 2, Scene 3

SEBASTIAN and VIOLA, twins, are separated by a shipwreck. VIOLA dons male clothing and serves DUKE ORSINO, who uses the services of the supposed youth to advance his courtship of OLIVIA.

OLIVIA falls in love with VIOLA, who in turn is enamoured of the Duke. MALVOLIO, OLIVIA's steward, is so conceited that a practical joke is played on him by means of a supposed love-letter from OLIVIA. When MALVOLIO follows the directions in the letter, OLIVIA believes that he has lost his mind.

SIR ANDREW AGUECHEEK, a suitor of OLIVIA, is annoyed by OLIVIA's attention to VIOLA and challenges her to a duel, which is prevented by officers.

SEBASTIAN, who resembles VIOLA closely, also comes to the same country and, on being challenged by SIR ANDREW, beats him soundly. When OLIVIA meets SEBASTIAN, mutual protestations of love are made and they are married secretly.

When OLIVIA encounters VIOLA in the presence of the Duke and addresses her as her husband, the Duke is enraged. VIOLA denies the ceremony, but the priest affirms it. The problem is resolved by the appearance of SEBASTIAN. OLIVIA discovers her real husband, and the Duke falls in love with VIOLA.

THE TWO GENTLEMEN OF VERONA
O, they love least, that let men know their love.
Act 1, Scene 2

VALENTINE and PROTEUS are intimate friends, living in Verona. VALENTINE is leaving to make his way in the world at the court of the court of the Duke of Milan. PROTEUS is deeply in love with JULIA, a lady of Verona. Soon after VALENTINE'S departure, PROTEUS' father decides it is time his son also made a name for himself, and decides that he shall follow VALENTINE.

In Milan, VALENTINE has fallen in love with SILVIA, the Duke's daughter, who is resisting her father's wish that she should marry THURIO, a clownish courtier. PROTEUS is highly recommended to the Duke by VALENTINE and is warmly welcomed. At first sight of SILVIA he forgets JULIA, who has followed him from Verona, and begins scheming to get both VALENTINE and THURIO out of the way.

PROTEUS' first trick results in VALENTINE being banished from the court, so he next prepares an elaborate betrayal of THURIO.

JULIA learns of PROTEUS' perfidy, and SILVIA, rejecting both THURIO and PROTEUS, prepares to go on a search for VALENTINE.

PROTEUS follows SILVIA and rescues her from outlaws in the forest. She still rejects his advances, whereupon he threatens to force her to accede to his desires. All this has been overheard by VALENTINE, however, and he interrupts. PROTEUS is overcome by shame at all his scheming, and the timely arrival of the Duke and JULIA complete the scene for explanations, reconciliations, and betrothals.

THE WINTER'S TALE
Slander,
Whose sting is sharper than a sword's.

Act 2, Scene 3

    LEONTES, King of Sicily, requests his Queen, *HERMIONE*, to persuade *POLIXENES*, King of Bohemia, to prolong his stay in Sicily. Her success leads *LEONTES* to suspect intrigue between them. *CAMILLO*, a courtier, is induced to poison *POLIXENES*, but the former relates the plot to *POLIXENES* and flees with him to Bohemia.
    HERMIONE, confined to prison, gives birth to a daughter, who is disavowed by the King and is ordered exposed. The infant, taken to Bohemia, is found and reared by a poor shepherd.
    LEONTES, ignoring an oracle which upholds the honor of *HERMIONE* and *POLIXENES*, is informed of the death of *HERMIONE* and her only son. In his grief he vows daily penance.
    Sixteen years later, attentions paid by *FLORIZEL*, son of *POLIXENES*, to a shepherd's daughter lead the King to interfere between his son and the girl, *PERDITA*, who is really *HERMIONE*'s daughter. *CAMILLO* suggests a refuge and welcome for the pair in Sicily. Pursued thither by *POLIXENES*, *PERDITA* is found to be the daughter of *LEONTES*. Reconciliation between the two kings is followed by the marriage of their children. Subsequently, *HERMIONE*, who has been living in retirement, is restored to *LEONTES*.

HISTORIES

KING HENRY IV, PART I
The better part of valour is discretion.

Act 5, Scene 4

    HENRY IV, formerly *HENRY BOLINGBROKE*, has usurped the throne of *RICHARD II*. He wishes to do penance for *RICHARD'S* death by going on crusade, but is prevented from doing so by an uprising of the Scots who are defeated by *HENRY PERCY, "HOTSPUR,"* son of the *EARL OF NORTHUMBERLAND*. *HENRY* demands custody of the prisoners, but as he is unwilling to ransom *PERCY'S* kinsmen, *HOTSPUR* releases the prisoners and plots to overthrow *HENRY*.
    HENRY's son, also named *HENRY*, Prince of Wales, is placed in command of a wing of the army in the campaign against *HOTSPUR*. The Prince's friend, *SIR JOHN FALSTAFF*, a braggart soldier, accompanies the army.
    After a parley at Shrewsbury, battle is joined. *HOTSPUR* is killed by the Prince and the rebels are defeated.

KING HENRY IV, PART II
Uneasy lies the head that wears a crown.

Act 3, Scene 1

    Undaunted by the victory of the *KING* at Shrewsbury, a new coalition is formed against him, including the *ARCHBISHOP OF YORK* and *LORDS MOWBRAY* and *HASTINGS*. The *EARL OF NORTHUMBERLAND*, father of *HOTSPUR*, is persuaded by his wife and *HOTSPUR'S* widow not to join the rebels until there is some indication that they will succeed. The uprising is further weakened by the death of the Welshman, *GLENDOWER*. The *KING* sends his third son, *JOHN OF LANCASTER,* and the *EARL OF WESTMORELAND* against the rebels.

PRINCE HAL still grieves his father by his association with the gang of which *FALSTAFF* is the leading spirit, and much of the play is devoted to the doings of this riotous crew.

Under a promise that their grievances will be remedied, the rebel leaders disband their army, but as soon as this is done they are all treacherously seized and executed. The *KING,* feeling death approaching, is worried over the future of England with the irresponsible *PRINCE HAL* as monarch. The *PRINCE* receives a long lecture from his father and promises to reform.

News reaches *FALSTAFF* that the *KING* is dead, and feeling that his fortune is made, now that his friend *HAL* is *KING,* he hurries to court. There he is disillusioned. *PRINCE HAL,* now *KING HENRY V,* apparently intends to keep his promise to his dying father, and he turns from his former dissolute companions to the men upon whom his father had relied for advice and support.

KING HENRY V
They sell the pasture now to buy the horse.
Act 2, Prologue

KING HENRY seeks a sanction for his claim upon certain French provinces against his title to which the Salic Law is quoted by the French. The *ARCHBISHOP OF CANTERBURY,* to gain the *KING'S* favor, and to obtain the defeat of a proposed law which would reduce the power of the church, in a lengthy argument upholds *HENRY'S* claim, and war is declared upon France.

FALSTAFF dies, cursing wine and women, but his old companions carry on his function of enlivening the drama. The *KING* diverts himself by occasionally mingling with this crew, but not to the point of neglecting serious affairs.

The English army invades France, but at the Battle of Agincourt wins a decisive victory. The *DUKE OF BURGUNDY* brings together *CHARLES,* the King of France, and *HENRY,* and *HENRY'S* claims are recognized. Permanence is to be given to the treaty by *HENRY*'s marriage to *KATHARINE,* daughter of *CHARLES.* The play closes with *HENRY'S* amusing courtship of *KATHARINE,* carried on against the handicap of neither understanding much of the other's language.

KING HENRY VI, PART I
She's beautiful, and therefore to be woo'd;
She is a woman, therefore to be won.
Act 5, Scene 3

The first part of the *HENRY VI* trilogy consists of a series of scenes which have only the slightest relation to each other. They begin with messages arriving in England of disasters to the armies in France. The Dauphin, *CHARLES,* who is attempting to raise the English siege of Orleans, accepts the offer of *LA PUCELLE,* commonly known as *JOAN OF ARC.* She weakens the English strategically as well as numerically by persuading the *DUKE OF BURGUNDY* to forswear his alliance with England and join the French cause. The factional differences in England which are to result in the Wars of the Roses begin to appear. The ambitious

EARL OF SUFFOLK arranges a marriage, supposed to bring peace, between MARGARET of Anjou and KING HENRY, and expects to become the actual ruler of England through his influence over the queen.

It is generally believed that very little of this play was the actual work of Shakespeare

---

KING HENRY VI, PART II
Thrice is he armed that hath his quarrel just.
                                        Act 3, Scene 2

With the arrival in England of MARGARET of Anjou to be HENRY's queen the intrigues of the court are multiplied. SUFFOLK is created Duke by the grateful monarch, and starts plotting the downfall of the KING'S uncle, the DUKE OF GLOSTER, who is himself faithful to the KING, although it is true that ELEANOR, his wife, is scheming to have her husband seize the throne. SUFFOLK brings about the betrayal of ELEANOR, and GLOSTER's enemies immediately combine to encompass his complete ruin.

GLOSTER is murdered at the instigation of SUFFOLK, and BEAUFORT, Bishop of Winchester, dies of remorse at his part in the plot. SUFFOLK has aroused the enmity of the people and the KING orders his banishment, being further urged to it by evidences of a love affair between him and the QUEEN. SUFFOLK is murdered by sailors.

Meanwhile the star of RICHARD PLANTAGENET, Duke of York, is rising rapidly. He wins the support of the powerful EARLS OF SALISBURY and WARWICK, the latter of whom is to become famous as the Kingmaker. YORK is sent to Ireland to put down a minor uprising, and he returns to England with a strong force, claims the crown, and wins his first engagement, the Battle of St. Albans.

KING HENRY VI, PART III
The smallest worm will turn, being trodden on.
                                        Act 2, Scene 2

The victorious DUKE OF YORK moves on from the Battle of St. Albans to seat himself on the throne. The weak KING agrees to a compromise, proclaiming YORK his successor, thus dispossessing his own son, EDWARD, Prince of Wales. The QUEEN refuses to recognize this agreement, however, and leads an army against YORK, defeats him and herself stabs him to death.

His sons EDWARD and RICHARD, assisted by WARWICK,, attack the royal forces at Towton and win a complete victory. KING HENRY escapes to Scotland, QUEEN MARGARET to France, EDWARD is crowned KING EDWARD IV and RICHARD becomes DUKE OF GLOSTER.

WARWICK goes to France to arrange a marriage between BONA, sister of LEWIS XI, and KING EDWARD, but in his absence EDWARD, carried away by an infatuation, marries LADY GREY. WARWICK is furious, and meeting MARGARET at the French court, takes up her cause.

EDWARD has made the deposed KING HENRY prisoner, but WARWICK surprises him, frees HENRY and imprisons EDWARD. EDWARD escapes to Burgundy, raises a new army, and turns the tables on WARWICK, seizes HENRY and again takes the throne. HENRY is sent to the Tower.

Pursuing his advantage, *EDWARD* surprises *WARWICK* at Coventry and finally defeats and kills him at Barnet. *MARGARET* is beaten at Tewks-bury, and her son, *PRINCE EDWARD,* murdered in her presence by the *DUKE OF GLOSTER,* who then hurries to the Tower and kills *HENRY. MARGARET* is ransomed by her father, the *KING OF SICILY,* and *EDWARD IV* looks forward to peace and "lasting joy."

KING HENRY VIII
Farewell, a long farewell, to all my greatness!
Act 3, Scene 2

This play follows the course of three of the important advisers of *HENRY VIII,* the *DUKE OF BUCKINGHAM, CARDINAL WOLSEY* and *ARCHBISHOP CRANMER.* The ambitious *WOLSEY* convinces the *KING* that *BUCKINGHAM* has designs upon the crown, in the event that *HENRY* should have no children, and *BUCKINGHAM* is executed. *HENRY,* meanwhile, has become enamored of *ANNE BULLEN,* and pretending that his conscience troubles him because he has married his dead brother's wife, though that marriage was never consummated, has *WOLSEY* try to persuade *QUEEN KATHARINE* to consent to an annulment. Failing in this, the *KING* demands that *WOLSEY* obtain the *POPE's* consent to a divorce, and when the *CARDINAL* opposes this, has him executed and appropriates his property. The more pliable *CRANMER* now becomes *HENRY's* trusted adviser or rather instrument of *HENRY'S* wishes. *HENRY* marries *ANNE* and the play ends with *CRANMER's* glowing prediction of the future greatness of *ANNE's* daughter, *ELIZABETH.*

Serious doubts have been cast upon Shakespeare's part in the authorship of any considerable portion of this play, at least half of which, it has been established, was by Fletcher.

KING JOHN
In sooth, I would you were a little sick,
That I might sit all night and watch with you.
Act 4, Scene 1

JOHN is King of England. An ambassador from France announces that *KING PHILIP* demands Ireland and the greater part of England's continental territory on behalf of *ARTHUR,* son of *JOHN's* elder brother *GEFFREY,* the late Duke of Bretagne. *JOHN* refuses and tells the ambassador to warn the *KING OF FRANCE* to prepare for war.

The two kings meet before the walls of Angiers, which is in the disputed territory. The young *PRINCE ARTHUR* is present, with his mother, *CONSTANCE,* who has induced *PHILIP* to take up her cause. *KING JOHN* is accompanied by his mother, *ELINOR,* and these two women engage in bitter wrangling. The citizens of Angiers propose a compromise that *BLANCH,* daughter of the *KING OF SPAIN* and niece of *JOHN,* shall marry the *DAUPHIN,* and unite the two monarchies, giving *ARTHUR,* for consolation, the Dukedom of Bretagne.

This satisfies everybody except *CONSTANCE,* but the agreement is soon disrupted by *PANDULPH,* a papal legate, who brings an ultimatum from Rome. The *POPE* demands that *JOHN* cease his opposition to *STEPHEN LANGTON,* Archbishop of Canterbury. *JOHN* defies the church, and not only is himself excommunicated, but the threat of excommunication is also issued to any king who is his ally. *PHILIP* then withdraws from the treaty and a battle ensues in which JOHN is victorious and takes ARTHUR prisoner to England, ordering his chamberlain, HUBERT DE BURGH, to kill the boy secretly.

HUBERT is unable to carry out the KING'S order, having become very fond of PRINCE ARTHUR, but JOHN believes the boy is dead and so informs certain lords who have told him that there is much discontent over ARTHUR'S imprisonment. France invades England. Needing public support, JOHN regrets ARTHUR'S death, and when he learns that he is alive orders him set free. Meanwhile, however, ARTHUR has committed suicide.

JOHN yields to Rome and the legate PANDULPH tries to call off the DAUPHIN, who is leading the invaders, but now that ARTHUR is dead, LOUIS through his marriage to BLANCH is heir to the English throne, and says that the war shall continue. The French are defeated, but KING JOHN dies of poison administered by a monk, and his son succeeds him as HENRY III.

KING RICHARD II
There is no virtue like necessity.
Act 1, Scene 3

BOLINGBROKE, son of the wealthy and powerful JOHN OF GAUNT, Duke of Lancaster, accuses THOMAS MOWBRAY, Duke of Norfolk, of treason. They are about to settle their quarrel in single combat when KING RICHARD intervenes and banishes both, being especially glad to be rid of BOLINGBROKE because of his power and growing popularity with the people. The KING needs money to quell a rebellion in Ireland, his own funds being exhausted. JOHN OF GAUNT dies and the KING seizes his property, raises an army and sets out for Ireland. BOLINGBROKE hears of the KING'S action, raises an army and returns to England. His forces are joined by a number of lords who are disgusted with RICHARD. The KING returns and finds himself in BOLINGBROKE's power, and while the latter says all he wants is the return of his father's possessions, RICHARD knows the end has come. He goes before Parliament and abdicates and BOLINGBROKE is crowned HENRY IV. The new KING has RICHARD murdered.

KING RICHARD III
A horse! a horse! my kingdom for a 'horse!
Act 5, Scene 4

Between RICHARD, Duke of Gloster, and the throne, there now stand his brother, KING EDWARD, EDWARD'S two sons, and another brother of the KING, the DUKE OF CLARENCE. But the hunchbacked RICHARD deliberately sets out to remove these obstacles. First, he cynically but successfully proposes marriage to ANNE, widow of the PRINCE he killed at Tewksbury. He then hires assassins to murder the DUKE OF CLARENCE.

The KING dies a natural death, and now only the two young princes remain in the path the unscrupulous RICHARD is carving toward the throne. These he kills, and also procures the execution of nobles who oppose him. He obtains the consent of the MAYOR OF LONDON and the populace to his coronation by pretending a religious fervor, and making a pretense of reluctance.

Meanwhile, there are uprisings against RICHARD throughout England, and the EARL OF RICHMOND, whom HENRY VI had said would one day reign, leads a united force against the KING and himself kills RICHARD on Bosworth Field.

TRAGEDIES

ANTONY AND CLEOPATRA
Age cannot wither her, not custom stale
Her infinite variety

Act 2, Scene 2

MARC ANTONY, one of the Triumvirate governing Rome -- ANTONY, CAESAR and LEPIDUS – has gone to Egypt and has fallen under the spell of CLEOPATRA. He pays no attention to affairs of state or to dispatches from Rome. At last he receives news of the death of his wife, FULVIA, of civil war in Italy, of a threat from Pompey and other difficulties menacing the state. With a supreme effort he separates from the Egyptian queen and returns to Rome.

In Rome, ANTONY frankly admits his faults to CAESAR, and the triple alliance is sealed by his marriage to CAESAR's sister, OCTAVIA. When CLEOPATRA hears this, she has to be restrained from killing the messenger. An advantageous peace with Pompey is signed and all seems well, but it is clear that ANTONY still feels the tug toward Egypt.

ANTONY goes to Athens, with OCTAVIA, to take command of the Roman forces in the east. His generals are successful. He is indignant at the news that CAESAR has deprived the third triumvir, LEPIDUS, of power and made war upon Pompey. OCTAVIA returns to Rome to try to make peace between CAESAR and ANTONY, but ANTONY gathers forces for an attack upon CAESAR. CLEOPATRA has joined ANTONY with a strong sea force, but at a critical moment her fleet deserts, and CAESAR is victorious. ANTONY flees to Alexandria with CAESAR following and demanding that CLEOPATRA surrender her lover. ANTONY has CAESAR's messenger whipped and sent back as his answer.

In a battle before Alexandria, ANTONY beats back CAESAR, but again he is betrayed by CLEOPATRA, who fails to support him. ANTONY denounces CLEOPATRA, who has a report sent to him that she died through grieving over his defeat. ANTONY falls on his sword, and is then borne to CLEOPATRA'S hiding place, and dies.

CAESAR sends word to CLEOPATRA that he will treat her honorably, but she has reason to believe that he proposes to drag her through the streets of Rome, and she kills herself by pressing poisonous asps to her body.

CORIOLANUS
O, a kiss
Long as my exile, sweet as my revenge!

Act 5, Scene 3

CAIUS MARCIUS is a Roman noble, with nothing but contempt for the mob. The citizens, complaining of the price of corn, decide to make an example of him as their principal enemy. MENENIUS AGRIPPA, a friend of MARCIUS, encounters a rabble and argues with them, but MARCIUS arrives and berates them. News is received of an impending attack by the Volscians, and MARCIUS' services are needed. He leads the Romans to Corioli and gains a complete victory, personally overcoming his ancient rival in arms, TULLUS AUFIDIUS.

Returning to Rome in triumph, MARCIUS is christened CORIOLANUS in commemoration of his victory. He finds that the weak Tribunes have given in to the demands of the populace and sold them corn at their own price. CORIOLANUS' popularity is such that his friends demand he shall be made Consul, but in asking for the votes of the people he insults them to such a degree that the Tribunes, jealous of his power, arouse the rabble against him, and he is exiled.

CORIOLANUS goes to Antium, where AUFIDIUS is planning a new campaign against Rome, and offers to join him. The mere word of this alliance, before a blow is struck, terrifies the Romans. To the Volscian camp, a short distance from Rome, CORIOLANUS' patrician friends come begging for peace at any price, but he refuses to listen. Not until his mother, wife and son appeal to him does he consent to a treaty.

AUFIDIUS has become jealous of the popularity of CORIOLANUS with the army, and when they return to Antium he organizes a conspiracy, denounces CORIOLANUS, and has him murdered.

CYMBELINE
*There's no motion
That tends to vice in man but I affirm
It is the woman's part.*
Act 2, Scene 5

CYMBELINE, King of Britain, exiles POSTHUMUS, who has married IMOGEN, daughter of the King. In Rome, POSTHUMUS meets IACHIM0, who wagers that he can compromise IMOGEN. Unable to do so, IACHIMO returns to, POSTHUMUS with fraudulent evidence of the accomplishment of this act. POSTHUMUS, misled, orders his follower, PISANIO, to kill IMOGEN. PISANIO, however, does not carry out the order, and advises IMOGEN to disguise herself and to go in search of POSTHUMUS.

In her journey across Wales, IMOGEN encounters BELARIUS, a nobleman disguised as a peasant, who had abducted the KING'S two sons twenty years earlier. The PRINCES, ignorant of their true status, welcome IMOGEN, who is fearful of her step-mother, the QUEEN, and her son, CLOTEN.

CLOTEN is killed in a duel by one of the princes. IMOGEN, who takes a potion and falls into a stupor, is placed near the headless body of CLOTEN. When IMOGEN awakens, she mistakes CLOTEN's body for that of POSTHUMUS. In her grief she joins a Roman army invading Britain. IACHIMO and POSTHUMUS are also with this army which engages in battle with CYMBELINE's forces. POSTHUMUS, BELARIUS, and the two princes fight for CYMBELINE.

Reconciliation takes place between BELARIUS and CYMBELINE. IACHIMO, taken prisoner, confesses. IMOGEN is restored to POSTHUMUS, who is welcomed by CYMBELINE. The QUEEN dies of frustration.

HAMLET, PRINCE OF DENMARK
To be, or not to be: that is the question.
Act 3, Scene 1

HAMLET, Prince of Denmark, learns from his father's ghost at the castle at Elsinore that HAMLET's uncle, CLAUDIUS, had poisoned the KING. CLAUDIUS has assumed royal power and has married the Queen, GERTRUDE. HAMLET is sworn to revenge.

HAMLET, pretending madness, writes incoherently to his lady-love, OPHELIA, daughter of POLONIUS. He makes use of a play given by strolling actors, in which the plot resembles the events in Denmark, to watch the reactions of his uncle. When his suspicions are confirmed, HAMLET reproaches his mother for marrying CLAUDIUS.

HAMLET is banished for the accidental slaying of POLONIUS, but returns in time for the funeral of OPHELIA, who had become insane and had accidentally drowned. LAERTES, OPHELIA'S brother, regarding HAMLET as the source of his family's troubles, wishes to kill him. CLAUDIUS suggests a fencing match between them. LAERTES' foil is tipped with poison. The QUEEN unwittingly drinks of a poisoned cup of wine intended for HAMLET and dies. LAERTES, wounded with his own blade, confesses the plot and dies. HAMLET, also wounded by the poisoned blade, kills CLAUDIUS and then dies.

JULIUS CAESAR

There is a tide in the affairs of men,
Which, taken at the flood, leads on to fortune.
Act 4, Scene 3

JULIUS CAESAR, returning victorious over Pompey, is offered the crown by MARK ANTONY to climax the triumph. Although he refuses, his enemies, led by CASSIUS, conspire to kill him. BRUTUS, a noble-minded Roman, who is a friend of CAESAR, is induced to join the conspiracy on the grounds of patriotism.

CAESAR, warned by a soothsayer to "beware the Ides of March," is disturbed on that day by the ominous dreams of his wife, CALPURNIA. He wishes to remain at home but is persuaded by the conspirators to go to the Senate-house.

There CAESAR is murdered, each conspirator stabbing him. When BRUTUS uses his dagger, CAESAR murmurs, "And you, too, Brutus?" and dies.

MARK ANTONY requests permission to speak at CAESAR's funeral and is permitted to follow BRUTUS in his explanation of the reasons for the slaying. ANTONY arouses the citizens against the conspirators, who are forced to flee.

After CAESAR's death, there is war between two factions, one led by BRUTUS and CASSIUS, the other led by MARK ANTONY, OCTAVIUS CAESAR, and LEPIDUS. The armies meet at Philippi. CAESAR's ghost appears to BRUTUS and foretells a meeting on the battleground.

In the battle the triumvirate is victorious. BRUTUS and CASSIUS commit suicide.

KING LEAR

How sharper than a serpent's tooth it is
To have a thankless child.
Act 1, Scene 4

When LEAR, King of Britain, decides to divide his kingdom among his three daughters, GONERIL and REGAN profess their love for him in most generous terms. CORDELIA, the youngest sister, promises to love him in accordance with her duty. LEAR, enraged, divides the kingdom between GONERIL and REGAN, and banishes CORDELIA. The EARL OF KENT, who intercedes for CORDELIA, is also banished.

When LEAR is mistreated by his elder daughters, he leaves their courts for the open fields. Accompanied by his two remaining retainers, his jester and the returned EARL OF KENT, LEAR takes refuge in a hovel where they meet EDGAR, son of the EARL OF GLOUC-

ESTER. When the latter, in pity, takes care of LEAR, EDMUND, another son of GLOUCESTER, informs LEAR's daughters, and GLOUCESTER is blinded by CORNWALL, REGAN's husband. GLOUCESTER is found and is protected by EDGAR.

CORDELIA, now married to the KING OF FRANCE, learns of her father's plight. She brings in a French army which is defeated by EDMUND. CORDELIA and LEAR are taken prisoner. GONERIL poisons REGAN and then kills herself. EDMUND is killed by EDGAR.

CORDELIA is hanged in prison, and LEAR dies broken-hearted.

MACBETH
Sleep that knits up the ravelled sleave of care.
Act 2, Scene 2

MACBETH and BANQUO, generals of DUNCAN, King of Scotland, are told by witches that MACBETH will become King of Scotland and that BANQUO's sons will sit upon the throne.

Spurred on by this prophecy, MACBETH, together with his ambitious wife, murders DUNCAN, whose sons, MALCOLM and DONALBAIN, flee the country and are blamed for the murder. MACBETH ascends the throne. Remembering the second part of the witches' predictions, MACBETH, has BANQUO and his son, FLEANCE, waylaid. FLEANCE flees, but his father is killed and his ghost appears to MACBETH at the feast to which BANQUO has been invited.

In another session with the witches MACBETH is warned to beware of MACDUFF; he is promised that "none born of woman" shall harm him; he is advised not to fear until Birnam Wood shall come against him.

LADY MACBETH, now the Queen, is tortured by her conscience and finally dies, overcome by remorse.

MACDUFF, joining forces with MALCOLM, attacks MACBETH. Branches of trees from Birnam Wood are used to camouflage the advance of the troops. MACBETH, meeting MACDUFF in single combat, is told that MACDUFF was born by caesarian section, and is then killed. MALCOLM becomes King of Scotland.

OTHELLO
Trifles, light as air,
Are to the jealous, confirmations strong
As holy writ.
Act 3, Scene 3

OTHELLO, a Moorish general in the service of Venice, marries DESDEMONA, against the wishes of her father, BRABANTIO. IAGO, OTHELLO's aide, plots OTHELLO's ruin because of the promotion of CASSIO to a higher position desired by IAGO. CASSIO, involved in a drunken brawl by IAGO, is deprived of his position by OTHELLO.

At IAGO's suggestion, CASSIO tries to regain favor through DESDEMONA's intervention. By various hints and by arranging to have CASSIO possess a handkerchief given to DESDEMONA by OTHELLO, IAGO succeeds in convincing OTHELLO that his wife is unfaithful to him.

At OTHELLO's orders, IAGO tries to have CASSIO killed. DESDEMONA is smothered with a pillow by OTHELLO, who then learns of his wife's innocence. OTHELLO wounds IAGO

PERICLES, PRINCE OF TYRE
How courtesy would seem to cover sin!
                    Act I, Scene 1

PERICLES, Prince of Tyre, has the spirit of a knight errant, and goes on one adventure after another. In the first he accepts the challenge of the KING OF ANTIOCH to read a certain riddle. Success is to be rewarded with the hand of the KING'S beautiful daughter, failure punished with death. PERICLES discovers the secret of the riddle, and that it means the KING has committed incest with his daughter. PERICLES refuses to marry this princess and returns to Tyre. He is seen next relieving a famine at Tharsus, where he wins the enduring gratitude of the governor, CLEON, and his wife DIONYZA.

Now he is shipwrecked near Pentapolis, and finds himself among some fishermen who, drawing in their nets, discover PERICLE's armor in them. The PRINCE dons the armor and enters the lists at Pentapolis, wins first honors, and marries THAISA, daughter of KING SIMONIDES.

Sailing for home, THAISA apparently dies In childbirth and is buried at sea. PERICLES takes his daughter, MARINA, to Tharsus to be cared for by his old friends, CLEON and DIONYZA. THAISA is washed ashore alive at Ephesus. For some reason she believes PERICLES is dead, and takes the veil of chastity.

DIONYZA becomes jealous because MARINA so far surpasses her own daughter in beauty and intelligence, and arranges to have her murdered, but she is stolen by pirates and sold to procurers in Mitylene. She escapes violence by her purity and beauty, and becomes a teacher, to earn her living without sacrificing her honor.

PERICLES hears from Tharsus that his daughter is dead. His ship is driven to Mitylene, and there he is entertained by LYSIMACHUS, who sends for the now famous MARINA to divert the saddened and bereft PERICLES. The PRINCE recognizes his daughter, and the goddess DIANA appears to him in a vision, directing him to go to Ephesus. Here he finds his lost wife, THAISA, and the family is reunited.

ROMEO AND JULIET
What's in a name? that which we call a rose,
By any other name would smell as sweet.
                    Act 2, Scene 2

Although there has been a feud of long standing between the houses of Montague and Capulet in Verona, ROMEO, a Montague, disguises himself to attend a feast at the Capulet house. Here he falls in love with JULIET, heiress of the Capulets. TYBALT, a Capulet, learns ROMEO's identity and has to be prevented from dueling with him.

When ROMEO declares his love under JULIET'S balcony, she accepts him and they are married by FRIAR LAURENCE. Following the marriage, a quarrel ensues between TYBALT and ROMEO, who is accompanied by MERCUTIO. TYBALT kills MERCUTIO and in turn is slain by ROMEO, who is then banished from the city.

Forced to marry PARIS, JULIET is advised by FRIAR LAURENCE to drink a potion, which will induce a death-like state. JULIET does so and is placed in the family tomb.

When ROMEO learns of this, he goes to the tomb where he is confronted by PARIS. In a duel PARIS is killed. ROMEO then takes poison. When JULIET awakes and sees his body, she kills herself. This double tragedy brings about a reconciliation between the two houses.

TIMON OF ATHENS
Men shut their doors against a setting sun.
Act 1, Scene 2

TIMON, a wealthy Athenian, has been squandering his money in gifts, entertainments, dowries and all manner of extravagances. His steward, FLAVIUS, tries to warn him that he is exhausting his resources, but he will not listen.

Finally things reach a crisis, and FLAVIUS having no funds to meet the mounting debts, TIMON is forced to face the situation. He first rebukes FLAVIUS, then sends to all his former friends, who have been forever flattering him in order to share in his showers of gold, but they are unanimous in refusing to help him.

He then invites all these persons to a feast at his house, and when they sit down and uncover the dishes they find that they are being served only with warm water, which TIMON flings in their faces and leaves Athens, swearing never to return. ALCIBIADES, at this time, is banished from the city for his temerity in denouncing the Senate for refusing to pardon an offense of a friend of his, who has performed valuable services to the state in the past.

TIMON goes to live in the woods, and discovers a vast store of gold. He passes his entire time in cursing mankind. ALCIBIADES encounters him, and when TIMON learns that ALCIBIADES desires to attack Athens, but lacks funds to equip an army, TIMON supplies the gold. In fact, he gives gold to all who ask it, and with the gold a curse. Only FLAVIUS escapes his vituperation.

Artists and senators seek him out, pocketing their pride and begging for gold and the response is always the same gold and a curse. ALCIBIADES succeeds in intimidating the Athenian authorities, and they beg him to return. He demands the punishment of his enemies and those of TIMON and they agree. TIMON dies, having first written his own epitaph, which is a curse against all mankind.

TITUS ANDRONICUS
He lives in fame, that died in virtue's cause.
Act 1, Scene 2

This play is nothing more than a series of scenes of licentiousness and murder, and many devotees of Shakespeare are loud in their insistence that he had nothing to do with it, or at most merely polished up the verse.

TITUS ANDRONICUS returns to Rome from a successful campaign against the Goths. Two brothers, SATURNINUS and BASSIANUS, are in conflict over the succession to the crown. TITUS supports SATURNINUS and he is crowned with the understanding that he will marry TITUS' daughter, LAVINIA. The unsuccessful BASSIANUS, however, elopes with LAVINIA and marries her himself. SATURNINUS then marries TAMORA, queen of the Goths, who has been brought to Rome a prisoner, with *AARON*, her Moorish lover, and her two sons.

TITUS kills his own son, *MUTIUS*, who prevented him from pursuing the elopers. *TAMORA's* sons find *BASSIANUS* and *LAVINIA* in a forest, kill the former, and mutilate the latter after first ravishing her. This crime is charged against two other sons of *TITUS*, who allows a hand to be cut off as the price of their pardon, but *AARON* arranges for the execution of the sons after all. *TITUS'* son *LUCIUS* goes to join the Goths to fight his foes in Rome. *TAMORA* gives birth to a black child, and *AARON* murders the midwife and nurse to insure their silence.

TAMORA and her two sons go in disguise to *TITUS* to persuade him to have *LUCIUS* return. He pretends not to recognize them, induces *TAMORA* to leave the sons with him, and having previously learned the truth about their crime, kills them. He invites *TAMORA* and *SATURNINUS* to a banquet, at which he serves a pie made of the fragments of the bodies of *TAMORA's* sons. Then he kills *LAVINIA* and *TAMORA*. *SATURNINUS* kills *TITUS*. *LUCIUS* kills *SATURNINUS* and becomes emperor.

TROILUS AND CRESSIDA
One touch of nature makes the whole world kin.
Act 3, Scene 3

The scene is the siege of Troy by the Greeks. *TROILUS*, one of the sons of *PRIAM*, King of Troy, is in love with *CRESSIDA*, daughter of *CALCHAS*, a Trojan priest. She reciprocates his affection, but pretends the opposite, when her uncle, *PANDARUS*, praises *TROILUS*. The Greeks discuss the progress of the war, especially a challenge from *HECTOR*, another of *PRIAM's* sons, to fight the best man the Greeks can offer. *NESTOR* suggests *AJAX*, who is presented as an ignorant braggart, because *NESTOR* fears their champion, *ACHILLES*, is becoming too opinionated.

The Greek leaders, whose names are familiar in the roster of ancient heroes, bandy sneering remarks, for it seems they were anything but heroes to one another. *ACHILLES*, sulking, refuses to fight *HECTOR*, and the generals agree to *NESTOR's* choice of *AJAX*. The Trojans, in council, consider an offer from the Greeks to end the war. The cause of the conflict was the abduction of *HELEN*, wife of *MENELAUS*, by *PARIS*, son of the *KING OF TROY*. The Greeks' sole demand is that she be surrendered, but the Trojans refuse.

PANDARUS succeeds in breaking down *CRESSIDA's* pretended dislike of *TROILUS*, and they spend a night in *PANDARUS'* house. *CRESSIDA's* father, *CALCHAS*, who has deserted to the Greeks, asks them to exchange for his daughter a Trojan they have captured and they agree.

CRESSIDA first refuses to go to the Greek camp, then consents, but promises to be true to *TROILUS*. Arriving at the camp she is kissed by all the Greek generals except *ULYSSES*, who regards her as a trollop. The fight between *AJAX* and *HECTOR* comes to a draw. *CRESSIDA* falls to the lot of *DIOMEDES*.

ACHILLES finally decides to fight *HECTOR*. *TROILUS* fights with *DIOMEDES*, who merely takes his horse away from him and sends it to *CRESSIDA*. Instead of fighting with *HECTOR* in single combat, *ACHILLES* has his troops surround the Trojan, kill him, and tie his body to the tail of *ACHILLES'* horse. The entire play is a satire on the ancient heroes of Greek mythology.

www.ingramcontent.com/pod-product-compliance
Lightning Source LLC
Chambersburg PA
CBHW082034300426
44117CB00015B/2480